Government Export Promotion

Government Export Promotion (1990) focuses on an extremely important international trade and economic issue: the role and impact of government export promotion. The efforts of governments to support companies in both the developed and developing world are described, and the impact of this support on exporting activities and programmes. It examines the approaches and methods, as well as the underlying philosophies and strategies, of government export promotion worldwide. It reviews the economic and competitive context within which these efforts take place, and identify future challenges facing government officials and managers, suggesting how government export promotion can be made more effective in the public and private sectors.

Government Export Promotion

A Global Perspective

F.H. Rolf Seringhaus and Philip J. Rosson

Routledge Revivals
Routledge
Taylor & Francis Group

First published in 1990
by Routledge

This edition first published in 2026 by Routledge
4 Park Square, Milton Park, Abingdon, Oxon, OX14 4RN

and by Routledge
605 Third Avenue, New York, NY 10017

Routledge is an imprint of the Taylor & Francis Group, an informa business

Publisher's Note
The publisher has gone to great lengths to ensure the quality of this reprint but points out that some imperfections in the original copies may be apparent.

Disclaimer
The publisher has made every effort to trace copyright holders and welcomes correspondence from those they have been unable to contact.

A Library of Congress record exists under LCCN: 89032097

ISBN: 978-1-041-30131-8 (hbk)
ISBN: 978-1-003-77301-6 (ebk)
ISBN: 978-1-041-30132-5 (pbk)

Book DOI 10.4324/9781003773016

Government Export Promotion
A Global Perspective

F.H. Rolf Seringhaus
and Philip J. Rosson

Routledge
London and New York

First published 1990
by Routledge
11 New Fetter Lane, London EC4P 4EE

Simultaneously published in the USA and Canada
by Routledge
a division of Routledge, Chapman and Hall, Inc.
29 West 35th Street, New York, NY 10001

Filmset by Mayhew Typesetting, Bristol, England
Printed and bound in Great Britain by
Biddles Ltd, Guildford and King's Lynn

British Library Cataloguing in Publication Data

Seringhaus, F.H. Rolf *1942–* .
Government export promotion : a global
perspective. — (International business
series)
1. Exporting. Promotion
I. Title II. Rosson, Philip J.
III. Series
382′.63

ISBN 0–415–00064–5

Library of Congress Cataloging in Publication Data

Seringhaus, F.H. Rolf, 1942–
Government export promotion : a global perspective / F.H. Rolf
Seringhaus and Philip J. Rosson.
p. cm. — (International business series)
Bibliography: p.
Includes index.
ISBN 0–415–00064–5
1. Foreign trade promotion. 2. Commercial policy. I. Rosson,
Philip J. II. Title III. Series: International business series
(London, England)
HF1417.5.S47 1989
382′.63 — dc20 89-32097
CIP

This book is dedicated to
our parents, Rudolf and
Elfriede Seringhaus, and
Maurice and Rosina Rosson.

Contents

Part IV Conclusions

Figures

Figures

Tables

The authors

F.H. Rolf Seringhaus is Associate Professor of International Marketing at the School of Business and Economics of Wilfrid Laurier University in Waterloo, Ontario, Canada, where he is also chairman of the International Business Unit of the Laurier Institute for Business and Economic Studies. He studied at York University in Toronto where he received his MBA and Ph.D. in International Marketing. He has researched and published internationally in journals and books in the area of export marketing management, international marketing strategy, and government export promotion. Prior to his academic career, Dr Seringhaus spent twenty years in managerial positions in marketing and finance with major international corporations in Canada, Switzerland and Germany. Dr Seringhaus also consults to industry and government in matters of marketing strategy, export development, and export promotion.

Philip J. Rosson is Professor of Marketing at the School of Business Administration of Dalhousie University in Halifax, Canada, where he is also Director of the Centre for International Business Studies. He was educated in England, obtaining an MA and Ph.D. in Marketing at the Universities of Lancaster and Bath respectively. He has taught at universities in Scotland and New Zealand. His research interests currently embrace export methods and strategies in smaller firms and marketing in high technology environments. He has published widely in journals and book collections, and has two books to his credit, most recently *Managing Export Entry and Expansion*, published by Praeger in 1987. Dr Rosson has seven years of marketing experience with organizations in England and East Africa. He consults for government and business on export and technology marketing matters.

Foreword

This book focuses on an extremely important international trade and economic issue: the role and impact of government export promotion. The efforts of governments in both the developed and developing world are described, and conclusions drawn that will help lead to more effective export promotion programmes in the future.

Professors Seringhaus and Rosson argue that government export promotion programmes will be successful only when they take into account the economic development and export situation in the country in question, and meet the needs of user companies. I echo this view. Both macro (country) and micro (company) factors must be considered in export promotion policy, and the design and delivery of export programmes. Macro considerations include the country's economic, legal, social, and cultural situations and institutions. Micro factors include the company's goals, plans, its export management know-how, its drives, its structure, and so on.

Professors Seringhaus and Rosson show that government export promotion efforts in the developed world vary in sophistication and comprehensiveness, and reflect differing philosophies and strategic approaches. But that in the developing world, government efforts show a broad emergence of more formal approaches to export promotion. The latter frequently are modelled on other countries' experiences and are aided by international institutions. Because many developing country situations repeat themselves world-wide, lessons from one country frequently can serve as a useful guide to other countries. However, transfers of knowledge from one country's situation to another must be undertaken with care.

My research in Central America shows that companies in nearby countries can have very contrasting views about the export barriers they face.[1] For this reason, an export programme designed in one of these countries and applied to another, runs the risk of being inappropriate and, hence, ineffective. Nevertheless, parallels often can be drawn between companies in different countries. Studying Costa

Rican, Salvadorian, and US companies has convinced me that for companies with comparable products, and of comparable size, and comparable export experience, their export behaviour is more similar than different.[2] This suggests that certain export promotion programmes may be suitable for specific types of companies regardless of the country in which they operate.

Another point concerns programme evaluation and government export promotion research in general. The authors rightly state that much room exists for improving practice in these areas and provide some guidelines as to how better (more valid and reliable) approaches might be accomplished. I anticipate that considerably more attention will be paid to this topic in the future.

In conclusion, this is an important subject area and one that has attracted too little serious attention. Significant improvements can be made in the design and delivery of government export promotion programmes but this will be achieved only through careful study and the thoughtful transfer of knowledge. Professors Seringhaus and Rosson have provided a thorough, useful, and timely assessment of where we currently stand and how progress might best be made.

Warren J. Bilkey
Professor International Business
The University of Wisconsin-Madison

Notes and references

1. W.J. Bilkey, *Industrial Stimulation*, Lexington, Mass., D.C. Heath, 1970.
2. ibid.

Acknowledgements

We wish to acknowledge the contribution of the chapter on legal barriers to export promotion by Philip Raworth of the University of Alberta, which adds an important dimension to the discussion of government export promotion. We are grateful for the support provided by our universities, Wilfrid Laurier University and Dalhousie University respectively. We have received excellent co-operation during the research phase for this book from a number of institutions and organizations and wish to acknowledge them here:

Centre for the Promotion of Imports from Developing Countries, Rotterdam
Department of Export Promotion of Thailand, Bangkok
Department of External Affairs, Government of Canada, Ottawa
Economic and Social Commission for Asia and the Pacific, Bangkok
Import Promotion Office for Products from Developing Countries, Stockholm
United Nations Industrial Development Organization, Vienna
International Chamber of Commerce, Paris
International Trade Centre, UNCTAD/GATT, Geneva
Japanese External Trade Organization, Tokyo
SPR Associates Incorporated/National Mail Surveys Incorporated, Toronto

In addition, we are grateful to the following who have given permission for the use of copyright material:

McGraw-Hill Book Co. for material from *Countertrade, Barter and Offset*, by Pompiliu Verzariu, 1985.
Prentice-Hall Inc. for adapted material from *International Business – Environment and Management*, 2nd edn, by Christopher M. Korth, 1985.

South-Western Publishing Co. for material from *International Trade and Investment*, 4th edn, by Franklin R. Root, 1978.
International Marketing Review, MCB University Press
Irish Marketing Review, Irish Marketing Review Society

Finally, we wish to thank Elsie Grogan and her wordprocessing team at Wilfrid Laurier, and Maggy Lapp at Dalhousie, for secretarial assistance in preparing the manuscript. Rob Hyndman of Dalhousie University also deserves our thanks for his computer assistance.

Part I

Introduction

Chapter one

Government export promotion: an overview

Introduction

Today, as never before, governments are involved in supporting the export activities of companies. Sizeable budgets and numerous programmes have been put in place so as to help draw companies into exporting for the first time, and enable existing exporters to expand or consolidate their foreign market operations. This book is the first that we are aware of to focus on this subject: it describes the export promotion initiatives of governments around the world, and examines the role and impact of the programmes that have been established. In addition to reviewing recent experience, it attempts to look to the future.

This chapter provides an overview of government export promotion support activities. We view government export promotion as those public policy measures which actually or potentially enhance exporting activity at the company, industry, or national level.[1] The chapter begins by highlighting the importance of international trade to nations and companies. Many countries and companies are very dependent on exports for their well-being, whereas others plan to move towards greater involvement in global trade. The importance of exports is reflected in the commercial policies of governments around the world. Various means are employed to serve the end of improved export performance, and these are briefly described in the second section. While infrastructural, financial, and other factors obviously play a part in furthering export activity, the matter addressed in this book is those export promotion methods that assist companies in overcoming export marketing barriers. The third section of the chapter outlines these difficulties, while the fourth goes on to explain how government programmes attempt to combat them. Finally, having provided some context for the detailed discussion that takes place later, Chapter 1 concludes with a description of the plan of the book.

The importance of international trade

The importance of international trade is highlighted in this section, where a distinction is made between country (macro) and company (micro) levels. The two levels are clearly interrelated, but for the time being we treat them separately, discussing countries first, and companies second.

Countries

World trade has grown dramatically over the last two decades, its value climbing from $200 million to over $2 trillion. Not all types of economies, regions, or countries have shared equally in this substantial increase in export activity, but the importance of exports in economic development is universally accepted, and governments around the world actively pursue export growth. The importance of exports is discussed below, first for various country groups,[2] and then for individual countries.

Country groups

Three facets of international trade are looked at from a country group perspective: (1) relative contributions to world exports and imports; (2) export commodity structures; and (3) exports and economic development.

Exports and imports

The developed, western industrial nations dominate world exports, accounting for two-thirds of all exports in 1985. The USA, West Germany, and Japan are the leading export nations among this group, followed by the United Kingdom, France, Canada, and Italy (see Table 1.1). The second most important group of countries is the upper-middle-income developing countries.[3] Four nations that have pursued export-led growth figure prominently here: Hong Kong, South Korea, Brazil, and Singapore. Mexico is another important member of this group, which overall makes up 14 per cent of all exports. The non-market economies of Eastern Europe account for 9 per cent of world exports, with the USSR contributing more than half of this volume.

Three remaining country groups are least involved in export trading. The high-income oil-exporting countries' importance has waned as a result of oil conservation measures following price escalation after the 1973 embargo. In 1985 this small group of countries made up 3 per cent of world exports, with Saudi Arabia earning almost a half of these export dollars. Two oil-producing nations –

Table 1.1 Exports – country groups and major exporting nations

Country group	*Exports 1985 (US $ m)*	*No. of countries*	*Average exports/ country (US $ m)*	*Major exporting nations (% of country group exports)*
Low-income economies	52,704	37	1,424	China (52), India (19)
Middle-income economies				
lower	91,343	36	2,537	Indonesia (20), Nigeria (14), Hong Kong (10), S. Korea (10), Brazil (9), Mexico (8), Singapore (8)
upper	273,433	20	13,672	
High-income oil exporters	63,573	4	15,893	Saudi Arabia (43)
Industrial market economies	1,248,376	19	65,704	USA (17), West Germany (15), Japan (15)
East European non-market economies	175,907	7	25,129	USSR (50)

Source: World Bank, *World Development Report*, Washington, DC, 1987, Table 10, pp. 220–1.

Table 1.2 Origin and destination of exports, 1985 (%)

	Destination			
Origin	*Industrial market economies*	*East European non-market economies*	*High-income oil exporters*	*Developing economies*
Low-income economies	52	4	4	41
Middle-income economies	64	7	2	28
High-income oil exporters	59	0	1	40
Industrial market economies	71	2	3	24
East European non-market economies	na	na	na	na

Source: World Bank, *World Development Report*, Washington, DC, 1987, Table 13, pp. 226–7.

Indonesia and Nigeria – are responsible for more than 30 per cent of exports by the thirty-six lower-middle-income developing countries. Among the thirty-seven low-income developing countries,[4] exports are even more concentrated. Here China and India together contribute $7 out of every $10 of exports.

As well as being the major generator of exports, the developed industrial nations of the west absorb the greatest volume of exports (see Table 1.2). For every $10 worth of exports from the three groups, developing economies, high-income oil exporters, and industrial market economies,[5] between $5 and $7 are imported by developed western nations. Developing economies also account for substantial dollar import volumes, not surprising in view of the large number of countries (ninety-three) in this category, as well as their lack of self-sufficiency in most areas.

Export commodity structure

Various export trade structures are evident in Table 1.3. Most marked is that of the high-income oil producers, where fully 98 per cent of all export dollars are in the fuels, minerals, and metals category. Low- and middle-income economies generate more than 50 per cent of their exports from this same category and other primary commodities, but are diversifying their export base (rates of export growth for manufactures have outpaced those of primary goods over the last twenty years – see Table 1.4). Lastly the export emphasis for industrial market economies is on manufactured products, these making up almost 80 per cent of total export volume.

Exports and economic development

A clear relationship between exports and economic development is seen when the average exports per country group are charted. Four distinct groups are apparent in Figure 1.1: countries of the First World (average exports of $65.7 billion); the Second World ($25.1 billion); and two groups from the Third World: high-income oil exporters ($15.9 billion) and upper-middle-income economies ($13.7 billion); and finally, lower-middle-income ($2.5 billion) and low-income economies ($1.4 billion).

Summary

This discussion shows that the industrial market economies of the west dominate international trade. These countries are not only the greatest source of exports, but also the largest destination point for exports from other country groups. Developing countries, high-income oil exporters, and East European non-market economies all play a relatively smaller role in world trade, but countries within

Table 1.3 Structure of exports, 1985 (%)

Country groups	*Fuels, minerals, and metals*	*Other primary commodities*	*Machinery and transport equipment*	*Other manufactures*	*(Textiles and clothing)*[a]
Low-income economies	25	31	4	41	20
Middle-income economies	40	19	14	27	9
High-income oil exporters	98	0	1	1	0
Industrial market economies	11	13	40	37	4
East European non-market economies	na	na	na	na	na

Source: World Bank, *World Development Report*, Washington, DC, 1987, Table 11, pp. 222–3.
Note: [a] Textiles and clothing is a subgroup of other manfuactures.

Table 1.4 Export growth rates, 1965–85

Country group	*Annual change in export volume (%)*		
	1965–73	*1973–80*	*1982–85*[a]
Developing economies	4.9	4.7	4.6
Manufactures	11.6	13.8	8.2
Primary goods	3.7	1.2	1.9
High-income oil exporters	15.9	1.1	−15.9
Industrial market economies	9.5	5.6	3.9

Source: World Bank, *World Development Report*, Washington, DC, 1987, Table A.8, p. 175.
Note: [a] 1985 data are estimated.

Figure 1.1 Average exports per country (1985)

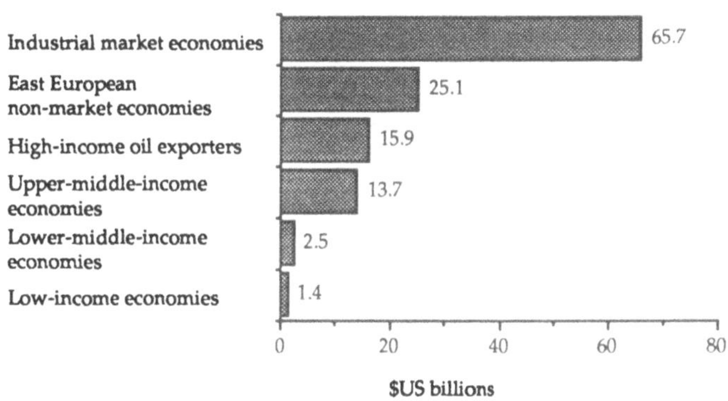

these groups are seeking ways to improve their export performance further. This is a particularly acute need for countries whose exports are concentrated in primary commodities and/or sold to a restricted number of markets. Despite their dominant position in international trade, developed western nations are also active in their export promotion efforts, as we shall see.

Individual countries

Passing reference was made above to the position of a number of countries in world trade. Here, we look in more detail at the importance of exports to the major trading nations for which data are available. Among the industrial nations, Belgium, Ireland, and the Netherlands earn more than a half of their GNP from exports, with most others earning 20 per cent or more of GNP from exports (see

Table 1.5 The importance of exports to major trading nations

Country	*Exports as a % of GNP 1985*	*Percentage of world exports 1985*
Industrial		70.0
Belgium	67.0	3.0
Ireland	61.3	0.6
Netherlands	54.1	3.8
Norway	33.0	1.1
Sweden	31.7	1.7
Denmark	30.6	0.9
Germany	29.4	10.3
France	30.3[a]	5.7
Canada	28.8	5.1
New Zealand	28.2	0.3
Finland	28.0[b]	0.8
Switzerland	27.5	1.5
Austria	25.9	1.0
Italy	22.2	4.4
United Kingdom	21.9	5.6
Spain	15.6[b]	1.3
Australia	13.9	1.3
Japan	13.3	9.9
USA	5.3	11.9
Africa		3.7
South Africa	32.7	0.9
Nigeria	17.9[b]	0.7
Asia		9.9
Singapore	119.0	1.3
Malaysia	51.0	0.8
S. Korea	35.8	1.7
Indonesia	23.3	1.1
Thailand	20.8	0.4
Philippines	17.7	0.3
China	11.6[c]	1.5
Pakistan	9.3	0.2
India	4.1	0.4
Hong Kong	na	1.7
Europe		3.5
Hungary	43.7[a]	0.5
Portugal	30.7[a]	0.3
Romania	23.5	0.7
Yugoslavia	22.7[d,e]	0.6
Poland	15.6	0.6
Greece	15.0	0.3
Turkey[a,b]	14.1	0.4
Middle East		5.9
United Arab Emirates	54.7	0.8
Kuwait	45.1	0.6
Saudi Arabia	43.7	1.2
Libya	41.0[a,b]	0.6

Table 1.5 contd.

Country	*Exports as a % of GNP 1985*	*Percentage of world exports 1985*
Israel	27.4	0.3
Egypt	11.3[b]	0.2
Iran	7.7	0.7
Western hemisphere		5.5
Venezuela	50.0	0.7
Colombia	33.2	0.2
Chile	22.1[e]	0.2
Peru	21.6	0.2
Ecuador	20.3	0.2
Mexico	13.7[b]	1.2
Argentina	13.6[a,e]	0.4
Brazil	13.2[b]	1.4

Source: Derived from *International Financial Statistics*, 1987 Yearbook, International Monetary Fund, Washington, DC, 1987.
Notes:
[a] Data for GDP
[b] Data for 1984
[c] Data for National Income
[d] Data for Gross Material Product
[e] Data for 1983

Table 1.5). Countries with small domestic markets (Norway, for example) are seen to be most dependent on exports. In contrast, the large home markets of Japan and the USA make exports less important to their economies. It must be remembered, however, that while less dependent on exports, these two nations generate the world's largest and third-largest export volumes.

It is not only in the industrial world that nations are highly dependent on exports. Confirming earlier discussion, the data show that exports are extremely important for many oil-producing countries. More than 40 per cent of GNP is accounted for by the (largely oil) exports of Malaysia, the United Arab Emirates, Kuwait, Saudi Arabia, Libya, and Venezuela. Other notably export-dependent nations include South Africa, Singapore, South Korea, Hungary, Portugal, Israel, and Colombia. Singapore deserves a special note since exports are 119 per cent of GNP and imports 135 per cent. These statistics are explained by Singapore's special role in world trade as an offshore assembly platform, with large volumes of imports supporting outward-focused production. The ten nations with the largest export/GNP ratios in 1985 are shown in Figure 1.2.

As well as recording the importance of exports to individual nations, Table 1.5 also shows how much these same nations (and their groupings) contribute to world-wide exports. Although the

Figure 1.2 Nations with largest export/GNP % (1985)

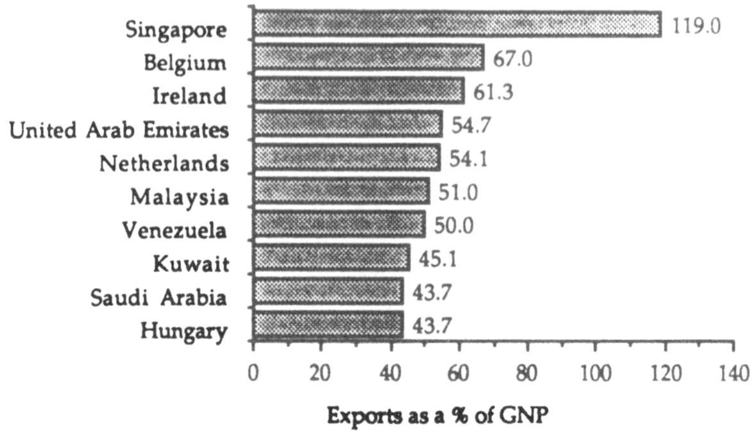

Figure 1.3 Largest export nations (1985)

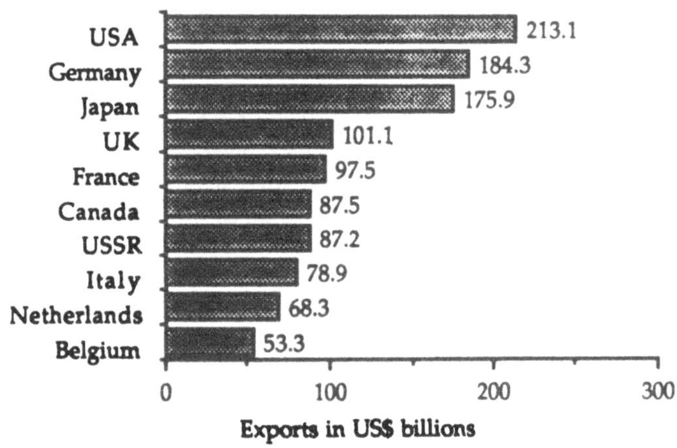

country groupings employed here are different from those of Table 1.1, once again the industrial western nations are seen to dominate world exports (70 per cent in 1985). This position is illustrated in Figure 1.3, where the world's ten largest export nations are charted.

While they dominate international trade, industrial western nations are also intent on improving their export performance further. The world's leading export nation provides an excellent example. US exports were \$213 billion in 1985 (or 11.9 per cent of total world exports), and the following statistics dramatize the importance of this activity:

1 One out of every four acres of US farmland produces for export.
2 One out of every nine US manufacturing jobs produces for export.
3 Eighty per cent of all new jobs in US manufacturing are linked to exports.
4 Every additional billion dollars of export business creates 40,000 jobs in the US.
5 Between 1970 and 1980 the dollar volume of exports grew 500 per cent, whereas over the same period the GNP rose by only 170 per cent.

As well as being the world's largest export earner, the USA also has the distinction of being its largest market. The size and affluence of the US market has acted like a magnet to foreign companies, so that in the mid-1980s one out of every five cars, nine out of every ten television sets, one-half of all shoes, two out of every three suits, and every video recorder sold in the US was imported.[6] Imports totalled \$362 billion in 1985, or \$152 billion more than exports.

This trade imbalance has created a dilemma for the US government. In the short-term it must attempt to reduce the trade deficit – through improved export performance, restricted imports, or a combination of both of these measures. However, given the trend to 'freer' world trade and the 'open' markets this brings, longer-term success will depend less on protectionist measures and more on the competitive ability of US companies – both in foreign markets and at home. Government support through various export promotion programmes will clearly be a major factor in this process.

Companies

Just like the countries that spawn them, companies of all kinds are involved in exporting. An amazing number and range of products are exported by numerous companies. In this discussion we focus on one feature of companies that is relevant from a government support standpoint, distinguishing between those that are large and small.

The importance of exporting to large companies is illustrated by analysis of multinational corporations' operations. Table 1.6 lists the world's twenty largest corporate exporters.[7] Several notable features of this listing deserve comment. First, only one US multinational makes the listing. This is not due to a lack of foreign market

Table 1.6 Largest corporate exporters

Rank	Company	Country	1981 Exports ($US million)	Exports as % of total sales
1	Nissan Motor	Japan	9,088	53
2	BASF	Germany	8,434	60
3	Renault	France	7,395	39
4	Toyota Motor	Japan	7,042	43
5	Daimler-Benz	Germany	6,813	42
6	Volkswagenwerk	Germany	6,536	39
7	Siemens	Germany	6,509	41
8	Boeing	United States	6,106	62
9	Honda	Japan	5,705	75
10	Peugeot-Citroen	France	5,323	40
11	British Petroleum	UK	5,223	10
12	Hoechst	Germany	5,028	33
13	Nippon Steel	Japan	4,877	34
14	Mitsubishi Heavy Industry	Japan	4,590	37
15	Matsushita Electric Industrial	Japan	4,553	29
16	Philips	Netherlands	4,250	25
17	Mannesmann	Germany	4,096	60
18	Brown Boveri	Switzerland	4,031	80
19	Bayer	Germany	3,733	25
20	Hitachi	Japan	3,715	24

Source: Derived from Table A of Stopford, John M., *World Directory of Multinational Enterprises 1982–83* 2nd updated and expanded edition, Detroit, Michigan; Gale Research Co., 1982–83, pp. 113–120. Figures for Boeing are from 'The 50 Leading [U.S.] Exporters', *Fortune*, August 9, 1982, p. 68.

orientation by these corporations but results from their preference to operate through overseas subsidiaries rather than exports. For example, Exxon and General Motors are the world's two largest corporations, and transact all of their overseas business through foreign subsidiaries. This leads to the second point. Fourteen of the corporations listed in Table 1.6 are either German or Japanese. In contrast to US multinationals, these corporations secure a higher proportion of their foreign sales as exports from Germany and Japan. A third feature of the listing of top twenty exporters is the prominence of companies with automobile (seven), electrical/electronic/industrial equipment (six), and chemical (three) interests. These data and others[8] show that exporting – as well as foreign investment – is a significant source of multinationals' earnings from overseas operations. Much more could be made of multinational corporations' exporting activities, but since these tend not to be the target of government export promotion efforts, the discussion will focus more on small and medium-sized companies (SMCs).

It is harder to demonstrate the numeric importance of exports to SMCs than multinationals, since data are much less readily available for the former. None the less, studies in numerous countries attest to the fact that smaller companies are often highly dependent on export markets. In Canada, for example, a survey of 116 exporters showed that small (C$2 million in sales or less) and medium-sized companies (C$2–25 million) generated 37 per cent and 34 per cent of their total sales from exports respectively, as opposed to 20 per cent by large companies.[9] The dependence of some small companies is even more marked. Among eleven SMCs that won Canada Export Awards in 1983–4, the contribution of exports to total sales averaged 77 per cent. One manufacturer of exclusive eyeglass frames was specifically established to export and earns 99 per cent of its sales overseas.[10] Much of Italy's growth in international trade has been achieved by SMCs. In the footwear industry leading exporters typically sell 80 per cent of their output abroad, whereas in the furniture industry the most prominent companies earn 50 per cent of their sales in foreign markets. In both industries the importance of exports to SMCs has grown in recent years.[11]

Export promotion: one form of commercial policy

Given the importance of exports, how do governments pave the way for improved performance? A panoply of different policy instruments impact on export activity, some more directly than others. It is recognized, for example, that domestic economic policy influences exporting as well as the more obvious foreign economic policies.[12] Policy instruments affecting exporting may also operate on the supply or demand side. Supply-side policies not only include initiatives for creating and expanding export production, but also involve the broader matters of transportation networks, port facilities, financial, tax and investment systems. Demand-side policies attempt to stimulate more sales, largely through promotional methods. As far as exporting is concerned, these initiatives include programmes to alert companies to the opportunities present in international markets, and to strengthen the commitment and skills of those already involved. Thus, in a general sense, we can see that governments influence export activity and performance at different levels: through shaping (1) the overall economic infrastructure, (2) specific industrial sectors, and (3) individual companies.

Through initiatives at these various levels, many companies have been encouraged to enter foreign markets to the point where exports are now an important source of their revenue. This is not to say that operating overseas is easy or that it is something every company should do. The majority of companies do not, and never will sell on international markets.[13] This may be because their products are not competitive, or alternatively, better growth prospects exist in the domestic market. Others may not export because of managerial indifference to overseas opportunities. These companies are unlikely to become exporters in the immediate future. Still others may recognize that export potential exists for their products and be interested in tapping this potential. They may never do this, however, because of certain export barriers. With assistance these barriers can frequently be overcome and export operations initiated or expanded. We describe the barriers next, prior to the programmes established to deal with them.

Export barriers

Three main categories of export barrier exist: (1) motivational; (2) informational; and (3) operational/resource-based.[14] Motivational barriers mostly stand in the way of companies that currently do not export, whereas informational and operational/resource barriers afflict both non-exporters and those expanding their overseas activities.

Regarding motivational barriers, non-exporters typically view exporting as more time-consuming, costly, risky, and hence less profitable than doing business at home. This is also the experience (although not so extreme) of companies that do export, confirming the challenging nature of marketing overseas. The fact that exporters endure these conditions, however, indicates that foreign markets – although difficult to tap – can produce useful returns, spread market risk, and provide an avenue for continued expansion.[15]

A lack of adequate *information* is another barrier to exporting. All companies require information so as to examine the viability of exporting but, perhaps, the need is most acute for those that are smaller. These companies are usually at a managerial and financial disadvantage, and this impacts on their ability to collect and analyze foreign market data.

Export markets are often tough to penetrate, especially those that are some distance away and/or culturally dissimilar. This invariably means a sizeable investment of time and money to develop knowledge and experience of foreign market conditions. Yet those are the *resources* in shortest supply, especially among smaller companies. As well, executives in these companies are more sceptical about obtaining export market skills than those in larger organizations.[16]

The implication of this discussion is obvious: unless these barriers to exporting can be reduced, considerable potential for exports will have to be forgone. Government export promotion programmes have been designed in an attempt to deal with these problems.

Government export promotion programmes

Government export promotion programmes include a variety of initiatives to deal with the barriers identified above. Some of these initiatives (advertising, local seminars) highlight the benefits of export involvement, thus providing a *motivational* boost to reluctant managers. Others (market reviews, overseas visits) help companies to assemble timely and inexpensive foreign market data, and so deal with the *informational* barrier. The third *operational/resource-based* barrier is also dealt with in various ways (bid preparation, trade fair participation), easing the burden facing many new or expanding exporters. As well as these direct thrusts, government programmes make an important indirect contribution. They attempt to create a pro-exporting attitude and to assist in making exporting a positive experience for the company. This, in turn, fosters a high level of export commitment – a necessity for success.

These barriers and resulting programmes can be usefully thought of in the context of decisions that companies make about exporting. There are a number of clearly demarcated steps in the export process (see Figure 1.4). Companies normally make the following sequential decisions:

1 Whether to expand their operations through exporting or

domestic market expansion.
2 If through exporting, which market(s) should be targeted.
3 How the selected market(s) should be entered.
4 How distribution, selling, and other operations should be managed.
5 Whether and how operations should be changed in light of company performance in the export market(s) in question.

Figure 1.4 The export decision process

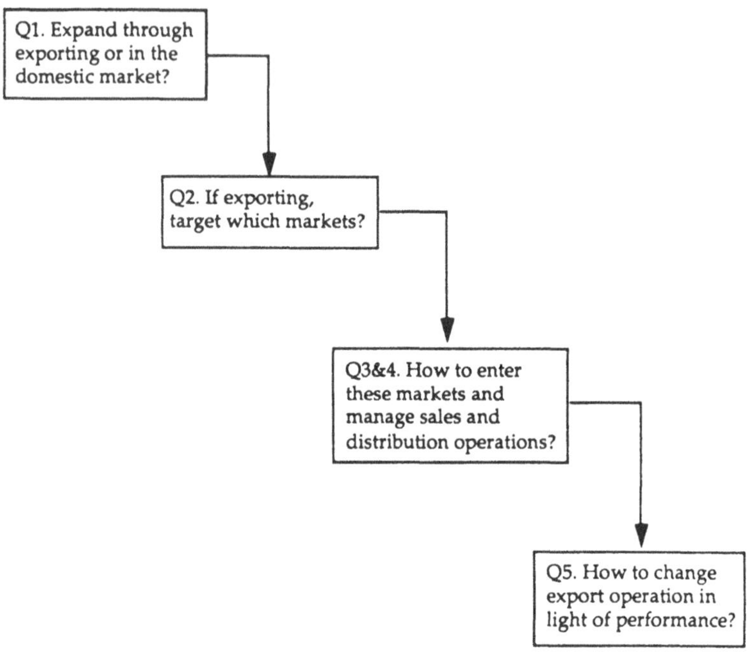

Source: Adapted from S.D. Reid and P.J. Rosson, 'Managing export entry and expansion: an overview', in P.J. Rosson and S.D. Reid (eds) *Managing Export Entry and Expansion: Concepts and Practice*, New York, Praeger, 1987, p. 6.

Not all companies proceed in such a logical manner. Numerous companies get involved in exporting through the appearance of an unsolicited order or because of a need to fill under-utilized production capacity. Such events tend to 'force' companies into exporting. Other companies – even though quite seasoned in the international arena – do no more than 'muddle through'.[17] However, in most cases, Figure 1.4 portrays company decision-making well and will be referred to in later chapters.

Table 1.7 Government export support in various nations

Country	*Government expenditure/$'000 of exports 1976 ($)*	*Comments*
United Kingdom	2.08	Very intensely and actively involved
Italy	1.65	Actively involved
France	1.43	Vigorous
Japan	0.90	One of the best
USA	0.56	—
Netherlands	0.46	Small government programmes
Canada	0.37	Modest but significant
Germany	0.15	Modest: depends on private sector
Switzerland	0.12	Little government participation

Source: Export Promotion Review Committee, *Strengthening Canada Abroad*, Ottawa, Supply and Services, 1979, p. 20.

Although governments recognize the need for improved export performance, the extent and nature of support provided varies dramatically from country to country. The data in Table 1.7 reflect variations among nine industrialized western nations.

The level of support ranges from a high of $2.08 to a low of $0.12 per $1,000 of exports by the governments of the United Kingdom and Switzerland respectively. This translates into values of $94 million for the UK and $2 million for Switzerland. The magnitude of the difference between these levels of support indicates contrasting ideas about and approaches by the governments. Of course, picking extreme values in this way serves to dramatize differences, but the other support levels in Table 1.7 reveal sharp variations by national governments. As well as these differing levels of export support, nations also vary in the aspects of exporting that they emphasize. For example, a study of nine developed and developing countries' export support programmes revealed the following principal areas of support: (1) export planning: no countries emphasize; (2) export production: no countries; (3) export marketing: Canada, Germany, Sweden; (4) export financing and guarantees: France, Italy, South Korea, UK, USA.[18]

Despite the fact that large expenditures of funds have been made on export support programmes in numerous countries, programme results are seldom well documented. Clearly the programmes are held to be useful, but how useful? This question is hard to answer. Aggregate programme evaluations usually reveal positive benefit/cost ratios. However, studies at the company level produce equivocal results, export support programmes being viewed positively in some cases, and critically in others.[19] Generally then, the impact of government export support programmes is not well understood. These points are expanded on in the following chapters and ideas developed for changing this situation.

Plan of the book

In this final section, we outline what the reader will find in the chapters that follow. This acts like a map, giving a sense of the terrain to be covered – what to expect, and when. We also suggest some alternative paths that might be followed, depending on the reader's major interest.

Chapter contents

As the title indicates, this book reviews the role and impact of government export promotion activities, and these topics structure the material that follows. Part II focuses on the role of government export promotion. The role played by governments in developed nations is described in Chapter 2. As might be suspected, comprehensive export promotion support is available in most countries. However, the approach taken does vary, reflecting different philosophies and strategies towards export promotion. Comprehensive reviews of export promotion programmes in three nations are highlighted and a number of trends noted.

Chapter 3 is concerned with export promotion approaches, institutions, and practices in the developing world. The International Trade Centre at UNCTAD/GATT plays a major role in export promotion for these nations, many of which lack the experience or resources to go-it-alone with the development, implementation, and management of their own programmes. ITC's operations are discussed, as are the export promotion efforts of various nations at differing levels of development. Through the establishment of organizations that encourage imports from developing counties, a number of industrialized western nations also play an important role in export promotion. The operations of three of these import organizations are described in an appendix.

Having outlined current export promotion activities in the developed and developing world, Chapter 4 alerts us to the fact that some forms of promotion support might be construed as 'subsidies' and therefore seen as illegal. Hence legal barriers to the use of certain forms of government export promotion exist and need to be recognized. Such barriers operate at international, national, and regional levels, and the appropriate rules for each of these are identified and discussed in some detail.

In Part III of the book, attention turns from the role played by government export promotion to the outcome these efforts produce. The argument developed in Chapter 5 is that export promotion will work best when the programmes offered and used closely match the needs of companies. This may seem obvious but there is evidence that this happens all too seldom. Government export programmes often do not stress the most appropriate support methods, nor do they involve the companies that will benefit most from support. In view of this situation, Chapter 5 provides a review of company needs at various export stages and, in light of this, how export promotion methods might best be targeted.

Chapter 6 makes the point that the impact of export promotion efforts must be measured at both the national (programme) and company levels. It reviews the manner in which evaluations are often done and concludes that present practice leads to (at best) imprecise results. The chapter concludes with recommendations for future evaluations of the impact of government export promotion activities.

The threads of the separate discussion of Chapters 5 and 6 are drawn together in Chapter 7. Given that many studies have been beset with problems, an example is provided of a recent evaluation which embodies many preferred features. The better methods enable the programme–company matching matter to be examined closely, and for programme impact to be measured more accurately.

Finally in Part IV, the emphasis switches from the present to the future. Trends in government export promotion support are highlighted. Budget pressure is one constraint that most governments face and this is causing a reassessment of activities. For some, this means retraction from export support. For all, export promotion support moneys must be spent more efficiently. This reinforces the argument concerning the need for better planning and evaluation of programmes.

Readers and the chapters

We envisage two main types of readers of this book. First, those involved in the design, delivery, and evaluation of government export promotion support, whether at the international, national, state, or provincial level (see Table 1.8). For those who are familiar with and experienced in government export promotion, Part II may be read only lightly en route to the more analytical discussion in Part III. Others that are newer to this field, as well as those who want to get a more global view, will probably do well to read the chapters in order, perhaps dwelling more either on Chapter 2 than 3, or vice versa depending on orientation. Researchers – whether academic or

Table 1.8 Book chapters, reader types, and suggested reading paths

Chapters	*Government programme officials*		*Academic researchers and consultants*
	Experienced	*New to field*	
1 Government export promotion: an overview	lightly	yes	yes
2 Export promotion in the developed world	lightly, depending on interest	yes, depending on interest	yes, depending on interest
3 Export promotion in developing world	lightly, depending on interest	yes, depending on interest	yes, depending on interest
4 Legal barriers to government export promotion	lightly	yes or lightly, depending on interest	yes or lightly, depending on interest
5 Company needs and government export promotion assistance	yes	yes	yes
6 Measuring impact of government export promotion	yes	yes	yes
7 The impact of government export promotion programmes: a case study	yes	yes	yes
8 Government export promotion: present and future	yes	yes	yes

Source: Prepared by the authors.

consultants – are the second major reader group and will also probably benefit from reading the chapters in sequence. Again, depending on interest, Chapters 2 to 4 may receive more or less emphasis. Naturally, we hope that many readers will proceed from cover to cover!

Notes and references

1 F.R. Root, 'The elements of export promotion', *International Trade Forum*, July–September 1971, pp. 118–21.
2 Here we use the groups employed by the World Bank in its *World Development Report*.
3 Middle-income countries are those with 1985 GNP per person of $401 or more, and are broken down into lower (e.g. Philippines: $580) and upper

(e.g. Mexico: $2,080) groups.

4 Low-income developing countries are those with 1985 GDP per person of $400 or less.

5 In this case the trade is between countries within the industrial market economies group.

6 The above statistics are drawn from A.R. Negandhi, *International Management*, Boston, Mass., Allyn & Bacon, 1987; R.W. Waldman, *Managed Trade: The Competition between Nations*, Cambridge, Mass., Ballinger, 1986.

7 Third World multinationals are excluded since their export ratios are not publicly available, thus ruling out any computation of export sales volumes.

8 P.J. Buckley, 'The role of exporting in the market servicing policies of multinational manufacturing enterprises: theoretical and empirical perspectives', in M.R. Czinkota and G. Tesar (eds) *Exporting Management: An International Context*, New York, Praeger, 1982, pp. 174–99.

9 P.W. Beamish, A. Goerzen, and H. Munro, 'The export characteristics of Canadian manufacturers: a profile by firm size', Working Paper Series 8384, School of Business and Economics, Wilfrid Laurier University, Ontario, 1984, p. 9.

10 P. Rosson, M. Brooks, S. Kamath, and D. Patton, *Excellence in Exporting: Advice and Comments from Canada Export Award Winners*, Ottawa, Department of External Affairs, 1985.

11 R. Varaldo, 'The internationalization of small and medium-sized Italian manufacturing firms', in P.J. Rosson and S.D. Reid (eds) *Managing Export Entry and Expansion: Concepts and Practice*, New York, Praeger, 1987, p. 207.

12 F.R. Root, *International Trade and Investment*, 4th edn, Cincinnati, Ohio, South-Western Publishing, 1978, p. 715.

13 Only 8 per cent of US companies sell outside their domestic market. Further it is estimated that a half of US manufactured exports are made by 100 companies and that 80 per cent are made by 2,500 companies: US Department of Commerce, Industry and Trade Administration, 'Seven surprising facts about exporting', Washington DC, Government Printing Office, not dated, p. 1; House Subcommittee on Government Operations, *Commerce and State Department Export Promotion Programs*, 95th Congress, 1st session, 1977, p. 23.

14 S.T. Cavusgil, 'Public policy implications of research on the export behaviour of firms', *Akron Business and Economic Journal*, 1983, vol. 14, summer, pp. 16–22.

15 M.R. Brooks and P.J. Rosson, 'A study of the export behavior of small and medium-sized manufacturing firms in three Canadian provinces', in M.R. Czinkota and G. Tesar (eds) *Export Management: An International Context*, New York, Praeger, 1982, pp. 39–54.

16 F.H. Rolf Seringhaus, 'The process, problem and management perspective of export involvement: a review of the export marketing literature', Working Paper Series 6.68, School of Business and Economics, Wilfrid Laurier University, Ontario, 1986.

17 S.T. Cavusgil, 'On the nature of decision making for export marketing', in *Proceedings*, Marketing Theory Conference, Chicago, Ill., American Marketing Association, 1982, pp. 177–80.
18 National Swedish Industrial Board, *Export Promotion by Government in Nine Countries*, Stockholm, 1984.
19 F.H. Rolf Seringhaus, 'Impact of government export marketing assistance on firms', *International Marketing Review*, 1986, vol. 3, no. 2, pp. 55–66.

Part II

Role of government export promotion

Chapter two

Export promotion in the developed world

Introduction

In this chapter export promotion philosophies and practices in the developed world will be discussed. The concept of export promotion has evolved to become a generally accepted means for enhancing export performance in industrialized market economies since the Second World War. Particular elements which today form part of a country's export promotion efforts, however, predate this time, a good example being the Trade Commissioner Service in Canada. The kinds of general export promotion activities developed countries engage in are broadly agreed upon under the General Agreement on Tariffs and Trade (GATT).

Export promotion was defined in Chapter 1 as public policy measures which actually or potentially enhance exporting activity at the company, industry, or national level.[1] The role of export promotion then is the creation of awareness of exporting as a growth and market expansion option; the reduction or removal of barriers to exporting; and the creation of promotion incentives and various forms of assistance to potential and actual exporters. Because countries differ in their philosophy of business–government relations and their intervention in the private sector, some offer loosely co-ordinated export promotion programmes, while others have strategically integrated programmes. Organizational arrangements to carry out these export promotion activities vary from pure government/public-sector approaches, mixed public/private-sector to quasi-private or wholly private-sector arrangements. These different approaches to export promotion are illustrated in the first part of the chapter through a brief discussion of efforts in selected countries.

Although the focus of this book is on government export promotion, a variety of institutions and organizations exist in developed countries that concentrate part of their efforts on the promotion of trade and specifically exports. These are described in the second part of the chapter. Often such efforts link up with, or support those of the formal export promotion agencies or programmes. Among the major non-governmental organizations are Chambers of Commerce, Industry, or Trade Associations as well as various other organizations such as banks, trading houses, and so on. These sources of export support are particularly useful for small and medium-sized firms, who typically form the largest constituent group and often have the greatest need for assistance and support on exporting matters. Chambers of Commerce, trading houses, and export trading companies are discussed in more detail as examples of private-sector organizations which have an impact on export promotion.

Finally, the chapter deals with the issue of the adequacy of countries' export promotion efforts. In this context, extensive recent reviews of export promotion activities undertaken by the USA, Canada, and Australia governments are summarized.

Commercial policy

There are four main areas of foreign economic policy whose broad purpose it is to regulate, restrict, promote, or otherwise influence the conduct of international trade and investment. These are commercial, investment, foreign aid, and balance of payment policies (see Figure 2.1).[2] Export promotion is but one area of activity within a country's commercial policy. Each of the four policy areas uses particular policy instruments through which government influences foreign economic policy. In theory a country, in pursuit of its national goals, has a range of choices available, from complete self-sufficiency and independence to absolute free trade and interdependence. Realistically governments cannot follow just any foreign economic or commercial policy, but must use their policy instruments to influence trade flows to conform to national goals. Clearly, shifts toward one policy extreme exacts a cost in terms of the other. There is no objective measure of what a country's overall national interest is or ought to be, as this lies in the realm of the political process. From the latter, however, broad directions emerge which find expression in the framework of foreign economic policy.

In industrialized nations, commercial policy is considered the most important of the foreign economic policy areas because of its direct influence on the flow of imports and exports. By the same token, it should be recognized that policy areas and instruments are not and cannot be independent of each other. For example, investment policy affects the international location of business enterprise and thereby not only causes changes in the industrial structure but also affects a country's domestic competitive environment as well as its participation in

Figure 2.1 Areas and instruments of foreign economic policy

Instruments	Commercial Policy	Investment Policy	Foreign Aid Policy	Balance of Payments Policy
Tariffs	●			
Non-tariff trade barriers	●			
Export promotion	●			
Foreign investment restrictions		●		
Foreign investment inducements		●		
Official grants and loans			●	
Fiscal				●
Monetary				●
Exchange-rate adjustment				●
Exchange control				●

Source: F.R. Root, *International Trade and Investment*, 4th edn, Cincinnati, Ohio, South-Western Publishing, 1978, Figure 5.1, p. 120, reprinted with permission.

the global trade arena.[3] The impact of investment policy is thus not only limited to capital but also involves management and technology as forces underlying company behaviour.

Similarly, foreign aid policy often entails a trade–aid linkage through which some portion of foreign aid is funnelled into domestic production dedicated to the aid recipient. Accordingly, any country, industry, or company's foreign trade involvement is directly affected by aid policy. Foreign exchange rates, which abandoned the relatively fixed relationships of the pre-1973 oil shock period, have enormous ramifications for a country's international trade position. Thus, balance of payments policy is also intricately involved in foreign trade and competitiveness issues.

The complexity of the foreign trade environment makes it one laden with conflicts. One central area of conflict concerns the diversity of goals. For example, a nation's pursuit of relatively free trade on one hand, and the desire at the same time to protect certain domestic industries from foreign competition are essentially incompatible.

Commercial policy is interventionist and combines both trade inhibiting and stimulating approaches. The former are tariffs on imports which were historically of great importance, and non-tariff measures of considerable diversity. While tariffs have been negotiated away under the various GATT rounds, a myriad of non-tariff barriers, such as quotas, health, safety and other product standards, buy national laws, and export restraint agreements are employed by governments to influence trade flows.[4]

Stimulation of trade by artificial means such as governments' attempting to encourage the exportation of goods and services is also interventionist in character. Strictly speaking, such trade stimulation is an obstacle to free and economically efficient trade. When gains from trade – in some measure – result from governmental support of marketing or production costs, then these costs are not part of the product price paid by the buyer, but rather borne by the sources of government revenue in the exporting country.[5]

Export promotion has evolved into a widely used, comprehensive instrument of trade stimulation in all major industrialized countries. Some forms of export promotion are generally accepted internationally (under GATT) such as those in Table 2.1. Others, for example direct subsidies (direct financial support by government for export), are in contravention of the GATT agreement. Legal barriers to export promotion are addressed in detail in Chapter 4.

Table 2.1 Major forms of government export promotion acceptable internationally under GATT

1 *Market research* Many governments provide information regarding export opportunities to exporters.
2 *International trade missions* Many regional and national governments support trade missions abroad to bring sellers and prospective buyers together.
3 *International trade shows* Many national or regional governments help to finance trade shows abroad that help promote products of the companies in that country or region.
4 *Trade-promotion offices* Permanent product-information offices in foreign countries can stimulate demand for exports of a country or region.
5 *Government-sponsored research* Government studies can lead to the development of exportable products, for example, the US space programme.
6 *Trade-financing programmes* A government agency can finance or guarantee exports, for instance, the export-import banks of Japan and the USA and the Export Credits Guarantee Department in the United Kingdom.
7 *Insurance programmes* Insurance is necessary to protect receivables from international trade; government agencies sometimes provide such protection.
8 *The rebate of indirect taxes* Indirect taxes are basically charged to domestic, but not foreign buyers; any indirect taxes that have already been paid can be rebated to the seller, for example, the **value-added tax** (VAT), which is prevalent in much of Europe. In contrast, **the rebate of direct taxes** (for example, taxes on profit or property) on exported items is not acceptable. This can work to the disadvantage of producers in countries where direct taxes represent the major share of tax burdens.
9 *Free-trade zones* These zones are areas where **imported** goods can be processed for re-export without paying duties, since they will not be used locally.

Source: C.M. Korth, *International Business-Environment and Management*, 2e, © 1985, p. 94. Adapted by permission of Prentice-Hall, Englewood Cliffs, NJ.

Approaches to export promotion

Direct and indirect means of export promotion

There are two broad categories of approach used by governments to promote exports – indirect and direct programmes. Indirect programmes focus on the production and supply side, while direct programmes concentrate on the market and demand side. Although viewed differently from a public policy perspective, these two approaches are not mutually exclusive. Indeed, at the company level they are highly interrelated. Production and supply factors are shaped by cues and stimuli from the demand side, while the company's market-oriented activities in turn are influenced by these production and supply factors.[6]

Indirect programmes and services include a variety of government support, dealing with

1 productivity,

2 research and development,
3 technology and innovation,
4 manpower planning,
5 regional and sectoral development,
6 fiscal measures such as tax and investment incentive policies,

at both the sectoral and firm levels.[7]

All of these services and programmes have the purpose of improving competitiveness and performance through structural and/or process changes at the company level. As the term 'indirect' implies, however, such change is not specifically for export activities. None the less, export benefits may be derived at some point in time.

Direct export promotion activities include an array of programmes and services that range from awareness-creating, interest-stimulating, research support, export preparation, export market entry, to export market development and expansion focused activities. All of such activities are either information, learning- and experience-intensive, or both. Thus, direct export promotion measures are aimed to influence positively a firm's export competitiveness.

In addition to the indirect and direct export promotion approaches mentioned, there are measures which do not neatly fit into either of these categories, yet can have substantial impact on a firm's export activity. Such measures include the trade–aid interface that occurs when aid recipient countries purchase commodities directly through donor-country suppliers, either through competitive bid or negotiated procurements.[8] Government agencies typically involved in such bilateral or multilateral aid arrangements or industrial co-operation arrangements are for example the Canadian International Development Agency (CIDA), and the Agency for International Development (AID) in the USA.

Some tax policies also play a more direct role than suggested earlier. Value-added tax, which is prominent as a main source of government revenue from indirect taxation in western Europe, Latin America, and other countries[9] is not applied to exports in countries such as France and West Germany.[10] In the international marketplace this creates a direct, price-competitive impact. Depending on the home country cost levels and the relative level of the exchange rate of its currency, such tax policies may enable the firm to reduce a price disadvantage and thus become more competitive.[11]

Subsidies constitute an area of conflict and potential threat to the flow of international trade. Subsidies or export bounties for the purpose of either decreasing reliance on imports or to become more competitive in exports have a history of at least four centuries (in Europe). Although subsidies *per se* are not prohibited under international trading rules, unless they are responsible for economic injury elsewhere, their role in export financing and insurance provided by government has caused considerable friction among some trading nations. Credit-Mixte, or providing an export finance interest rate below that which foreign competitors have to pay (through a mix of short- and long-term loans) can produce a competitive advantage. As the USA and Canada experienced in the late 1970s, subsidized foreign export credits are most injurious when market rates of interest are high (or a large differential across markets exists) and when the foreign exchange value of the dollar is relatively high. Buyers in the international market typically are more likely to turn to foreign products benefiting from such export subsidies.[12]

Philosophies and strategies of export promotion

Broadly speaking, export promotion programmes attempt to influence the firm in three phases. In phase one, companies should be motivated to become involved in exporting through awareness of opportunities and advantages to be derived from pursuing such opportunities. Awareness of the existence of support programmes also falls within the scope of this phase.

In phase two, companies' needs relative to export involvement must be understood and met by assistance programmes in an effective manner. This means providing the right information to the right firms at the right time. This involves not only objective information requirements such as those met by, for example, UK's computerized Export Intelligence Service (EIS),[13] but also various other services that assist in the planning and preparation of the export involvement process. Information-facilitating services which aim at improving managerial expertise and knowledge through learning and experience are equally as important.

The third phase generally addresses the process of introducing a firm's products in a foreign market. This is a more intensified extension of activities of the second phase described above. Information and knowledge acquired through learning and experience is the most critical part of a company's export-related needs.[14]

There is an implicit need to recognize that export promotion efforts and a company's export market involvement process have to be co-ordinated if this mode of business/government interface is to produce benefits. Figure 2.2 suggests such co-ordination.

As was noted earlier, common objectives of trade and international competitiveness provide the premise for countries' export promotion activities. Different programmes and services are broadly aimed at

***Figure** 2.2* Co-ordination of government and company activity for exporting

		Time / Experience →		
Export process in company	- conceptual:	attitudinal	structural	procedural
	- actual:	adoption process	implementation	export operations
Focus of government assistance		increasing export awareness	structural assistance	expanding foreign markets and sales

Source: Adapted from P.S. Linden. *Developing a Mode of Exporter Identification: An Attempt to Integrate U.S. Government Export Promotion Initiatives with Company Development*, Washington, DC, US Department of Commerce, March 1980.

different stages in a company's exporting process. A company in the export planning stage certainly has different needs form one about to enter a new market, or one already actively involved in export operations.[15] This idea is developed further in Chapter 5.

Figure 2.3 shows that export promotion programmes and services surveyed in twelve developed countries attempt to match specific export support to different parts of the exporting process.

In these developed countries, several distinct similarities in export promotion approaches are evident. Similarities include

1 information services, market research, contact-facilitating programmes such as trade missions and trade fairs,
2 programme focus on small- and medium-sized companies,
3 broad emphasis on planning for export involvement and export market entry.

Most types of programmes appear universally available across these countries. One major exception is assistance so that foreign buyers can visit the exporting country. This type of programme is not provided by Austria, France, West Germany, or Italy. The rationale for this may relate to the notion that exporters learn more about operating in a foreign market environment through visits to the market being considered.

In addition to the similarities in programmes and services a number of significant differences exist across these countries as to organization, strategy, and coverage. In terms of organization,

Figure 2.3 Export promotion in twelve developed countries

Stage of Exporting Process	Major Service Type	COUNTRY											
		AUSTRALIA	AUSTRIA	BELGIUM	CANADA	FRANCE	ITALY	JAPAN	NETHERLANDS	SWEDEN	UNITED KINGDOM	UNITED STATES	WEST GERMANY
Pre-Export	Export Motivation Programmes	●	●●	●●	●	●	●	●	●●	●	●	●	●
	Information Services	●	●●	●	●	●	●	●	●	●	●	●	●
Market Entry	Market Research Programmes	●	●●		●	●	●	●	●	●	●	●	●●
	Trade Mission Programmes	●	●●	●	●	●	●	●●	●	●	●	●	●●
Market Entry / Export Operations	Export Financing/ Insurance Programmes	●	●	●	●	●	●	●	●	●	●	●	●
Export Operations	Foreign Buyer Programmes	●		●	●			●	●	●	●	●	
	Trade Fair Programmes	●	●●	●	●	●	●	●	●	●	●	●	●

Note: ● programmes offered by public sector/government.
●● programmes available through or assisted by quasi-private institutions such as chambers of commerce, industry associations, etc.

Source: Adapted from F.H. Rolf Seringhaus, 'Export Promotion: The Role and Impact of Government Services', *Irish Marketing Review*, vol. 2, 1987, Exhibit 1, p. 107, reprinted with permission.

arrangements vary from mixed public-private (Sweden and Japan) and quasi-private institutions (West Germany) to almost wholly government-led export promotion programmes (France and Canada). Regarding strategy, some countries have systematic, integrated, and firm-strategic approaches to assisting firms in export market involvement (primarily Austria, Sweden, France), whereas others operate much more loosely (Australia, Italy). Finally, services and programmes vary from very extensive (UK) to much less extensive (Japan).[16]

Most of the countries use public-private or quasi-private organizations to deliver export promotion. This stems from the fact that the focus of such assistance is on the private sector. Extensive involvement of that sector therefore enhances the practical relevance of export promotion support.

In the USA and Canada, private sector organizations are relatively remote from the commercial policy formulation process and have only minimal influence on export promotion, when compared with similar institutions in European countries. Japan, with its close business–government relationships and trading companies' extensive role in international trade, must be regarded as a special case in this context.

The Japan External Trade Organization (JETRO), organizationally situated within the Ministry of International Trade and Industry (MITI), has as its chief purpose the support of trade between Japan and its trading partners. This means imports as well as exports. Indeed, with the ascent of Japan as a major global economic force, the necessity for export promotion has waned so that in recent years most of JETRO's efforts have been directed at the promotion of imports to Japan.[17] Furthermore, a special organization has been created, the Manufactured Imports Promotion Organization (MIPRO – see appendix for details), to lend strategic direction to foreign firms' access to the Japanese domestic market.

Although Japan's export promotion efforts are defined as falling into the mixed publicly-private sector form of organizational arrangements, the role of KEIDANREN (the Federation of Japanese Industries), which also includes the trading houses, is significant in the context of export promotion. Thus, when viewing export promotion activities in Japan, most of such activity actually transpires at this private-sector level.

Table 2.2 summarizes the different strategic approaches and the main forms of organizational arrangements employed to develop and provide export promotion in major developed countries.

The firm-strategic approaches such as those in Austria, Sweden, or France go beyond the traditional offering of a loosely co-ordinated set of programmes and services found in other countries. They emphasize a strategic application of programmes and services compatible with an individual firm's competitive competence. Such export promotion assistance is phased over a specific period of

Table 2.2 Characteristics of export promotion policies in developed countries

Organization arrangements	*Strategy approach*	
	Loose co-ordination	*Integrated, strategic*
Government/ public sector	co-operative approach to reduce conflict in objectives, programmes between federal and secondary levels of government; some consultation with private sector on programme development; strategic view within certain programmes but not on the overall export promotion effort (e.g. Canada, Australia)	clearly integrated strategic goal, task and responsibility assignment; specific firm, industry, market objectives which are guided, monitored, and evaluated (e.g. France)
Mixed public/ private sector	government involvement restricted, industry associations, chambers of commerce and trade promotion councils undertake co-operatively developed, contact-intensive foreign market activities (e.g. Netherlands, Italy)	partnership approach under specific trade policy and/or jointly developed objectives; extensive sharing of private/public resources to conduct export promotion; strategic planning to effect firm commitment and export involvement (e.g. Sweden, UK)
Private sector	extensive network of chambers of commerce and industry associations maintains close links with firms; provides information, research, and counsel in planning, preparation, and development of export trade at firm level; minor role of government in export information and promotion in foreign markets (e.g. West Germany)	similar in scope to above, except infrastructure links with firms are obligatory; strategic planning emphasis to preparing firms for support to ensure experienced exporters are up-to-date on opportunities (e.g. Austria)

Source: Adapted from F.H. Rolf Seringhaus, 'Export promotion, the role and impact of government services', *Irish Marketing Review*, 1987, vol. 2, p. 110, reprinted with permission.

foreign market development, and is closely co-ordinated and managed between firm and programme agency.

Countries following the loosely co-ordinated approach show no such evidence of a phased and integrated process of assistance. Rather, a range of individual export promotion programmes is made available and companies are able to make use of the programmes or services without needing to demonstrate that it is consistent with an overall export management approach.

Profiles of export promotion in selected countries

In an attempt to provide a more comprehensive perspective on these differences in approaches to export promotion, one country from each of the cells in the strategy matrix of Table 2.2 is profiled below.

Canada (loose co-ordination/government dominated)

Export promotion support at federal government level consists of three key elements. First, general support includes a diverse number of publications on market profiles, market strategy plans, market or sector-specific export policies and opportunities. Industry sector branches and computerized data banks (such as BOSS – Business Opportunity Sourcing System and WIN – World Intelligence Network) are other resources. Second, the Trade Commissioner Service has as one of its major tasks the promotion of export sales. It also acts as an export consultant in all phases of export marketing. Third, the Program for Export Market Development (PEMD) offers specifically designed sub-programmes. The overall objective of PEMD, namely to stimulate economic growth in Canada by increasing export sales, is pursued through two programme streams, one government-initiated, the other industry-initiated.

The government-initiated export assistance includes trade missions and trade fairs, where participation is by invitation only, usually with a specific industrial sector or product focus. To be eligible to participate, a firm must be judged to be export-ready. In addition to the organizational assistance, government shares a company's cost of participating in these events.

Industry-initiated support activities include participation in international trade fairs, individual visits to overseas markets or by foreign buyers to Canada, project bidding assistance, establishment of export consortia, assistance in setting up overseas sales offices, and several special activities for non-profit organizations. Industry-initiated export promotion support is repayable – generally over a period from six months to two years – if the participant is successful and generates sales as a result. A somewhat more systematic export promotion approach is attempted through co-ordinating several activities for a firm under a one- or two-year marketing agreement.

In addition to these export promotion activities, there are several federal crown agencies which provide export-related services, as for example export financing and insurance. Beyond the federal level are provincial government export promotion services with region-specific objectives. Such programmes generally complement federal programmes, albeit on a smaller scale.[18]

The Netherlands (loose co-ordination/public-private sector involvement)

Government export marketing assistance covers basic informational services as well as trade fair and mission programmes, albeit on a relatively modest scale. Industry associations and chambers of commerce are involved with government in a co-operative market planning approach to exporting; specific government support, in turn, is directed to small and medium-sized companies. The focus is on foreign market entry and subsequent support in solidifying market presence. Activity abroad is highly contact-intensive in the form of exhibitions and fairs, technical weeks, symposia, and other promotional meetings. Such activities are supported for individual companies, as well as for groups of companies, for example, those organized by industry associations. In addition to such government support, export marketing assistance is available to companies from the Nederlands Centrum voor Handelsbevorderung (NCH), a council for trade promotion which is supported financially by the government. Dutch chambers of commerce abroad generally serve in a complementary manner to these efforts.[19]

West Germany (loose co-ordination/private sector dominated)

The West German government chooses to play a minimal role in the promotion of its companies' exports. This means that the task is undertaken by the private sector. Only in isolated instances do foreign government posts become involved in foreign markets on behalf of industry. Commercial enquiries received by embassies or consulates are passed on directly to the appropriate chamber of commerce. Thus, export promotion differs from that of other countries both in philosophy and delivery of services. Domestically, the chambers of commerce and a multitude of industrial associations and organizations maintain the closest possible links with individual companies and provide information and counsel on exporting. The Federation of German Chambers of Commerce has created an organization of German Chambers of Commerce abroad (AHK) which are a catalyst for bilateral trade promotion. In terms of the earlier Canadian discussion, AHK can be viewed as providing a trade commissioner service, and industry sector branches, all rolled into one. For a fee, AHKs offer a comprehensive array of information, market research, and individualized counselling/seminar services on foreign market involvement. The interesting feature is that these services are available to domestic German companies wishing to export and to foreign companies who want to export to Germany. While there is minimal public funding support of the AHK (5 per cent of their budget comes from government, 95 per cent from the private sector), all German companies are required to be members in the chambers of commerce and thus finance these institutions. Their primary services are to provide information and enable contacts to be made. Export financing and export insurance services are provided respectively by the Ausfuhr Kredit Gesellschaft (AKG) – an export credit agency for the West German commercial banks – and HERMES Kreditversicherungs A.G. – a private insurance company which handles export guarantees backed by the federal government. Although the federal government maintains a *laissez-faire* attitude towards business, it is fundamentally committed to a highly internationally oriented private sector. Thus, it has assumed the role of guarantor – through HERMES – of export transactions.

Trade fairs have been a traditional mainstay in German export development and for this reason government shows an ongoing interest (through consultation with Chambers of Commerce) in the use of international trade fairs as an instrument for development of new markets, contacts, and maintenance of existing trade relations.[20] Various umbrella organizations are involved in providing organizational support and structure to the trade fair medium of export promotion, among them are Ausstellungs- und Messe-Ausschuss der Deutschen Wirtschaft (AUMA) which assists trade organizations in trade fair participation. Also, on a minor scale, some specific export counselling is available from government to small and medium-sized companies. These two types of assistance are available federally and from the regional government of North-Rhine-Westphalia, the German industrial heartland. While general information on foreign markets is also routinely available from the government office for foreign trade information (Bundesstelle fur Aussenhandelsinformationen), banks, which have traditionally been committed to the promotion of foreign trade, are another information source for a company.[21] Most company-specific information, however, is provided through the Chambers of Commerce, both domestically and abroad.

France (integrated/government dominated)

France has an extensive programme of export assistance organized at the federal government level. There is, however, input from the private sector into the planning of such activities through representatives on the administration council. Policy control for all services for exports rests with the Direction des Relations Economiques Exterieures (DREE) under the Ministry of Economic Affairs and Finance. Programmes are administered through semi-public autonomous organizations such as Centre Français du Commerce Exterieur (CFCE) or the Direction de la Promotion et du Comité

Français des Manifestations Economiques à L'Etranger (DM-CFME). CFCE provides export marketing assistance in terms of comprehensive information services and market research for key industries and market regions. The focus is on small and medium-sized companies with little or no export experience. Such companies are assisted in all aspects of opportunity analysis and export strategy formulation. DM-CFME, on the other hand, handles the promotion of products abroad through trade fairs; French Weeks; floating exhibitions; and the Promosalons programme. The latter provides organization support to promote buyer/seller contact and assists with marketing of French products. The consular service plays an important role in export marketing assistance generally and specifically where direct foreign contact is involved, as in the case of the substantial trade mission programme, and in the activities associated with Promosalons. A relatively minor role is played by the French Chamber of Commerce in foreign markets. Its activities are mainly complementary to the government efforts in promoting export involvement.[22]

Sweden (integrated/private-public sector involvement)

In terms of scope Swedish export promotion assistance is similar to that of Canada, the USA and the UK; however, the organizational set-up underlying Swedish support differs from these others. The Swedish Trade Council – an organization of 50 per cent private and 50 per cent government ownership – is the main agency conducting export promotion. The Trade Council's basic task is to provide competent, effective, and easily available service to exporters, that is to supplement and strengthen the companies' own export operations. Export promotion policy is the responsibility of the domestic organization of the Trade Council. This policy is implemented through the Council's foreign trade offices which act as consultants to the Swedish Trade Council, and by provincial Development Funds domestically. The Development Funds are regional offices with a mandate to assist small and medium-sized companies with marketing planning and strategy and occasionally with financing requirements. The trade commissioners for foreign offices are recruited from industry and return there after their tenure. The foreign offices are non-governmental but work closely with government and the Trade Council. The overall export promotion focus is on creating export involvement. Within this objective, Trade Council and Development Funds maintain close contact and they co-operate by advising companies on how to become exporters. This involves screening of companies as to their competitive capability. Then, two to six foreign markets are identified that offer good exporting prospects.

This process involves the respective trade offices which synchronize their assistance to the firm with that of the Development Fund. The specific promotional tools, such as fairs, trade missions, study trips, are chosen jointly after the screening process is completed.

The systematic approach used by the Swedes is company-specific. Companies are expected to show a high degree of commitment to export involvement (they have the option to back out at any stage). The process of export development at company level from initial contact with the assistance programme to market entry and first sales takes about one to one-and-a-half years.[23]

Austria (integrated/private sector dominated)

The Austrian government provides no export marketing assistance whatsoever: all export promotion activity is handled through the Bundeskammer. This institution is similar to a Chamber of Commerce; however, it plays a substantially more important role in the Austrian business setting and foreign market/trade involvement. Business links with the Bundeskammer are ongoing and regular and, in the case of exporters, importers, and all industry or trade associations, obligatory. Considerable emphasis is placed on assistance to companies in the pre-export stage; that is the export planning and preparation phases. In this context, managerial training in export activity as well as in technical matters, such as export documentation, is looked upon as a key to creating pro-exporting attitudes and export motivation, especially among small and medium-sized firms. The Bundeskammer and the trade commissioners abroad provide concentrated support to companies seeking foreign customers. One role of trade commissioners is to act in an advisory capacity based on their specific knowledge of market opportunities. There is also an ongoing assistance service for experienced exporters with emphasis on objective information that tends to be country-, industry- or technology-specific.[24]

A question of effectiveness

A pertinent question arises from this discussion of strategic/organizational approaches. Would we expect the strategic/private approach to out-perform the loose/public approach? On the one hand, it can be argued that the private sector should accomplish business tasks – such as promoting exports – more efficiently and effectively than a public sector bureaucracy. On the other hand, some public sector approaches (such as France) have introduced a strategic planning focus and appear very effective, while others (such as Canada) seem to achieve good export promotion results without a strategic approach. Finally, a joint public-private approach can be advantageous in that it combines the goal-oriented business management approach with the macro view, organizational and resource network strength of government.

More precise comparisons or evaluations of the relative effectiveness of different strategic approaches and organizational arrangements are currently not possible. The reasons are that first, export promotion systems in different countries evolve with a certain consistency: that is a country with a public sector export support system does not suddenly turn this activity over to the private sector or vice versa. Second, the business culture varies across countries and promotion initiatives tend to be matched to such characteristics. Thus, a system that works well in one setting may not do so elsewhere. Third, evaluation and impact measurement of export promotion activity is in its infancy, so that uniform or broadly comprehensive comparisons of different export promotion systems are not currently feasible. (Chapter 6 deals in detail with the issue of impact and effectiveness of export promotion.)

Summary

Three factors explain differences in the comprehensiveness of export promotion programmes in various countries. First, the economic size of the respective country and its foreign trade sector. Thus, in Austria or Sweden a relatively small number of companies are involved in the countries' large foreign trade dependence. This allows for greater focus and strategic approach to export promotion, whereas in the USA, with a large domestic market and small number of companies in the foreign trade sector, a lesser degree of importance is given to the area of export promotion. Second, the attitude of the private sector toward foreign market involvement. Companies in countries with small domestic markets are more likely to consider foreign markets for growth and expansion and have a need for export support. Often, however, interest in and initiative for foreign market involvement need to be stimulated. Third, ability and willingness to recognize and respond to the areas of greatest need (or obstacles) in the development or enhancement of competence for such involvement abroad. Overall, the extensiveness and similarity of programme portfolios suggests that developed countries

1 attempt to cover the full spectrum of export market involvement,
2 differentiate services and programmes over different export phases according to perceived need,

3 recognize the relatively greater need for external assistance among small and medium-sized companies.

Export promotion in the private sector

Overview of role and activities of non-governmental organizations

Various non-governmental organizations play a role in the promotion of exports. This role varies in importance given countries' differing philosophy of export promotion. Private sector organizations whose aim it is to contribute to the development of exports do so in conjunction with government. Generally this is not a competitive or confrontational co-existence but one that is complementary.

The following list of private sector organizations which engage in export promotion provides an overview:

1 Chambers of commerce
   - local chambers of commerce
   - national chambers, national and international associations of chambers
   - national chambers abroad and bi-national chambers

2 Industry and trade associations
   - national, regional, and sectoral industry associations
   - associations of trading houses
   - mixed associations of manufacturers, traders, and other bodies

3 Other organizations concerned with trade promotion
   - organizations concerned with export training
   - organizations carrying out export research
   - regional export promotion organizations
   - world trade centres
   - geographically oriented trade promotion organizations
   - export associations and clubs, international business associations, world trade clubs
   - organizations concerned with commercial arbitration

4 Export service organizations
   - banks
   - organizations in the transport sector (airlines, shipping lines)
   - freight forwarders
   - trading houses
   - export trading companies

Companies involve themselves in export markets to pursue sales and profits. Private sector organizations, through a variety of export promotion activities, directly or indirectly, assist associated companies in the pursuit of export market development and export-related profits. These organizations generally develop and provide export promotion to companies on a not-for-profit basis. Their orientation is towards the company. This is in contrast with government-supported or sponsored export promotion which seeks to achieve trade balance objectives through the enhancement of competitive competence at the company level. Thus both private and public sector organizations aim to accomplish improved export performance, the difference being one of approach. Overall, if a programme benefits a company, then it is also deemed to be good for the country.

Recognizing the under-resourced nature of many small and medium-sized companies, government export promotion focuses on their needs. This does not mean that there is no room for others to play a role, indeed certain private sector organizations do a useful job in providing individual services developed to satisfy the requirements of associated companies. One important task is to raise export consciousness among the general membership of non-exporters. With growing foreign competition in domestic markets, campaigns aimed at changing the attitudes of member companies towards export market involvement are vital to survival and growth.

Private sector organizations offer substantial resources from which companies can draw. Among the types of assistance provided are:[25]

1 Information and publications
  - information on export incentives and facilities, customs and foreign trade regulations, international finance
  - bid and sell opportunity information
  - periodicals, directories, and reference handbooks
  - newsletters and trade summaries
2 Education and assistance
  - trade awareness and opportunities
  - export documentation
  - advisory, consultative services on export marketing problems
  - joint assistance schemes for small firms
  - access to official export promotion programmes
3 Activities at home
  - congresses, publicity to foster export orientation
  - encouragement of direct contacts abroad
  - dissemination of information about available services
4 Promotional activities abroad
  - promotion of country/product image through exhibitions and publicity
  - assisting firms to make business contacts via trade fairs, joint

booths, trade missions, trade representation
 – facilitating export operations
5 Structuring export promotion activities within the organization
 – advice and counselling at firm level

This listing contains activities which government programmes also cover and, thus, raises the question of duplication and co-ordination. This is an issue not only between government and private sector organizations, but also within each. For example, there may well be export promotion overlaps between government departments and at different levels of government (federal versus state). Equally there may exist a duplication of effort between chambers of commerce and industry associations.

UNCTAD/GATT, in its report on private sector export promotion, addressed the issue of diverse sources of promotion support:

> In almost all countries there is a certain overlapping in the export promotion activities carried out by public and private sector agencies. This is in many cases difficult to avoid. Chambers of commerce, industry and trade associations and similar bodies are membership organizations whose members pay a regular subscription and expect certain services in return: these services include assistance in understanding and penetrating export markets. These organizations are usually smaller than government trade promotion services, and for this reason a more intimate and personal rapport is often established between the member firm and the associations secretariat, than is possible between the firm and a government department or agency. In addition there is often a certain complementarity in the services provided. While they may broadly look the same, there may in fact be differences in their precise nature: this is often true in the information field. The information on export markets furnished by official commercial services abroad, by banks, by chambers of commerce and by industry associations, tends to vary in each case. Each type of organization has its own contacts and its own particular slant and interests. Therefore when many different types of organization engage in export promotion it is difficult to say *a priori* whether this constitutes a wasteful duplication in effort, or whether the different efforts reinforce and strengthen one another; in certain cases competition in the provision of services is a useful stimulus to greater efficiency. Whatever the ideal may be with respect to a rational division of labour in the export promotion field, it is not realistic to suppose that this ideal can be attained in any absolute way: a certain untidiness is bound to persist.[26]

Some co-ordination of export promotion efforts across private sector institutions may seem sensible. However, too much structuring and centralization will almost certainly negate the many benefits local or regional and institution-specific programmes hold for members. Two aspects are important: first the effectiveness of promotion measures from the company's perspective, and second the appropriateness of a given service to a member's needs from the organization's view. Both aims may best be achieved in a setting of direct and close interaction based in a member–organization relationship and not necessarily through more centralized and less personal supra-local or supra-regional organization.

Consultation and co-ordination between public and private sector activities on trade and export promotion matters is not only desirable but also essential in the developed market economies. Co-operative efforts are recognized as valuable and numerous examples attest to this:

> In the late 1960s in West Germany, the Harwarth Commission urged closer collaboration of German Chambers of Commerce abroad with federal government's overseas diplomatic and commercial representatives.[27]
>
> An Export Trade Development Board was set up in 1980 in Canada to strengthen the consultative process and co-ordinate export support services through private sector involvement in the framing of priorities.[28]
>
> In the Netherlands the council for trade promotion (Nederlands Centrum voor Handelsbevorderung – NCH) and the Dutch Chambers of Commerce at home and abroad maintain close co-operative ties with the federal government on export promotion support for private sector firms.[29]
>
> In France private sector input through the administrative council influences the broad planning of export promotion activities. Programmes are administered through semi-private organizations such as Centre Français du Commerce Exterieur – CFCE process.[30]

Private sector organizations often are a structural element in the system that delivers export promotion assistance to companies. In developed countries where government has assumed an active role in the promotion of exports, private sector organizations generally play a lesser and often complementary role. Those countries whose trade promotion philosophy favours minimal government involvement have evolved with an export promotion infra-structure primarily based in private sector organizations.

Chambers of commerce and their role in export promotion

As was shown in the discussion of philosophies and strategies of export promotion, private sector organizations play a significantly larger role in countries where government provides minimal or no export promotion support to business. Austria and West Germany are two cases in point. In the former, the Bundeskammer is of singular importance to the business community in all exporting and foreign market involvement matters. In West Germany the role of chambers has several dimensions; these merit a brief discussion.

The Federation of Chambers of Commerce – the Deutscher Industrie- und Handelstag (DHIT) – heads some sixty-nine chambers of commerce (IHK) in West Germany (with about 1.5 million members) and forty-two German Chambers of Commerce abroad (AHK) (with about 32,000 members). As far as business development is concerned, German business has traditionally been independent from government. The German Chambers of Commerce abroad evolved out of such self-reliance and self-help to aid German business activities abroad shortly after the turn of the century. Their role has since broadened and their focus is bilateral. This means that their activities encourage, promote, and support economic relations and trade between Germany and the respective host country with equal commitment.[31] Not only do IHKs and AHKs maintain close working relationships (because IHKs represent and are closely connected with regional business) but also maintain direct contacts with various organizations in Germany, among them industry associations, trade fair organizations, regional associations, economic development institutions, as well as the business media.[32]

Trade promotion activities of AHKs are functionally oriented and include:[33]

1 contact development between potential business partners,
2 information and advice on business conditions and environment,
3 market research and market studies,
4 contact establishment and liaison with country authorities,
5 information on, representation at trade fairs and exhibitions,
6 assistance for financial transactions,
7 assistance for co-operative arrangements such as joint-ventures, licensing and technology transfer.

Importance of chambers of commerce

In the context of export promotion, chambers of commerce (CC) introduce producers to exporting. The business community is thereby encouraged to explore, develop, and expand foreign market opportunities specifically and to contribute to trade development generally. Chambers in the developed world have a different task from those in developing countries. In the former case, chambers have evolved with industry to support business activities and to help communications within the business sector and with institutions and government. They also perform a lobbying role with government on a variety of issues of concern to business. Depending on the export promotion approach of a country, chambers might play a relatively minor, supporting role for business (as in Canada) or play a widespread and comprehensive role in all aspects of domestic and export business activity (as in Austria).

In developing countries (the subject of the next chapter), chambers are set up as integrating mechanisms, that is they are looked upon as facilitating and building business development and trade development. Chambers are, as a rule, long established and well organized in developed countries. Their position in developing countries however is still emerging and emphasis is being placed, by organizations such as the International Trade Centre (ITC) of UNCTAD/GATT, on strengthening the capability of national chambers of commerce.

Often, relations between government and chambers of commerce in a developing country leave a lot to be desired. Through its work in developing nations, the ITC has come to some general conclusions concerning chambers of commerce:[34]

1 The organization, policies, legal status, etc., of chambers vary from country to country, even within a subregion.
2 Whereas most chambers provide a range of basic services to the business sector, including acting as its representative *vis-à-vis* the government, comparatively few provide extensive services in trade promotion.
3 Where governments organize and manage national trade promotion programmes, the chambers' role in these programmes tends to be unclearly defined. This minimizes the contribution that these chambers, which normally group together the country's most powerful and wealthiest business interests, can make to trade promotion programmes.
4 Similarly many chambers do not perceive for themselves a large role to play in national trade development and particularly in trade promotion programmes, and consequently limit their participation in these. Many chambers have expressed their willingness to participate more fully in trade promotion activities.
5 Chambers often have inadequate organizational structures and

limited legal status, financial resources, and memberships. These adversely influence the range and types of technical services provided.

6 There is evidence, however, that governments and chambers of commerce are beginning to adopt a more constructive attitude towards co-operation in trade promotion.

It would seem logical and necessary for government and chambers of commerce to view each other as mutually beneficial. Developing nations which also have export promotion organizations may also show a more enlightened attitude towards chambers and integrate them into the business development system. One approach suggests that the export promotion organization is responsible for export marketing strategy and research, while chambers concentrate on tasks such as import-export regulations, trade information, assisting with market contacts perhaps through jointly organized trade missions.[35]

International and regional chambers of commerce organizations

Associations of national chambers of commerce such as the International Chamber of Commerce (ICC) or the Association of European Chambers of Commerce and Industry (Eurochambers) essentially fill an umbrella role. Sometimes they act in advisory roles to national chambers, while at other times they attempt to reach consensus on business problems or regulatory complexities.

The ICC is concerned primarily with a range of policy issues for business. It is responsible for the elaboration of many guidelines and codes for both the harmonization and standardization of global business practices. Particular achievements include the development of Incoterms, uniform customs practices for documentary credits, and the ATA carnet system. The ICC acts as liaison and lobbyist with international bodies such as GATT, on issues of taxation, international trade and investment, and insurance. It publishes a range of reports and studies on these topics.[36] The ICC's co-operative efforts with ITC has resulted in several projects that benefit export promotion efforts in developing countries directly.[37]

Eurochambers, in contrast, have as a primary focus problems linked to European integration. This organization seeks to define a common position on the general interests of its members and to create what is called concerted action policy. While its full members are the eleven countries who are EEC members, it maintains associate members among those currently aspiring to EEC membership (Cyprus, Turkey) and correspondence members, some of which belong to the European Free Trade Association (EFTA).[38]

Eurochambers work through committees and working groups. The former address issues of regional policy, including transport, customs, and legal affairs. The working groups engage themselves quite specifically in business and trade development activities. For example, the Foreign Relations Group communicates with European institutions on the views of the business community on trade relations with non-EEC countries. In the case of the EEC's co-operation agreements with the Association of South-East Asian Nations (ASEAN), Eurochambers bring together business interests from the two regions and have created an EEC/ASEAN Business Council. Another concern of Eurochambers lies in the area of promoting the development of European small and medium-sized businesses, particularly through trade and technology, and numerous events and fairs are organized annually toward this end.

Chambers of commerce thus play a useful role in export promotion. Supra-national chambers (such as the ICC or Eurochambers) contribute at the policy level and sometimes at the more applied multilateral country contact level. National chambers have the greatest direct impact on the promotion of exports, although their particular role is tied to a country's philosophy and strategy of international trade. Chambers' function in developed economies is well defined; however, in developing countries it is still emerging, although efforts are underway that could make chambers a more important and effective export support vehicle.

Trading houses and export trading companies

Two types of private enterprise organizations also play a role in the promotion of exports. Their motivation, however, is commercial and profit-oriented in contrast with governmental export promotion which pursues macro objectives. Both aim, in the final analysis, to benefit the firm. Trading houses have a long history of trade involvement and are closely tied to the generic concept of trade. Export trading companies (ETC) are, by comparison, a recent mechanism to foster exports. It is clear that the role of trading houses and export trading companies goes beyond facilitation and is concerned primarily with carrying out exporting. For this reason they are generally not classified as export promotion organizations. As they devote some part of their activity to the promotion of exports, these two important non-governmental organizational forms merit some discussion.

Trading houses

Throughout history, trading houses have been involved in developing international trade flows. Large Japanese trading houses have long been cited as examples of successful promoters of trade. They have been the focus of much recent discussion, largely because of their highly regarded international competitive capability and their ability to adjust to the dynamics of international trading patterns.[39] That is not to say other nations do not have successful trading houses as well (Finland and Sweden have large trading houses, while Canada has a broad trading house sector); however, none equals the prowess of Japanese trading houses.

Japanese trading houses have developed a distinct advantage in territorial knowledge through intra-company international communications channels. This strength serves to overcome the lack of knowledge of what are usually regionally oriented small and medium-sized companies. Thus, trading houses promote exports through their facilitating role.[40] Japanese trading houses trace their history back to the 1870s when Japan's self-imposed two centuries of isolation came to an end.[41] Japan's trading houses, however, were actually preceded by some of Europe's.

The first European trading power in the general form of a trading house was the Hanse whose extensive trading network dates back to the thirteenth century and which continued its major role for nearly six hundred years.[42] Similarly the powerful trading house, Fugger, operated in Germany from the late fourteenth to the early seventeenth century.[43] The East India Company was Great Britain's major organization to enter India, as the Cie Français de l'Afrique Occidentale or the Ste Commerciale de l'Ouest Africain were important to France's trade in Africa.[44] A recent definition states a trading house to be:

> a company engaged in exporting, (and in many cases importing), goods produced by others on a commission, retained or merchant basis and who looks on international marketing business as a significant source of revenue.[45]

A trading house, then provides expertise to its constituent firms.

A national trading corporation concept, based on the philosophy of the successful Japanese trading houses, was recently considered in Canada as a possible structure to enhance exports, particularly as a vehicle to draw smaller firms into exporting. Australia also considered an Overseas Trading Corporation (OTC) which could play a role in situations where government-to-government negotiations are prerequisites to trade and in counter-trade arrangements.[46] Such a national trading corporation would complement the already existing trading house sector, focus on the new growth markets in the Pacific Rim, Latin America, and Middle East, and also engage in third party trade and secondary manufacturing of products as well as providing specialized capital projects services. The key advantage cited would lie in a portfolio concept, which would spread the risk over a range of services. By contrast, private trading houses operate with risk-based approaches. The latter approach each export contract as a single project and generally provide, depending on the firm, a particular kind of service, such as exporting goods to an independent importer in the target market. The portfolio concept employed by a government trading corporation may provide an extensive direct sales and service network, offer pre-export research and market development services, provide better access to marketing to foreign governments, and involve existing facilities such as the Canadian Commercial Corporation.[47]

Export trading companies

The export trading company concept evolved in the USA as an adjunct to an extensive review of export promotion policy in 1980. The recent Export Trading Company Act established in the USA in 1982 is an attempt to capture the spirit of Japanese and Korean trading houses which have contributed significantly to the foreign trade performance of their respective countries. Export trading companies are encouraged to handle broad, multi-product lines. They are intended to eliminate the risks and uncertainties implicit in foreign trade for small and medium-sized companies. Thus they act as entrepreneurial organizers of foreign trade in goods and services.[48] A typical structure of an ETC includes a bank, manufacturers, service firms, or a trading house. These members contribute resources to pursue export opportunities by matching trade needs of suppliers and end users.

The actual configuration of an ETC, as shaped by the purpose defined by its members, may take into account

1 geographical criteria
   - sourcing exports from specific domestic regions or targeting particular foreign markets
2 product criteria
   - trading with a range of compatible products, by specializing in certain industrial sectors, by providing export support services, etc.
3 client criteria
   - specific joint ventures, turnkey projects, matching long-term sourcing needs of foreign importers

The role of an ETC is solely to strengthen export performance in the private sector, however, with a profit-making interest in contrast with government's macro concerns. Three characteristic functions of

Table 2.3 Characteristic functions of an export trading company

Market research and development	*Trade finance*	*Trade flow management*
Market or project analysis and selection; intelligence gathering	Credit risk assessment and related information gathering	Management of product sales, promotion and distribution
Matching the ETC resources (personnel, technology, products) with market objectives	Pre-shipment financing Export or project financing	Packaging, labelling, insurance, customs clearance, and preparation of documentation
Assessment of market entry modes and needed support assistance	Distributor financing Billing, collection, and payments management	Overseas shipping and inland transportation
Selection of product-promotion techniques, channels of distribution and servicing	Foreign exchange management Risk layoff (insurance and government guarantees)	Management of customer services and relations Management of product inventory and spares
Monitoring and adjustments	Performance guarantees (bonds or standby letters of credit)	

Source: P. Verzariu, *Countertrade, Barter and Offsets*, New York, McGraw-Hill, 1985, Table 10, p. 141, reprinted with permission.

an ETC focus on market research and development, trade finance, and trade flow management, as seen in detail in Table 2.3.[49]

Trading houses and ETCs differ in basic activities, as outlined in Table 2.4. It is noteworthy that, in the US example of ETC discussed here, the ETC concept is being adopted by firms and consortia as a mode of export entry and expansion. These ETCs are set up parallel to an existing trading house sector.

Summary

Private sector organizations, both non-profit, e.g. chambers of commerce, and commercial, e.g. trading companies, are seen to play a relatively minor role in export promotion, but one that needs recognition since it is concerned with facilitation of international trade.

While chambers of commerce and trading companies have been discussed in some detail, a variety of other trade- and export-

Table 2.4 Some basic differences between a large trading house and an ETC

Activity area	*Trading house*	*Export Trading Company*
Legal	Operates under existing legislation	Operates under new, untested legislation. Needs government certification.
Organizational	Capabilities span one or more of the following functions: export and import marketing, including representation, transportation, finance including investment, manufacture	Predominant functions are: Export marketing; Export financing
	Is a global firm organized to trade goods from any country	Is essentially a US firm organized to promote American exports
	Has proven and well-integrated multinational organization with sophisticated marketing and communication networks	Effectiveness of ETCs is dependent on the commonality of goals of its members and on its membership structure
	Goal is to import and export	Goal is primarily to export. Most ETCs have limited capability to absorb countertraded goods
Financial	Has untied credit lines	Usually no discretionary lending is available from banks. Financing of individual transactions is reviewed by lending bank.
Commercial	Deals mostly in goods from low-growth industries, e.g. commodities, textiles, machinery	Deals mostly in exports of industrial goods and services, inclusive of high-technology exports. Has potential to process or assemble goods abroad.
	Has as assets established market positions and a staff of import–export traders	Has usually a staff of export (not import) salesmen
	As middleman, operates on high volume and low profit margins	As principal, operates on higher profit margins
	Is at present increasing its representation functions for client manufacturers	Engages as principal in direct manufacturers' sales
	When not registering profits on both exported and imported goods, may be amenable to register an overall net profit in a market over several trade transactions	Normally required set profit margins for individual transactions. May have to use and subsidize brokers to market countertraded goods.

Source: P. Verzariu, *Countertrade, Barter and Offsets*, 1985, New York, McGraw-Hill, Table 12, pp. 144–5, reprinted with permission.

supporting organizations exist in the private sector, all of which have a reservoir of resources potentially of use to companies. Chambers of commerce at the international and regional levels have primarily a co-ordinating role. Their efforts go towards smoothing and simplifying the trading environment. At national levels, chambers are seen to operate at varying levels of intensity and involvement as far as exporting is concerned. In countries such as Austria and West Germany their role is integral and substantial in exporting, while in other nations, e.g. Canada, their efforts are at best peripheral to companies' foreign market activity. Trading companies, whether the traditional trading house or the export trading company, take on a facilitating role for smaller firms who are under-resourced for direct export market involvement.

Reviews of export promotion efforts

Country reviews of export promotion

Export promotion programmes have existed in various developed countries for a considerable time. Today's environment requires that on the one hand nations co-operate economically, while on the other hand governments attempt to increase the competitive competence of their home companies. Thus co-operation and competition is part of their policy agenda. Consequently over the last ten years export promotion programmes have become a larger factor in fostering companies' international orientation and capabilities. Several governments have undertaken formal and extensive reviews of their export promotion activities in light of the changing environment, needs, and objectives.

The most comprehensive examination of available export stimulation mechanisms as well as comparisons of programmes and services among other major trading nations has been undertaken in the USA. In Canada the Export Promotion Review Committee critically examined export promotion at the federal government level. Another extensive evaluation was undertaken in Australia and the report published by the National Export Marketing Strategy Panel. In the UK, with its comprehensive and long-established export promotion efforts, a study published by the Betro Trust Committee of the Royal Society[50] looked at export from a firm-strategic perspective. A key conclusion of this study was the British exporters' attempt to serve too many markets with too few and insufficiently focused resources. This reinforces the need for greater focusing and export promotion support programmes for companies.

To illustrate the nature and thrust of such overall reviews of government's export promotion activities,[51] the US, Canadian, and Australian reviews are summarized and their key conclusions given.

USA

The stimulus for the review lay in the perception that US firms were not exporting to their potential and the simple fact that most firms were not involved in exports at all. Inertia is created in part by the availability of an enormous home market and the psychological barriers in the form of foreign languages and business practices. One major obstacle to a wider export orientation is a lack of knowledge of foreign market opportunities and the skills to successfully pursue these.

Government export promotion programmes aimed at overcoming these problems are[52]

1 Department of Commerce programmes to provide information and direct marketing assistance to exporters.
2 Department of Agriculture programmes to promote agricultural exports.
3 Small business programmes of the Small Business Administration and the Department of Commerce focus on small business and minority-owned firms.
4 Other promotion programmes through a variety of agencies targeted at service industries.
5 Financial and tax incentives such as programmes by the Export-Import Bank, Overseas Private Investment Corporation (OPIC), Commodity Credit Corporation (CCC), Domestic International Sales Corporation (DISC), etc.

A series of regulatory export disincentives was also listed, such as export and re-export controls for national security or foreign policy reasons, code of conduct regulations, or environmental and safety programmes.

This review of export promotion was the most comprehensive ever undertaken by the US government[53] and led to a series of recommendations made by the President's export council:

1 The nation is to become export-conscious and export-oriented, and increase national export consciousness through[54]
   (a) adoption of a National Export goal,
   (b) establishment of a permanent National Export Council,
   (c) increase role of private sector advisory committees in on-going trade negotiations and implementation of trade agreements,

(d) increased export promotion activities of federal, state, and local governments and district export councils and greater accessibility by the private sector,
(e) greater co-operation among government, industry, consumers, and labour to promote, and common national interest in expanding, US exports.

2 Strengthen and integrate the federal government's international trade functions.[55]
An effective national export programme requires a highly competitive domestic trading sector working with a supportive public sector.

3 Eliminate or reduce export disincentives.[56]
Laws and policies which unreasonably or unnecessarily operate as unilateral, self-imposed disincentives on US exports should be eliminated or administered more reasonably.
Among these are:
(a) taxation of Americans working overseas,
(b) extra-territorial application of US anti-trust laws,
(c) foreign Corrupt Practices Act,
(d) US Anti-boycott Laws,
(e) export controls.

4 Improve US export incentives.[57]
Strong encouragement and support to enable US exporters to be competitive through improved assistance in
(a) export financing,
(b) export insurance,
(c) tax benefits,
(d) trading companies.

5 Reduce foreign trade barriers to US exporters through[58]
(a) monitoring and enforcement of US trading rights as provided for in the GATT Tokyo-Round trade agreements,
(b) press for further trade liberalization in markets where US exporters are barred or access restricted,
(c) uphold the principle of free/fair competition in world trade and enforce US and GATT laws against unfair or disruptive imports,
(d) resist domestic protectionist pressures and instead engage in national reindustrialization to increase US competitiveness.

6 US position on East/West trade is supported and a general process of normalization of trade relations with the Soviet Union, other East European non-market economies, and the People's Republic of China is recommended.[59]

7 Increase support for agricultural exports through[60]

- (a) the Commodity Credit Corporation,
- (b) the Department of Agriculture's foreign market development programme,
- (c) improved transportation facilities recommended by the Rural Transportation Advisory Task Force.

8 Improve overall industrial competitiveness through programmes that will foster greater investment which, in turn, will lead to greater competitiveness, productivity, and innovation. A tax system that encourages investment instead of consumption is recommended.[61]

Canada

A review of export promotion by the federal government was motivated by a desire to improve the Canadian balance of trade, while also realizing that companies faced a changing international environment in which to conduct business. Manufactured exports were regarded as essential to improved performance, yet Canada's loss of world share of these products during the expansionary 1970s was a major cause for concern among policy-makers. It was felt that through making export services equal to or better than those other nations offer their firms, manufactured exports could be increased. Three main criticisms of the federal export promotion programmes were pointed out:[62]

1. export financing is not competitive with that of other major trading nations,
2. export promotion programmes are impeded by regulatory procedures,
3. co-ordination is deficient (business-government, between federal agencies, and between levels of government).

These factors combine to hold back the development of exports from desired levels. The review recognized that industrial and taxation policies play an integral role in raising the competitiveness of the private sector. Thus an innovation-encouraging climate, export-supportive taxation, and import substitution policies, while outside the scope of export promotion, are seen as areas requiring review and positive change.

Eight main recommendations resulted from this first formal review of Canada's export promotion programmes:[63]

1. *Fundamental commitment to exports* High-profile public commitment supporting exports – through a supportive federal government with co-ordinated and focused export support services – to foster renewed will to invest in export market

development. Private sector firms should seek international skills and expertise.

2 *Formation of an export trade development board*[64] The purpose of the board is to supervise a focused and co-ordinated approach to export support services. A majority of members are private sector executives. This ensures development of international marketing strategies, identification of priority needs, and co-ordinated delivery of export services.

3 *Tax incentives for innovation and exports* An export-friendly tax system to redress disadvantage compared to other trading nations. The lack of innovative capacity and in-house product design and engineering capability inhibit downstream economic and employment benefits. Thus tax incentives to encourage the development or enhancement of this innovative capability are required.

4 *Export marketing* Encourage greater commercial awareness and involvement in the diplomatic missions abroad. Better manpower management in the trade commissioner service to deepen their trade and economic knowledge. Faster response to areas of growing commercial significance. Streamlined administration procedures for export programmes such as PEMD. Improve ease of access for less experienced firms.

5 *Export financing and insurance* Lack of export competitiveness can be caused by unfavourable financing costs. The agency with its mandate to provide export financing needs to restructure its medium and long-term financing to offer domestic firms rates of international competitive parity. Its insurance coverage needs to be made broader and more flexible, and the agency needs to enter export contract negotiations earlier to assist the exporter in covering the financing/insurance needs.

6 *Trade-aid interface* Trade-aid is an exporting opportunity for Canadian firms. Aid agencies tend to overlook the domestic sourcing option and a fundamental reorientation and co-ordination of aid and domestic sourcing is needed. Aid agency staff need to develop awareness of and expertise in export capabilities and mechanisms (such as export support) to play an effective role in export development. Linked parallel financing of such exports is one aspect that should contribute to bridging divergence between aid policy and commercial capability.

7 *Capital projects abroad* Major turn-key capital projects require consistent high-level ministerial support, as these projects often have a political dimension. To encourage firms to bid on large-scale projects – whose risks are often a threat

to the firm – the creation of public-private facility is recommended to evaluate and assume major risks in procurement and delivery of such capital projects for export markets. The proposed export trade development board would act as a supervising body for this facility.

8 *Export and small business* Small firms with typically limited managerial and financial resources have needs different from large firms. The firms require short-term financing for exports, simpler export credit insurance procedures. Many firms are unaware of export support programmes or intimidated by red-tape and currency risks. Export support programmes should place greater emphasis on the needs of smaller firms and provide incentives for them to overcome problems related to export entry in order that internationally competitive firms can exploit opportunities abroad.

Australia

Similar to the motivation underlying the Canadian review, the Australian assessment of export promotion activity was rooted in economic realities. A growing current account deficit, slipping participation in global expansion of manufactures trade, and a relatively inward orientation among corporate management provided the motivation for the recommended re-focusing and restructuring of export promotion efforts. The review panel described the major goal to be aimed for as the creation of necessary conditions and incentives for a technology-conscious and export-driven manufacturing and services sector.[65]

Key criticisms of existing export support programmes include:

1 Poorly designed and controlled export incentives.
2 A lack of performance orientation in export incentives.
3 Poor co-ordination of government policy and decision-making adversely affecting economic performance in general.
4 Under-utilized government sourcing through aid and offset programmes.
5 Strategic focusing and application of government marketing and promotion resources to markets and products of greatest promise.
6 New technologies development has not been supported as a vital factor in competitiveness.
7 The taxation system lacks reward for risk taking.

Overall, the review panel summarized the role of government in export marketing as (1) co-ordinating the export promotion policy and decision-making and imparting some stability to the measures adopted, and (2) targeting the limited resources on products and markets in order to derive an optimal return on export promotion dollars. Product targeting would require identification of products/industries offering the best prospects for increased export returns and subsequent support for these.[66] Markets would be identified and selected through a product/market approach and funds would be concentrated on those combinations with the best chance of increased returns.[67] Assistance then would be company-specific; however, poor export performers should not be singled out for support, neither should be the top export performers. The former may not generate the return, the latter already have the wherewithal to succeed. One unresolved issue arising from this approach is this: should companies follow government's identified export strategies for particular products/industries or should government assistance focus on and support companies' specific marketing opportunities and initiatives?

Specific recommendations emanating from the review are summarized:[68]

1 Greater co-ordination of government policy and decision-making should be pursued through a newly created Trade Subcommittee.
2 Export incentives, such as export market development grants, require immediate and significant reform so as to eliminate abuse, make them performance-oriented and an inducement to the genuine exporter in a cost-effective and measurable way.
3 Government purchasing through aid and offset programmes is not used to capacity and greater emphasis is to be placed on tied-aid.
4 Export promotion resources need to be allocated in a focused and targeted manner on those product/market opportunities that offer the best chances of success.
5 Capital goods and services industries are to be supported more effectively to pursue significant opportunities overseas.
6 Export development policy should continue to emphasize market maintenance and expansion for existing export products. The New Technologies Export Fund must play an effective role in enhancing competitiveness of products and processes abroad.
7 Governments should encourage direct foreign investment by Australians in support exports.
8 Shipping and logistical arrangements, which currently disadvantage liner users, need to be altered through subsidies to shipping companies.
9 Restructuring of the taxation system to provide incentives and

rewards for risk taking; thus private sector investment would revitalize industry and allow a lowering of protection levels.

Summary

A common thread runs through the export promotion programme reviews and evaluations:

1 A pro-exporting attitude and commitment to exporting are essential.
2 There is a need to motivate firms into export action, that is to motivate companies to become exporters, to maintain, or increase their export commitment.
3 Government's contribution is to stimulate the exporting process while the main commitment of marketing resources would remain with private sector companies.
4 The recognition that countries are interdependent in their trading relationships and that the need for competitiveness is a basic one.
5 A recognition that scarce resources available for export promotion initiatives need to be rationalized and focused on opportunities which deliver the best results in terms of export development and return from supported activities.

Conclusions

Export promotion in developed countries exhibits considerable sophistication and comprehensiveness. Although there is a spectrum of government involvement in export promotion efforts (government-public sector dominated or primarily private sector activity), as well as strategic approaches (loosely co-ordinated to strategic and integrated), export promotion *per se* is an important instrument in commercial policy. In this sense it has a direct impact on a country's import and export activity and affects the overall foreign economic policy.

Export promotion as an artificial trade stimulant is widely used in the industrialized world. There is a broad understanding, under GATT, of those forms of trade promotion that are acceptable and those which are not. The overview of export promotion programmes in selected developed countries reflects, in general, a thorough understanding by the export promotion organizations and agencies of the need to tailor assistance to the changing requirements of a firm over the exporting process. It is apparent that the requirement for export competitiveness in global markets is universal. Thus there is considerable similarity in export support programmes offered while the government philosophy and strategy as well as the programme delivery can differ.

Whether or not one system is better than another remains open to question. Evaluation and impact measurement of export promotion must be much further developed before such comparisons can be made with any validity or reliability.

Although the thrust of this book is on government export promotion, it is recognized that private sector organizations including chambers of commerce, trading houses, and export trading companies can and do play a contributory role in export promotion. The latter two organizations, although privately owned and profit-seeking in contrast with government efforts which have macro objectives, have recently been considered by governments in Canada and Australia as possible additional mechanisms to assist smaller firms in foreign market involvement. In a similar vein, an Export Trading Company Act has been passed in the USA to support export. These commercial organizations, however, lie at the fringe of export promotion as we view this.

Chambers of commerce have long had involvement in export promotion activities, the extent of which is closely linked with the role of government. In Austria the government has all but relegated export promotion to the Bundeskammer, while in Canada chambers are clearly of minor importance. At the international level, the ICC and Eurochambers, for example, provide useful roles at the policy level and sometimes in more direct ways as in helping trade relations.

Several countries have recognized the increasing importance of intensifying global trading relationships and saw the necessity for wide-ranging reviews of their respective export promotion activities. Reviews in the USA, Canada, and Australia point to similar conclusions. Namely firms may need to be motivated into export involvement, export promotion support cannot and should not attempt to substitute for private enterprise commitment and resources, and government export promotion needs a strategic thrust, that is limited resources should be where the most beneficial results for export development can be expected.

Notes and references

1 F.R. Root, *International Trade and Investment*, 4th edn, Cincinnati, Ohio, South-Western Publishing, 1978, pp. 118–21.
2 ibid., p. 115.
3 ibid., p. 119.
4 C.M. Korth, *International Business – Environment and Management*, 2nd

edn, Englewood Cliffs, NJ, Prentice-Hall, 1985, pp. 95–7.
5 ibid., p. 93.
6 F.R. Root, 'The elements of export promotion', *International Trade Forum*, July–September 1971, p. 14.
7 G.P.F. Steed, *Threshold Firms – Backing Canada's Winners*, Science Council of Canada, Canadian Government Publishing Centre, Supply and Services Canada, Ottawa, 1982, Background Study 48, pp. 28–30.
8 *A Basic Guide to Exporting*, US Department of Commerce, International Trade Administration, US Government Printing Office, Washington, DC, September 1986, p. 32.
9 D.K. Eiteman and A.I. Stonehill, *Multinational Business Finance*, 3rd edn, Reading, Mass., Addison-Wesley, 1982, p. 688.
10 M.C. Schitzer, M.L. Liebrenz, and K.W. Kubin, *International Business*, Cincinnati, Ohio, South-Western Publishing, 1985, p. 199.
11 ibid., p. 199.
12 P. Hartland-Thunberg and M.H. Crawford, *Government Support for Exports – A Second-Best Alternative*, Lexington, Mass., Lexington Books, 1982, p. 66.
13 *Export Promotion by Governments in Nine Countries*, National Swedish Industrial Board, Stockholm, Liber Tryck AB, 1985, p. 145.
14 F.H. Rolf Seringhaus, 'Government export marketing assistance to small and medium-sized manufacturing firms: the role and impact of trade missions on firms' off-shore market involvement', unpublished Ph.D. dissertation, York University, Toronto, 1984, p. 55.
15 Chapter 6 will discuss in detail the exporting process and firm needs.
16 F.H. Rolf Seringhaus, 'Export promotion: the role and impact of government services', *Irish Marketing Review*, 1987, vol. 2, pp. 112–13.
17 *Export Promotion by Governments*, p. 93.
18 Program for Export Market Development, *PEMD Handbook*, Department of External Affairs, Ottawa, 1987, pp. 2–14; Seringhaus, 'Government export marketing', pp. 44–53.
19 *Export Stimulation Programs in the Major Industrial Countries: The United States and Eight Major Competitors*, Congressional Research Service, 95th Congress, 2nd Session, Washington, DC, 6 October 1978, pp. 223–42; Ministerie Van Economische Zaken, *Regelingen Voor De Export*, The Hague, Augustus, 1980.
20 O.W. von Amerongen, 'Maerkte Oeffnen und Faehigkeit am Wettbewerb Ueberpruefen', *Welt Report*, Heft 28, 14 December 1983, p. 11.
21 *Export Stimulation Programs*, pp. 131–55. H.L. Weisberg and C. Rauch, *A Comparative Study of Export Incentives in the United States, France, the United Kingdom, Germany and Japan*, Chamber of Commerce of the United States, International Division, Washington, DC, 1979, pp. 8–12, 22–5, 33–7; U. Schwarting, C. Thoben, and M. Wittstock, *Nachfrageverhalten Kleiner and Mittlerer Unternehmen nach Aussenhandelsinformationen und Beratung*, Beitraege zur Mittelstandsforschung, Göttingen, Verlag Otto Schwartz, 1982, Heft 83;

Export Promotion by Governments, p. 44.

22 *Export Stimulation Programs*, pp. 103–30; Weisberg and Rauch, *A Comparative Study*, pp. 8–12, 22–5, 33–7; DM-CFME, *Promosalons*, undated; French Chamber of Commerce, *French Chamber of Commerce in Canada*, undated; *MOCI* 'L'accueil au CFCE', no. 533/13 December 1982, p. 49; *MOCI*, 'Une assistance sur mesure', no. 533/13 December 1982, 51–3; *MOCI*, 'Les informations en libre acces', no. 533/13 December 1982, pp. 59–68; *MOCI*, 'Promotions sur les marches porteurs', no. 533/13 December 1982, pp. 73–7; 'Services publics de l'exportation', no. 537/10 January 1983, pp. 25–8, 34–5; personal interview with Jean-Pierre Filippi, Deputy Commercial Counsellor, Consulate General of France, Toronto, 4 March 1983.

23 *Introduction to a New Export Market*, Swedish Trade Council, 1981; Swedish Trade Council, *Annual Report 1985/86*, Stockholm, 1986; personal interview with Niklas Lidskog, Acting Trade Commissioner, Swedish Trade Office, Toronto, 4 March 1983.

24 Bundeskammer der Gewerblichen Wirtschaft, *Export Services – Ein Leitfaden durch das Service für Exporteüre*, Wien, Ungar Druckerei GMBH, 1982; personal interview with Dr Heinz Paumgarten, Deputy Trade Commissioner, Austrian Consulate General, Toronto, 22 December 1982.

25 *Export Promotion by Private Sector Organizations*, International Trade Centre, UNCTAD/GATT, Geneva, 1971, pp. 25–38.

26 ibid., p. 39.

27 ibid., p. 41.

28 Industry, Trade and Commerce, 'Update on government response to EPRC (Hatch) Report recommendations', Department of Industry, Trade and Commerce, September 1981.

29 *Export Stimulation Programs*, pp. 223–42; *Regelingen voor de Export*, pp. 40–8.

30 MOCI, 'L'accueil au CFCE', *Promosalons*, no. 533/13, p. 49.

31 *Deutsche Aussenhandelskammern – Informationen, Anschriften*, Deutscher Industrie- und Handelstag, Bonn, Mai 1982, pp. 5–11.

32 ibid., p. 10.

33 ibid., p. 7.

34 *The Role of Chambers of Commerce in Trade Facilitation*, International Trade Centre, UNCTAD/GATT and International Chamber of Commerce, Geneva, 1984, p. vii.

35 ibid., p. ix.

36 Written communication from Susan Room, Public Information Office, International Chamber of Commerce, Paris, 23 November 1987.

37 Three recent studies are *Making the Most of Trade Fairs – How Chambers of Commerce can Assist Members in Participating in International Trade Fairs*, International Trade Centre, UNCTAD/GATT, Geneva, 1982; *Trade Information Services of Chambers of Commerce*, International Trade Centre, UNCTAD/GATT and International Chamber of Commerce, Geneva, 1984; *The Role of Chambers of Commerce in Trade Facilitation*, International Trade

Centre, UNCTAD/GATT and International Chamber of Commerce, Geneva, 1984.
38 *Eurochambers*, Association of European Chambers and Industry, Brussels, undated, pp. 2–3.
39 A.K. Young, 'Internationalization of the Japanese general trading companies', *Columbia Journal of World Business*, 1974, spring, pp. 74–85.
40 Y. Tsurumi, *Multinational Management – Business Strategy and Government Policy*, 2nd edn, Cambridge, Mass., Ballinger, 1984, p. 117.
41 JETRO, *The Role of Trading Companies in International Commerce*, Jetro Marketing Series, 1976.
42 D. Zimmerling, *Die Hanse – Handelsmacht im Zeichen der Kogge*, Düsseldorf, Econ Verlag, 1976.
43 E. Ortner, *Glück und Macht der Fugger*, Munich, Ehrenwirth Verlag K.G., 1977; G. Ogger, *Kauf Dir einen Kaiser, Die Geschichte der Fugger*, Munich, Drömer Knaur, 1977. S.B. Clough and C.W. Cole, *Economic History of Europe*, 3rd edn, Boston, Mass., D.C. Heath, 1952.
44 P.J. Nulty, 'Predecessors of the multinational corporation', *Columbia Journal of World Business*, May–June 1972.
45 Government of Canada, *Directory of Canadian Trading Houses*, 1986 edn, Distribution Services Division, Service Industries Branch, Department of Regional Industrial Expansion, Ottawa, December 1986, p. 4.
46 *Lifting Australia's Performance as an Exporter of Manufactures and Services*, Report of the National Export Marketing Strategy Panel, Australian Government Publishing Service, 1985, pp. 67–8.
47 House of Commons, *Proceedings of the Special Committee on a National Trading Corporation*, First Session of the Thirty-Second Parliament, Supply and Services Canada, Hull, 1980.
48 Tsurumi, *Multinational Management*, pp. 102–6.
49 P. Verzariu, *Countertrade, Barter, and Offsets*, New York, McGraw-Hill, 1985, pp. 139–41.
50 Betro Trust, *Concentration on Key Markets*, 2nd edn, Royal Society of Arts, London, December 1975.
51 US Department of Commerce, *Report of the President on Export Promotion Functions and Potential Export Disincentives*, US Government Printing Office, Washington, DC, 1980; US Department of Commerce, *The Export Imperative*, Report to the President submitted by the President's Export Council, December 1980, vol. I; Export Promotion Review Committee, *Strengthening Canada Abroad*, Department of Industry, Trade and Commerce, Ottawa, 1979; *Lifting Australia's Performance as an Exporter of Manufacturers and Services*.
52 US Department of Commerce, *Report of the President*, pp. 1–2 to 1–3.
53 ibid., p. 12.
54 US Department of Commerce, *The Export Imperative*, p. 16.
55 ibid., pp. 16–17.

56 ibid., pp. 17–18.
57 ibid., pp. 18–19.
58 ibid., p. 20.
59 ibid., p. 20.
60 ibid., pp. 20–1.
61 ibid., p. 21.
62 Review Committee, *Strengthening Canada*, p. 9.
63 ibid., pp. 10–12.
64 The Export Trade Development Board has since been disbanded.
65 *Lifting Australia's Performance*, pp. 2–3.
66 ibid., p. 17.
67 ibid., p. 21.
68 ibid., pp. 3–4.

Chapter three

Export promotion in the developing world

Introduction

Developing countries are becoming increasingly important players in the global trading system. Long important as a source of raw materials, in recent decades their industrialization policies have led to impressive gains in manufactured goods exports. Two statistics dramatize this point. First, Figure 3.1 shows that the share of manufactured goods exports accounted for by developing countries almost tripled between 1963 and 1985. Second, in 1986 the export earnings which developing countries gained from manufactured items for the first time were greater than those from agriculture and mining.[1] Thus developing countries are seen to be pursuing economic growth and stability through technology, specialization, and trade.[2] Two factors that could block such development, however, must be recognized. First, future industrial development could be retarded by lower levels of investment resulting from the indebtedness of many of these countries. Second, in order for further trade gains to be made by developing countries, they must find ready access to buyers in the developed world. There are signs, and signals being made to western governments at GATT talks, that the Generalized System of Preferences through which developing countries should have improved access to developed markets is being restricted. Such barriers work against developing country exports.[3]

In this chapter we present first an overview of the export situation in developing countries, followed by a section on the International Trade Centre UNCTAD/GATT which is the most important international organization as far as developing and promoting exports in developing countries is concerned. Two particular aspects of the International Trade Centre are described in more detail: first, the enterprise-level approach which makes ITC services available to export organizations; second, the extensive information services which benefit export development efforts. The next section discusses

Figure 3.1 World exports of manufactures, 1963 and 1985 (percentage shares)

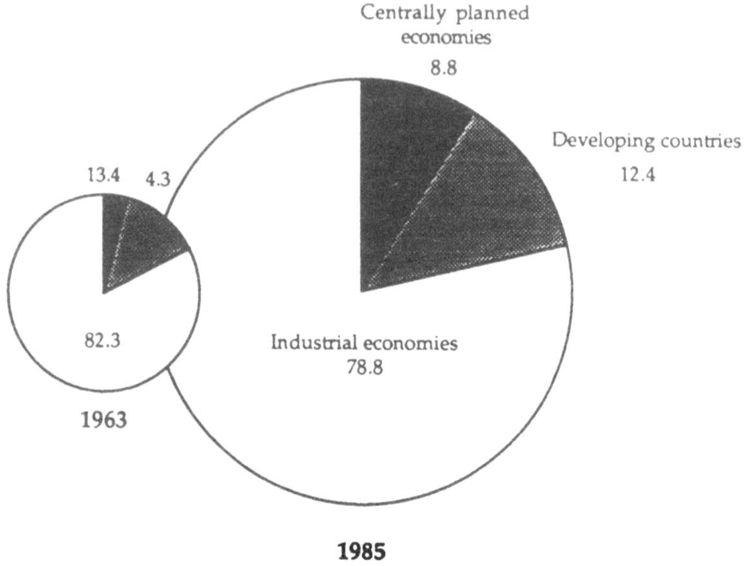

Source: *World Development Report 1987*, New York, Oxford University Press, 1987, Figure 8.3, p. 147. Reproduced with permission.
Note: Industrial countries include Australia, Japan, New Zealand, South Africa, and Western Europe. Developing countries include Africa (excluding South Africa), Asia (excluding China and other centrally planned economies), Latin America, and the Middle East. CPEs include China and other Asian centrally planned economies, Eastern Europe, and the USSR.

export promotion organizations in developing countries by drawing on a survey of the International Trade Centre. The focus is on explaining the role of export promotion organizations and their integration and operation in these countries.

This section is followed by a presentation of several examples of export promotion organizations. The characteristics and functioning of such institutions are given in some depth for the Latin American/ Caribbean region and South-East Asia, where the respective approaches used by Thailand and Sri Lanka are profiled. The chapter ends with the conclusion that, within the unique setting of the developing world, comprehensive export promotion efforts are underway and making an impact on developing countries' participation in global trade.

The export situation in developing countries

As touched on briefly in Chapter 1, some notable changes have occurred in the export situation of developing countries in recent years. Because of growth rates almost twice those of developed market economies,[4] these countries have expanded not only their share of world manufactured goods production but also, more significantly, their share of manufactured exports (see Table 3.1). The changing composition of developing country exports is shown clearly in Table 3.2, with a marked decline in labour-intensive and resource-based exports, and a corresponding increase in non-traditional manufactured exports.

These statistics show that, over time, three basic forces of economic development – technological change, specialization, and trade – combine to boost output and the importance of manufacturing to GDP.[5] Although the above trends describe the pattern of development within the developing countries group, individual countries show differing experiences. The impact of government policies on development plays a key role in explaining these differences and was the subject of a recent World Bank Study.

The World Bank, in a recent study of some forty-one developing countries, between 1963–73 and 1973–85, indicated that although the links between trade strategy and macroeconomic performance are not fully understood, a country's respective outward or inward orientation offers some useful insights into the dynamics of economic and industrial development.[6]

Strongly outward-oriented countries do not have a policy bias toward production for domestic demand, exchange rates are not overvalued, and if some import barriers exist these would at least be matched by export incentives.

Moderately outward-oriented countries show some bias toward production for the domestic market supported by some measure of protection across industrial sectors. Direct controls and licensing may be used. While export incentives exist they tend not to offset the import protection.

Moderately inward-oriented countries have extensive and high rates of effective protection and thereby have an incentive structure that favours production for the domestic market. A distinct bias against exports exists and an overvalued exchange rate further inhibits the competitiveness of exports that do occur.

Strongly inward-oriented countries follow full-fledged import substitution policies characterized by high effective protection, direct import controls and licensing disincentives to non-traditional exports, and significantly overvalued exchange rate. Changes in

Table 3.1 Production and exports of manufactures 1965 and 1985

	Developing countries (%)	*Industrial[a] countries (%)*
Share in production		
1965	14.6	85.4
1985	18.4	81.6
Share in exports		
1965	7.5	92.5
1985	17.7	82.3

Source: *World Development Report 1987*, New York, Oxford University Press, 1987, Table 3.1, p. 47.

Note: [a] industrial market economies.

Table 3.2 Structure of manufactured exports from developing countries, 1970–84

Description	*Share of developing countries' exports[a]*		*Growth rate[b]*
	1970	1984	1970–84
Traditional manufactured exports			
Labour-intensive	36.0	30.0	12.4
Textiles and apparel (84 and 85)	31.3	24.8	11.8
Footwear (85)	1.8	2.9	18.2
Other labour-intensive (61 and 83)	2.9	2.3	11.6
Resource-based	5.2	3.5	12.2
Wood and cork (63)	3.6	1.5	6.9
Paper manufactures (64)	0.8	1.1	17.6
Other resource-based (52 and 56)	0.8	0.9	14.5
Non-traditional manufactured exports[c]	58.8	66.5	15.1
Electrical machinery (72)	16.1	16.7	14.1
Chemicals (51)	8.3	9.9	15.3
Non-electrical machinery (71)	4.2	8.7	20.1
Transport equipment (73)	2.6	5.2	20.0
Iron and steel (67)	6.2	6.5	14.2
Other non-traditional[d]	21.4	19.5	12.9
Total	100.0	100.0	14.0

Source: *World Development Report 1987*, New York, Oxford University Press, 1987, Table 3.3, p. 47.

Notes: Figures in parentheses are the SITC categories for the respective product group.

[a] Developing countries' exports of the listed product as a share of developing countries' total exports of manufactured products defined as SITC categories 5, 6, 7, and 8, less 68.

[b] The rate of growth of developing countries' exports of the listed product during 1970–84 in constant dollars.

[c] Total manufacturing exports less traditional manufacturing exports.

[d] Rest of non-traditional exports.

Table 3.3 Classification of forty-one developing economies by trade orientation, 1963–73 and 1973–85

	Outward oriented		*Inward oriented*	
Period	*Strongly outward oriented*	*Moderately outward oriented*	*Moderately inward oriented*	*Strongly inward oriented*
1963–73	Hong Kong, Korea, Republic of Singapore	Brazil Cameroon Colombia Costa Rica Côte d'Ivoire Guatemala Indonesia Israel Malaysia Thailand	Bolivia El Salvador Honduras Kenya Madagascar Mexico Nicaragua Nigeria Philippines Senegal Tunisia Yugoslavia	Argentina Bangladesh Burundi Chile Dominican Republic Ethiopia Ghana India Pakistan Peru Sri Lanka Sudan Tanzania Turkey Uruguay Zambia
1973–85	Hong Kong, Korea, Republic of Singapore	Brazil Chile Israel Malaysia Thailand Tunisia Turkey Uruguay	Cameroon Colombia Costa Rica Côte d'Ivoire El Salvador Guatemala Honduras Indonesia Kenya Mexico Nicaragua Pakistan Philippines Senegal Sri Lanka Yugoslavia	Argentina Bangladesh Bolivia Burundi Dominican Republic Ethiopia Ghana India Madagascar Nigeria Peru Sudan Tanzania Zambia

Source: *World Development Report 1987*, New York, Oxford University Press, 1987, Figure 5.1, p. 83.

countries' policy directions over 1963–73 to 1973–85 are shown in Table 3.3

A number of important conclusions emerge from the World Bank study. Not only do real GNP per capita, real GDP, and manufactured exports grow more rapidly in outward-oriented countries, but their employment in manufacturing also achieved faster growth.

There are suggestions why outward works better than inward. Import protection burdens an economy in several ways. Consumption is lower since consumers have to pay higher prices for goods inefficiently produced. Producers shift resources into goods they would otherwise not have made. Economies of scale are more difficult to achieve and firms might become monopolies in their own truncated markets. In addition to the wastefulness of control- and intervention-oriented bureaucracies and private sector efforts to cope with an administrative maze, inward orientation ignores a pragmatic managerial dimension of competitive importance:[6] 'exporting firms can glean a lot of knowledge from their customers in rich countries, especially in production engineering and in design marketing'.[7] Linkage with international markets and competitive pressures may also reduce technological backwardness.

Economic development and exporting are not independent choices and both are influenced by the direction of public policy. Because of these relationships and the importance of exporting to developing countries, the International Trade Centre as one major international organization focuses its efforts on export development.

The role of the International Trade Centre

Rationale and emphasis of assistance

The International Trade Centre (ITC) is the focal point in the United Nations organization for assisting developing countries with trade promotion. ITC works with these countries to develop national trade promotion programmes with the view of creating more effective strategies, institutions, and operations for trade. ITC was created in 1964 by GATT and since 1968 has been operated jointly by UNCTAD/GATT.[8]

ITC's orientation has been shaped by the changing trade environment. Its thrust from the late 1960s to the late 1970s focused on training and information support for export promotion planning in both public and private sectors of developing countries. ITC emphasized activities to strengthen countries' capacity to deal with their export promotion needs. Since then ITC efforts have evolved towards export development on a broader scale. This has meant, among other activities, more emphasis on least developed countries, specialized trade promotion services, a broadening of the target audience as well as greater focus on small and medium-sized companies. These efforts then reflect both an awareness of the need to shape pro-export attitudes and the necessity of linking any systematic export promotion efforts with the broadest possible commercial sectors of an economy.

There are six sub-programmes within ITC's overall trade promotion and export development programme:[9]

1 *Institutional infrastructure for trade promotion at the national level* Priority is given to the creation of national trade promotion strategies. Economic development goals of national authorities provide the framework for such strategies, creating and strengthening national trade promotion agencies, and integrating other organizations such as chambers of commerce are part of this effort.

2 *Export market development* A broad approach is taken to identify and develop export potential through projects creating a suitable export supply base, involving adapting existing products and developing new non-traditional products, systematic contact with trade-related institutions, and their link with private firms.

3 *Specialized national trade promotion services* The need for specialized marketing and trade promotion assistance is met through services covering quality control, export packaging, physical distribution, costing and pricing, trade fairs and publicity, legal aspects of trade, export financing, trade information.

4 *Manpower development for trade promotion* Export development and expansion require qualified staff, both at the institutional and business level, creation or improvement of training programmes in international marketing, and trade promotion under an appropriate training strategy. Following a needs survey, existing training institutions are integrated into this process.

5 *Import operations and techniques* Improved import management through appropriate information back-up including sourcing techniques and expertise is the goal of ITC for administration of imports. Particular emphasis is placed on least developed countries in an effort to preserve foreign exchange.

6 *Special programme of technical co-operation with least developed countries* These countries often have the greatest need for export earnings and import management. Often strategies to improve these areas are non-existent, hence special assistance is offered beyond ITC's regular range of services. Such special efforts include product development suggestions, export-oriented investment projects, commodity promotion, as well as creating awareness in government and business of the need for organized approaches to trade.

Government export promotion

ITC has recognized that institutional frameworks and training programmes are critically important to export development and the six sub-programmes reflect this view.

ITC assists developing countries through specific technical co-operation projects within each of these six sub-programmes. Such projects are typically undertaken at the request of a developing country and can take any form from broad policy advice on the nature of possible export involvement to highly specific and focused efforts on, for example, export packaging alternatives appropriate for specific export goods. The extent of ITC involvement varies as well and may range from the complete development of an export promotion organization and infrastructure, to assistance in developing an information data base on export opportunities. The scope of projects may be national, sub-regional, regional, or inter-regional.

ITC's services then can be viewed as applying three levels: first, the institutional level, namely export promotion organizations to provide the strategic and administrative structure; second, the industry or business community level, namely linking export supply with export demand through institutions and technical co-operation projects; and third, the enterprise level, which links specific export development efforts to particular enterprises.

Two aspects of ITC's activities will be discussed in more detail. The enterprise-level approach brings ITC services to bear at the commercial, private sector level. Before this change, integration and actual involvement of companies had been the task of the institution benefiting from ITC assistance. The other aspect discussed is that of ITC's information services. Trade information has been a cornerstone of ITC activity. Its importance to exporting is the underlying reason why trade information services permeate the six sub-programmes discussed earlier.

ITC's enterprise-level approach

ITC has recently introduced a method of providing an integrated package of assistance for a selected number of enterprises that may cover both supply and demand aspects of export development and is offered in a sustained and comprehensive manner within the framework of an export expansion plan for each participating company. This novel results-oriented approach at the enterprise level was developed in 1986 and has since been used in several of ITCs export promotion projects.[10]

There are two broad reasons for emphasizing the direct involvement of the firm in export development. The first reason is that while small and medium-sized firms (SMF) typically play a vital role in the economic system of most developing countries and often engage in substantial export trade, their export potential is generally inadequately appreciated and remains largely untapped. Developing countries often lack any strategy to bring such companies into the export fold. This frequently means that export promotion organizations fail to develop this potential by not focusing on the issues of concern to SMFs.[11]

The other reason stems from ITC's move towards an emphasis on programme results. The desire to measure the impact of its efforts more closely, suggested a new focus at the level of the enterprise, where objectives can be set and performance is more easily discernible.

For an export orientation to emerge in developing countries, management at the enterprise level requires motivation and a pro-export attitude. Export promotion efforts of governments cannot be carried out effectively without support and co-operation from the business community.[12] These enterprise-oriented projects should be seen as demonstration projects. For an organization such as ITC it is important to spread the benefits of the approach to companies that have, for one reason or another, not been selected to participate in a given project. This can be achieved through a variety of means such as dissemination workshops and opening some project activities to a large number of company representatives while respecting the confidentiality of company-specific commercial information.

This enterprise-level approach should not be seen as a complete departure from ITC's previous work in developing countries, which mostly took the form of export potential studies and market surveys, marketing missions, or advice on product adaptation, but rather as a focusing and strengthening of this work.

In particular, ITC defines this enterprise-oriented approach as

> projects in which technical co-operation is provided direct to enterprises on both supply and demand-related aspects of export development in a sustained and comprehensive manner within the framework of an export expansion plan and tailor-made technical co-operation project both specific to the enterprises for the attainment of a set of results and export targets.[13]

This approach, however, is not universally useful to all export promotion projects undertaken in developing countries. Suitability of the approach for a particular country is established through environmental and enterprise-specific screening criteria. Such criteria are flexible in light of the diversity of developing country situations. An example of such criteria is the following.[14]

Environmental criteria	Enterprise-specific criteria
1 relative value of domestic currency 2 availability of export incentives or finance 3 export procedures and regulations 4 attractiveness of domestic market 5 physical infrastructure (telecommunications, roads, shipping lines, air cargo, etc.)	1 quantifiable export potential (target within firms' export expansion plan) 2 commitment criteria (accept and implement recommendations on production, marketing, finance to demonstrate managerial, technical, and financial capability) 3 export readiness criteria (e.g. updating production and sufficient capacity) 4 cost-effectiveness (level of export target to justify cost of project assistance) 5 size criteria (e.g. medium-sized firms with some exporting experience)

Thus if the initial assessment finds a basically favourable macro-environment but substantial weaknesses in the business community which might inhibit the success of an export promotion project or programme, then ITC's new approach at the enterprise level may be appropriate. In any event, before an enterprise-specific export expansion plan can be drawn up and agreed to by individual companies, criteria such as those described above are thoroughly examined.

The logic of integrating the exporter into the framework for export development and expansion is compelling and offers the prospect of building a pro-export attitude at the firm level. It is important to recognize that the attitude or commitment issue is not unique to less developed countries. Indeed, a pro-exporting attitude and management commitment to exporting has been found imperative to export success in studies of exporters in industrial countries.[15]

ITC's information services

Since its inception, ITC has expanded its informational programmes for developing countries in substance and content. For example, work in this field now includes the development of technical and methodological tools for trade information development and analysis, advisory services as well as training on trade information matters to trade promotion organizations.

The trade information services provided by ITC can be viewed at three activity levels:[16]

1 Trade information supply
  - Inquiry/reply service
  - Market news service
  - Traders' data base
  - Foreign trade statistics
  - International trade forum
  - Market surveys
  - Packaging information service
  - Export quality control note
2 Technical and methodological tools
  - Manuals and guides
  - Directories
  - Bibliographies
  - Applications software
3 Trade information advisory and training
  - Advisory services
  - Training services

While such a classification is convenient for presentation, often the services are interlocked due to the nature of assistance projects in developing countries. A brief elaboration is offered on several of these services to convey their comprehensiveness and diversity.

Market news service

This inter-regional, multi-product programme assists developing countries maximize their foreign exchange earnings from commodity exports of a non-traditional nature. It arose out of particular needs of those countries that had limited industrial capacity and thus relied particularly on commodities for their export earnings. Countries lacked current and accurate market information. For example, exporters unaware of the current market situation might ship their products to markets with depressed prices rather than high prices. Growers did not have up-to-date price information on importing markets, thus did not know if they were receiving the best or at least fair prices. The need for technical assistance was recognized and the mere provision of market information was insufficient in resolving commodity export-related problems. Market information had to be properly disseminated to both exporters and growers. Assistance in developing communication systems, quality control, and overcoming logistical problems (often plantation and shipping points are far apart) therefore is quite important. Finally, the need for exporter–importer contact was seen as critical. Such contact will not only build relationships but also provide the exporter with an understanding of how distribution in the import market works and helps the importer appreciate the problems on the supply side.

The Market News Service has been developed to meet these specific needs: it transmits to participating countries up-to-the-minute market information on their key importing markets, its technical assistance enables products to be upgraded to international standards and transported properly, and it provides for contact between exporters and importers and distributors in target markets.[17]

Traders' data base

This is a computerized data base of some 9,000 company profiles of exporters and 17,000 importers world-wide. Although far from exhaustive (the data are collected through mail survey), this data base provides an additional resource to both exporters and importers. It furthermore acts as a stimulus for developing countries to build their own, more comprehensive data bases.

Market surveys

These are detailed market research reports prepared either in the context of particular export development or expansion projects in specific countries, or are carried out more generally on present or potential market opportunities for export products from developing countries. Several major market surveys on specific product groups and leading supply and import markets are prepared each year. These are supplemented with short market surveys that focus on a specific market.

Trade data analysis at enterprise level

The enterprise-level approach discussed earlier also has particular relevance as far as trade information is concerned. Overall, trade data analysis (TDA) at the enterprise level analyzes the trade performance of individual companies or groups on the basis of customs statistics. This approach grew out of the need for 'more detailed analysis of trade flows . . . of individual firms'.[18] This has implications for export promotion organizations (EPO), who need a thorough understanding of the foreign trade sector of their economy. For EPOs to formulate and implement export promotion activities effectively, they ideally require information on trade performance by company. This, of course, also helps an EPO's ability to evaluate the effectiveness of its activities.[19]

Conventional methods of company-level information acquisition, such as direct contacts, surveys, chambers of commerce or trade associations, while suffering from various shortcomings (time-consuming, costly, non-representative, difficult to update, etc.) are and will continue to be indispensable for EPOs. Recent advances in customs data processing, however, offer a faster and more reliable approach to company-specific trade analysis. Customs-based trade data offer centralized information trade flows showing the trading activity of individual companies and product groups, on the basis of which rankings and trade profiles can be determined. This information, which could otherwise be obtained only through time-consuming and incomplete surveys, can be of great benefit to national trade promotion activities.[20] While the system is only emerging, it has merit for use in developing countries where

1 an export promotion organization exists and foreign trade plays a significant role in economic development,
2 EPOs encounter difficulties in developing company-specific trade data,
3 data processing of customs and trade statistics is sufficiently modernized and comprehensive.

A detailed approach to trade data analysis cannot be discussed here. Its appropriateness for a developing country depends on the extent to which it can benefit the EPO in carrying out its mandate. Table 3.4 offers a summary of major factors that are likely to bear on the level of benefit a trade data analysis system can provide.

Summary

ITC is seen to be a major source of assistance and expertise in the export development process underway in the developing world. It is dedicated to trade promotion as a means for narrowing the economic gap between the developing and developed countries. Its activities are grouped under six comprehensive sub-programmes through which the export development and promotion needs of developing countries are addressed.

The recent enterprise-level approach which brings ITC services to the company as well as institutional level is a response to the need to integrate more effectively the export suppliers (the business community) into the development process. Information services play an important part in ITC's activities and four key trade information services were highlighted.

Export promotion organizations in developing countries

Development of an export base and export markets

A common pattern still found in many developing countries is that production and exports are concentrated in a few primary commodities with a small share of exports of non-traditional

Table 3.4 Factors determining the benefits of trade data analysis at enterprise level

Low benefits	*High benefits*
Foreign trade plays a minor role in economic development.	Foreign trade plays a major role in economic development.
There is a little government intervention and regulation in the economy.	There is a considerable extent of government intervention and regulation in the economy.
The economic structure is rather homogeneous, i.e. there are hardly any differences in the performance between public and private sector, local and foreign sector, traditional and modern sector, etc.	The economic structure is not homogeneous, i.e. there are notable differences in the performance between public and private sector, local and foreign sector, traditional and modern sector, etc.
The institutional structure of the foreign trade sector is clear and specific.	The institutional structure of the foreign trade sector is not clear or specific.
The number of companies involved in trade is small.	The number of companies involved in trade is large.
There is no special foreign trade policy.	Foreign trade policies are differentiated.
There is no trade promotion organization.	A trade promotion organization exists.
Comprehensive, up-to-date directories of exporters and importers exist.	Comprehensive, up-to-date directories of exporters and importers do not exist.
Evaluation of trade promotion activites is carried out effectively.	Evaluation of trade promotion is not yet satisfactory.
No special efforts are undertaken to promote exports of small and medium-size companies.	Special efforts are undertaken to promote exports of small and medium-size companies.
Overseas marketing is not a major problem for export producers.	There is considerable room for improving export marketing.
Transfer pricing is uncommon.	Transfer pricing practices are wide-spread.

Source: Trade Data Analysis at Enterprise Level for Trade Promotion, International Trade Centre UNCTAD/GATT, Geneva, December 1986.

products. Expansion of the export base entails either increasing the production capacity of companies which currently supply only their domestic market, or creating entirely new production units primarily dedicated to export. Export market development requires that two activities be carried out in parallel: competitive products must be developed and markets identified and nurtured for these products. Thus the development of export supply must be closely tied to the development of export demand which requires knowledge and

Figure 3.2 Export supply and demand process for developing countries

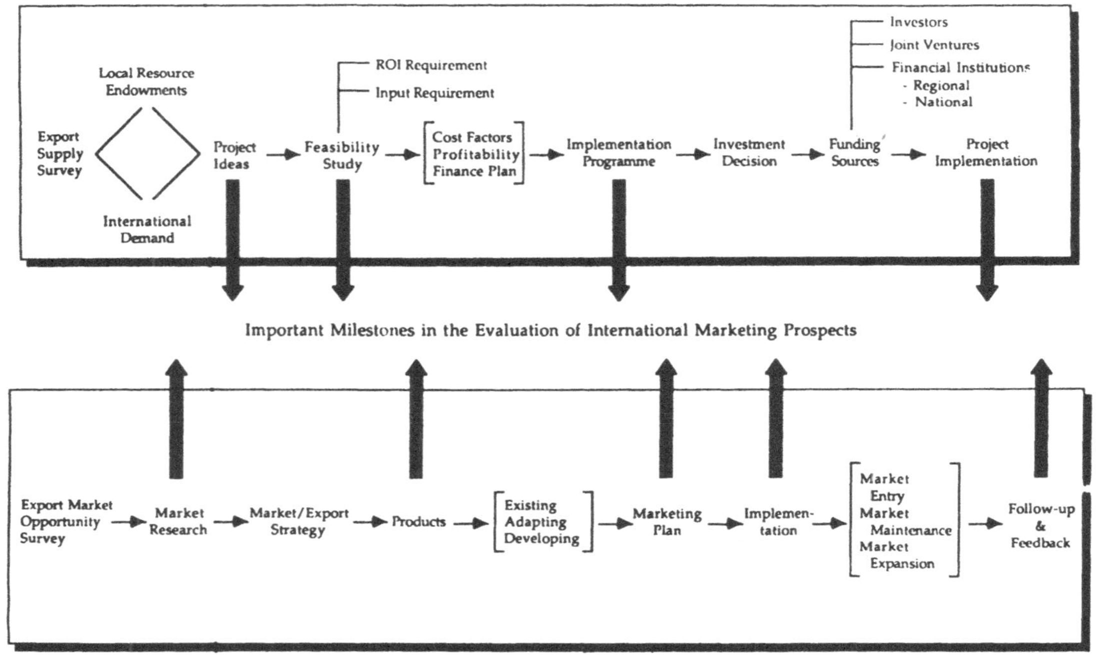

Source: Prepared by the authors.

experience in market research. The conception, planning, and implementation phases of the process for the expansion of the export base in developing countries and the simultaneous market development process are shown in Figure 3.2.

Role and organization of EPOs

Because management skills and experience are generally lower, and in light of institutional/infrastructural shortcomings, governments in the developing world tend to play a more critical role than those in the industrial countries. Various kinds of export promotion organizations (EPOs) have been created by government either on their own initiative or with assistance from external organizations such as the International Trade Centre UNCTAD/GATT, or both. Of considerable importance to the creation and operation of an EPO are, first, its position in the national hierarchical structure, second, its organizational character and affiliation, third, its involvement in policy matters, fourth, its objectives, and fifth, its function. These considerations are now dealt with in turn.[21]

EPO in the national hierarchical structure

The effectiveness of an EPO is, to a large extent, determined by its relative position within the hierarchical structure of a developing country. A clear definition of the role of an EPO, in essence operating as a service organization helping the business community, is necessary if it is to function within the governmental structure. If the EPO's role is obscure and lacks authority to carry out its responsibilities, this indicates that government accords low priority to trade development and trade promotion activities. Therefore, the degree of influence an EPO is able to exert over other governmental organizations is severely curtailed if its role is not clearly defined and its position in the hierarchy is low and its efforts to co-ordinate and carry out trade promotion activities are likely to be frustrated.

EPO organization and affiliation

As we show later on, the organizational character of EPOs is diverse and depends on the circumstances of a given country. Some of these differences stem from confusion in certain developing countries regarding policy-making and policy implementation. Two very general types of organizational arrangements are EPOs situated within a ministry or set up as an entity separate from a ministry. The reason for creating an EPO as a division or section within a ministry of trade, as in some Latin American countries, was the experimental nature of a country's early export promotion efforts. The underlying logic of easy creation (absence of complicated legislative measures) and quick funding (via normal ministerial budget), however, has drawbacks. The EPO unit generally lacks autonomy to carry out trade promotion activities and is tied to the same bureaucratic method of functioning as the rest of the ministry.[22] Furthermore, because promotion and control activities are intermingled in this setting, the EPO is often pulled in two directions simultaneously.

An autonomous or semi-autonomous EPO appears to be a better approach. Its legal status is well defined, and it can operate more effectively outside of ministerial bureaucracy. EPOs in the form of councils and boards, as those found in several Asian and African countries, comprise high-level government officials supported by technical secretariats. Other forms, although they may be attached to a ministry for control purposes, have a board of directors with public and private sector representatives. Their link with a ministry is for funding purposes and to satisfy public administration procedures, while they carry out their function relatively autonomously. An important element in the success of an EPO is the active participation of the export community on its board. The more operations resemble those of a business enterprise the more successful EPO operations tend to be.[23]

EPO and policy matters

Whether EPOs should be involved in formulation of economic policy is a moot point. Economic policy areas where EPOs could play a role include: national development plans, foreign trade programmes, export development strategies, and export incentive schemes. In a sense, EPOs owe their creation to development and trade policy decisions. They are then instruments of such policies, with a mandate to carry out export strategies. On the other hand, EPOs are often well positioned to know the needs and requirements of the business sector, and the measures that can facilitate sales in foreign markets. While EPOs lack large technical research staff to study the economic conditions domestically and abroad, valuable recommendations to policy-makers and thus contributions to the policy process can nevertheless be made. A number of EPOs play such a role and are a source of policy recommendations while policy initiatives mainly emanate from ministries, the central bank or, as in several Latin American and Caribbean countries, formal foreign trade councils.

EPO objectives

EPOs have as their charge successful export development. Developing countries' traditional exports are usually handled by organizations such as marketing boards. As traditional exports tend not to require the support of another institution, EPOs are generally given the exclusive task of promoting non-traditional exports. However, in some countries the export base is so narrow that the distinction between traditional and non-traditional exports is not meaningful. In such cases EPOs promote all exports.

Often the mandate given to the EPO is quite broad, and generally not shared with other private or public institutions. For example the EPO may implement any activity considered useful for, and beneficial to, the development and promotion of exports. Under this mandate the EPO can decide on activities it should undertake to achieve its objectives. This approach provides considerable latitude to the EPO. Not all countries see this as the best approach. Some authorities define their EPO's mandate in precise and comprehensive terms. Neither approach is ideal nor can one clearly say that one is more effective than the other. A broad mandate provides the flexibility to adapt activities to changing circumstances. A detailed approach could be misleading in that it suggests trade promotion aspects are completely covered. This is clearly not possible since first, not all of the activities are necessary all the time, and second, no single EPO would possess the resources to carry them out. Experience and knowledge is gained in some functions which might then provide the basis to carry out others.[24]

EPO functions

Although EPOs can be engaged in many activities, the actual range and intensity of trade promotion activities undertaken depends on available human and financial resources, the needs and requirements of exporters, the nature of the products to be exported, the characteristics of foreign markets, and the experience and expertise of the EPO. Activities can be grouped thus: (1) product and market identification and development, (2) trade information services, (3) specialized support services, (4) promoting activities abroad, and (5) provision of support to other institutions (see Table 3.5).

The first group of activities focuses on product and market identification and development since developing countries often lack a clear knowledge of the range and assortment of products they should be promoting and the characteristics and needs of the target markets. The second group of activities addresses one of the most frequently

Table 3.5 Activities of a trade promotion organization for developing countries

Product and market identification and development
- Determination of export supply and identification of constraints to the export trade
- Preparation of product profiles
- Preparation of company profiles
- Identification of foreign market opportunities
- Preparation of market profiles
- Acquisition of samples of foreign products
- Market studies
- Export promotion programmes on product basis

Trade information service
- Establishment of a trade information service

Specialized support services
- Technical assistance on export procedures
- Technical assistance on export financing
- Technical assistance on transportation
- Technical assistance on quality control
- Technical assistance on export packaging
- Technical assistance on marketing
- Technical assistance on costing and pricing
- Technical assistance on product adaptation
- Technical assistance on legal matters

Promoting activities abroad
- Commercial representation offices abroad
- Participation in trade (sellers) missions
- Participation in trade fairs
- Invitation to foreign buyers
- Sub-contracting for exports

Provision of support to other institutions
- Training of the export community
- Promotional campaigns
- Studies on export climate
- Pre- and post-shipment financing
- Export incentives
- Export credit insurance
- Joint export mechanisms
- Establishment of free zones
- Import rationalization
- Trade representation through foreign service
- Quality control programmes
- Co-operation with packaging institutions
- Preparation of investment profiles
- Investment promotion
- Financing of new investment

Source: *Trade Promotion Institutions: Monograph on the Role and Organization of Trade Promotion*, International Trade Centre UNCTAD/GATT, Geneva, 1986, pp. 51–96.

Table 3.6 Participation of EPOs of developing countries in policy recommendation/formulation and implementation of promotional activities

	Extent of participation		
	None (%)	*Medium (%)*	*Total (%)*
1 Type of participation in policy recommendation/formulation			
Policy recommendation	8	60	32
Policy formulation	37	45	18
Formulation of export development strategy	10	35	55
Formulation of foreign trade programmes	16	55	29
Formulation and planning of export incentives	28	39	33
Formulation of national development plan	52	40	8
2 Type of export promotion activity implemented			
Export incentives administration	49	32	19
Direct credit granting for export	79	13	8
Export credit insurance	79	13	8
Export development activities	3	31	66
Investment promotion	44	46	10
International trade negotiations	27	54	19

Source: Adapted from 'Participation of TPOs in various aspects of policy formulation', International Trade Centre UNCTAD/GATT, Geneva, December 1987.

mentioned constraints to exporting. Lack of adequate information can be overcome through, first, the collection and creation of appropriate information, and second, the selective dissemination of relevant information to users. Centralized information systems at the EPO or at other organizations, such as chambers of commerce, are at the beginning of export promotion efforts. Information needs of exporters must be systematically identified and understood so that an information service can be designed to respond appropriately. The third group of activities aims to build technical expertise in the export community. The objective is to enhance the competitiveness of products in international markets. Consultation with the export community is a very important part of the process of choosing those technical assistance services that are of greatest benefit in achieving improved competitiveness.[25]

The fourth activity group provides services that help with direct market contact and exporters' interaction with prospective buyers. Often close working relationships with a country's commercial representative abroad are developed which help the export community with communications, market contact, and tend to make the work of an EPO more effective. Additionally EPOs provide a host of support activities to other institutions. The expertise within an EPO thus is a valuable resource to bodies concerned with export financing, promotion of investment, or trade representation for example.

A profile of the activities undertaken by EPOs in developing countries gives a better sense of typical projects and tasks.[26]

Profile of EPOs

A recent ITC survey of EPOs in developing countries reveals what activities they are actually involved in.[27] The first part of Table 3.6 deals with EPOs' involvement in foreign economic policy formulation.

Nearly all EPOs make policy recommendations. Of those who do, about two-thirds participate to some extent, while one-third participate fully by making recommendations. Policy formulation, on the other hand, is not engaged in by 37 per cent, while 45 per cent have some participation, and 18 per cent participate fully. It is instructive to consider in what type of policy formulation EPOs are likely to participate. The most frequent level of participation is in the formulation of export development strategy, where 90 per cent of EPOs participate and over one-half do so totally. EPOs as a rule have least involvement in the formulation of national development plans (over one-half are not involved). Of those who are participating over four-fifths do so only to some extent.

The second part of Table 3.6 highlights the extent to which EPOs participate in export-related activities. It is apparent that typically their mandate does not encompass the provision of financial aspects of export promotion to any major extent. Although export incentives, financing, or insurance are not independent from non-financial export promotion activities the former do require different expertise and often separate institutional set-ups. Of the listed activities, export development, which is concerned with export supply, is clearly of importance to the otherwise export market demand-oriented functions of an EPO. Nearly all EPOs participate in this activity, with two-thirds being fully involved. The role of an EPO in international trade negotiations, such as the GATT rounds, shows that while not a major concern, this area offers an opportunity to relate some of the local concerns of the export community and the EPO to the negotiating bodies. The promotion of investment also involves EPOs to some extent. Their role here would relate most often to domestic investment associated with export development such as capacity creation or expansion at the enterprise level.

Table 3.7 Implementation of export promotion activities by EPOs in developing countries

	% of EPOs
1 Global responsibility for	
– Non-traditional products	41
– All products	59
2 Product and market promotion and development	
– Export supply studies	98
– Identification of export constraints	100
– Preparation of product profiles	96
– Preparation of market profiles	98
– Foreign market opportunity analysis	93
– Complete market studies	78
– Purchase of foreign samples	19
– Identification of export potential for development	87
– Export promotion programmes (product specific)	87
– Trade information services	100
– Selective information dissemination	91
3 Specialized support services to exporters	
– Export procedures/documentation	73
– Transportation (information)	50
– Guidance for export financing	56
– Marketing	85
– Costing and pricing	44
– Quality control	33
– Product adaptation	59
– Export packaging	44
– Publicity	72
– Legal advice	46
– Direct training	63
– Export of services	41
4 Promotional activities abroad	
– Participation of foreign trade fairs	98
– Organization of trade missions	91
– Invitation of foreign buyers	72
– Subcontracting of production	15
5 Support activities to other institutions	
– Training programmes	80
– Support to medium/small enterprises	87
– Promotion of joint export mechanisms	69

Source: Based on *Selected Export Promotion Organizations: Structures, Functions and Activities*, International Trade Center UNCTAD/GATT, Geneva, 25 September 1986.

Table 3.7 focuses on what can be regarded as primary export promotion activities and shows how comprehensively EPOs in developing countries engage in them. It is clear that nearly all organizations surveyed recognize the importance of market research, whether this is product-specific, market-specific, deals with the identification and analysis of export opportunities, or involves the implementation of trade information systems. It is in this general area of information support that most of the EPOs support the export community and the export promotion efforts of a country.

Between two and four in five EPOs offer specialized services to the export community. About 60 per cent of the organizations offer marketing support. Here the breadth of EPO involvement varies and ranges from 44 per cent providing advice on export packaging to 85 per cent assisting with marketing. Among other areas of specialized support, assistance with export procedures (73 per cent) and direct training of enterprises in exporting matters (63 per cent) stand out as widely provided services.

Among the tools that provide direct customer and market contact for exporters, foreign trade fairs (offered by 98 per cent) and trade missions (91 per cent) are clearly seen as very important to export promotion, as indeed they are in developed countries. EPOs also provide support to other institutions, such as industry associations through training programmes (offered by 80 per cent) and support to small and medium-sized enterprises in particular (offered by 87 per cent).

On the whole, the survey data show a comprehensive range of export promotion activities among EPOs in developing countries, but they fail to speak of the effectiveness of these activities. A case in point is where some 93 per cent of EPOs indicate that they carry out foreign market opportunity analysis. The degree of usefulness of such activity depends, at a minimum, on sufficiently trained and experienced staff to select appropriate markets for analysis, consider and evaluate the respective domestic and third country competitors, accurately assess market and buyer characteristics, clearly determine aspects of competitive advantage or disadvantage, identify target market segments, evaluate market growth, accessibility and longevity, consider the impact of technology on the product, buyer, competitors, and so on. Such an analysis depends on information. That means access to information, the appropriateness of information, its accuracy, currency, and cost. It can be seen that the effectiveness of this particular activity, quite apart from the issue of any action (by EPO and enterprise) based upon it, depends on a great many factors.

The survey data thus do not reveal the critical dimension of the quality of an EPO's functions. Trade information, for example, is a vital function within an export promotion organization. Experience has shown that trade information services or systems are given very low priority (i.e. resources and support) in an EPO. Often EPOs set up a library consisting of some standard reference works or directories, which subsequently is hardly used and becomes rapidly outdated. Such a library often is not built into a practical support system. The mentality of 'library' does not seem useful or appropriate in a fast-paced information environment. With an abundance of commercially available data bases, some EPOs in developing countries have fallen victim to salesmanship and have purchased overly sophisticated or inappropriate data bases that have turned out to be of little or no use to their export promotion activities.[28]

Another example demonstrates the importance and impact of follow-up and communications between EPO and the business community. In one Arab country the export promotion organization functions as an autonomous institution assigned to the ministry responsible for industry and commerce. Exports of some products began to decline. The apparent reason for this decline was the quality of goods, but this was not known to the EPO because the exporters did not share follow-up information from events with the organization. If information from follow-up (such as customer dissatisfaction due to poor product quality) was shared, even though the latter ultimately is the exporter's responsibility, the EPO may have provided quality control help. Why was information between exporter and EPO not shared? The business community was unhappy because they had not been asked to participate in the EPO's advisory board and hence had no input into the export promotion policy. An atmosphere of distrust was created, which unchecked, threatened the export business.

Summary

Export development requires a co-operative approach between business and institutions which are either directly or indirectly linked with government. Developing countries' governments have established various kinds of export promotion organizations, often with the assistance of external organizations such as the International Trade Centre. This section described the role and functions of such EPOs and provided a discussion of some specific characteristics drawn from a survey of such organizations. A number of individual EPOs are more comprehensively profiled in the next section.

Region/country examples of export promotion organizations

Export promotion organizations in Latin America and the Caribbean

In 1983 ITC conducted a study of export promotion organizations in eight Latin American and Caribbean countries whose exports were showing an upward trend. The purpose of the study was to examine the experiences of the EPOs and how they affected these countries' export marketing activities. Furthermore, the Economic Commission for Latin American and the Caribbean (ECLAC) provided some economic development guidance. In the immediate period following the Second World War the focus of these efforts was characteristically on import substitution and economic development. In other words, inwardly oriented protectionist strategies were pursued by countries in this region. Economic development soon suffered from balance of payments constraints. By the late 1960s and early 1970s countries in the region had generally adopted export promotion strategies, albeit based on existing industries and available production capacities. During the late 1970s and early 1980s Latin American countries found that they were unable to develop and sustain high volumes of exports to global markets with the existing manufacturing sector. A further shift in strategy became necessary. New productive capacity needed to be developed for non-traditional products to meet world demand and thus focus on export development. It was recognized by many countries that co-ordination and guidelines were needed if they were to participate successfully in increasingly competitive export markets. The concept of a national export promotion system evolved and essentially became the *modus operandi* for the interaction of institutional export promotion, global export strategies, and the export community. Economic development plans had proved inadequate and, apart from providing general guidelines, were generally not used in these countries.[29] EPOs were compelled to assume a greater role in trade development.

Table 3.8 provides an overview of the basic services provided by the trade promotion organizations in the eight countries surveyed. Three areas will be briefly discussed to show the experience in these eight countries. First, national export development strategy, second, export promotion policies, and third, the scope of export promotion services.

National export development strategies

Most of these countries experienced difficulty in creating a national export development strategy. There appear to be two underlying reasons for this. First, the responsibility for trade strategies is generally outside the realm of the EPO and within the purview of either the Ministry of Economy/Development, or the national planning or programming office and tends to be developed jointly with the central or development banks. Second, those responsible for the strategy have taken an increasingly short-term perspective in their economic management to the detriment of medium- and long-term

Table 3.8 Trade promotion organizations: basic services

Servicing unit	*Brazil*		*Colombia*	*Dominican Republic*	*Guatemala*
Service	*ITAMARATY*[a]	*CACEX*[b]	*PROPEXPO*	*CEDOREX*	*GURTEXPRO*
Export promotion	Commercial promotion department	DEPEM/CEPEX[c]	Development division	Technical assistance and promotion department	Statistics and trade commissioner services division
Trade information	Trade information service	DEPEM/CEPEX	Information department	Trade information department	Trade information services division
Market studies and development	Market research division	DEPEM/CEPEX	Technical assistance and training department	—	Statistics and market development department
Technical assistance	—	—	Technical assistance and training department	Technical assistance and promotion department	Technical co-operation and training
Product development	—	—	Promotion department	Technical assistance and promotion department	Technical co-operation and training
Trade policy and negotiations	Economic department	—	—	Economic research department	Market research section
Commercial offices abroad	Trade promotion section	Banco do Brazil offices	Technical assistance and training department	Technical assistance and promotion department	Support services abroad
Planning and programming	Trade promotion programmes division	—	Technical assistance and training department	Economic research development	Programming control and evaluation department
Financing	—	GEFIN[d]	Financial division	—	Export incentives and financing
Export incentives	—	—	—	Incentives department	Export incentives and financing
Export of services	Trade promotion division	DEPEM	Export of services division	—	—

Table 3.8 Trade promotion organizations: basic services (contd.)

Servicing unit *Service*	*Jamaica* *JNEC*[e]	*Mexico* *IMCE*[f]	*Peru* *FOPEX*	*Uruguay* *DGCE*
Export promotion	Promotions and trade commissioner services division	Internal promotion and market analysis	Internal and external promotion divisions	Promotion and development division
Trade information	Trade information services	Internal promotion and market analysis	Technical division	Trade information services
Market studies and development	Promotions and trade commissioner services division	Internal promotion and market analysis	Technical analysis	Promotion and development division[g]
Technical assistance	—	Technical assistance and training	Internal promotion division	Promotion and development division
Product development	Development division	Regional offices	Internal promotion division	Promotion and development division
Trade policy and negotiations	—	Legal advisory services	Technical division	Trade policy and negotiations divisions
Commercial offices abroad	Promotions and trade commissioner services division	Export programmes	Office of the general manager	Offices abroad
Planning and programming	—	Programming and control	Office of the general manager	—
Financing	—	—	—	—
Export incentives	—	Projects and studies	—	—
Export of services	—	Internal promotion and market analysis	—	—

Source: *Institutional Systems for Export Promotion in Latin America and the Caribbean: A Comparative Analysis*, International Trade Centre UNCTAD/GATT, Geneva, 1984, p. 79

Notes:
a Trade promotion department of the Ministry of Trade
b Banco do Brasil's Foreign Trade Department
c DEPEM is department responsible for trade promotion matters. CEPEX is the export promotion centre co-ordinated by DEPEM.
d GEFIN is the financial control under CACEX concerning export financing.
e Has two affiated trading companies (JAMCO and JETCO).
f Has an investment promotion unit.
g By sectoral units.
— Not provided.

strategic direction for export development. It appears logical that EPOs can positively affect the strategy formulation process through independently or jointly produced policy papers, seminars, workshops, or conferences focused on medium- and long-term export strategy. Apart from a jurisdictional problem there is also an inter-agency communications problem to be overcome.

Export promotion policies

EPOs consider a number of criteria in the promotion policy process: the international economic environment, national economic policies or development plans (where they exist), plans for external trade, investment and finance, the country's international commitments (i.e. debt servicing or trade agreements), and prior export promotion performance.

A key element that permits the EPO to develop such promotion policy is the authority vested in the board and its executive director. When high government officials participate in the board, such as in Colombia, Mexico, and the Dominican Republic, the policy directives on export promotion and development tend to be clear and authoritative with correspondingly precise guidelines for the technical activities of the EPO. On the other hand, when the board comprises low-level officials its policy process is typically weak and the internal direction as to export promotion activities inadequate. When higher authorities are involved in matters of trade policy, the directives may deal with macro-economic and broad foreign trade policy. It falls upon the EPO board to interpret these and correspondingly formulate export-specific policies.[30]

Foreign trade policy and export promotion policy, while closely interrelated, are generally formulated and implemented by separate institutions. Exceptions in this group of countries are Brazil and Uruguay, whose EPOs are involved in implementing both types of policies. Generally an EPO's independence from the broader trade policy process and ministries responsible for it is desirable, since it lets the EPO focus exclusively on export promotion. Such independence, on the other hand, reduces any influence of the EPO on the trade policy formulation. An EPO, however, can still maintain influence in other public sector institutions, such as the Ministry of Economy, without formal dependency. The executive director or other board members can maintain close contacts with both private and public sector institutions. Indeed a key qualification for executive directors is their ability to communicate and deal with officials in the relevant institutions.[31]

Scope of export promotion services

The array of services provided by the EPOs is comprehensive, although it is affected by several country-specific factors. Services vary according to the resources, the extent to which non-traditional exports are developed, the position and priority accorded to the EPO and export development. Thus, in general, the importance of individual services summarized in Table 3.9 varies by country.

Traditionally export promotion has been oriented strongly towards international marketing rather than the export supply side. Promotional activities themselves have often focused on foreign venues rather than the domestic business community. For reasons outlined below this orientation has meant certain weaknesses for the export promotion effort.

When export promotion concentrates on the existing export supply, and in this context on the most dynamic export companies in the community, by definition it neglects the imperative long-term view of export potential and development. As EPOs are conceived as instruments to help export expansion and development over the long term, their effectiveness is not adequately measured by the performance of current activities (say the success of the foreign trade fairs), but by positive changes brought about in the broadening of export capacity, increases in the breadth and depth of non-traditional exports, expanding the community of exporters, increasing the competitive competence of exporters, building and diversifying market acceptance of products in foreign markets. It appears reasonable that, as well as the services concerned with the demand side, EPOs should be involved in the creation of national production policies, which help to shape the export supply side.

The notion of broader EPO involvement may not be easily implemented, because of jurisdictional constraints and an obfuscation of goals, objectives, and responsibilities. There is merit in a clearly focused mandate for EPOs, even if this means a less than all-encompassing or perfect mandate. The issue of export incentives in the Latin American experience is conflicting. Some EPOs responsible also for the allocation of financial incentives have on the one hand increased their interaction with firms requiring export credit, but on the other hand have lessened their emphasis on direct and indirect export promotion activities. Some EPOs have managed to combine these activities fairly well but as a result have become more bureaucratic, thus discouraging exporters from using their services altogether. Another concern has been ambivalence on the part of the business community to request export promotion assistance from an organization which (through access to firms' financial data from export credit and financial incentive applications) has

Table 3.9 Trade promotion organizations: level of involvement in export promotion activities

Service	*Brazil*	*Colombia*	*Dominican Republic*	*Guatemala*	*Jamaica*	*Mexico*	*Peru*	*Uruguay*
Identification of export supply	M	H	M	H	M	H	H	H
Trade information	H	H	H	M	H	H	H	M
Market studies	H	M	L	L	M	M	M	M
Studies of export potential	M	H	L	L	L	H	H	M
Trade fairs	H	H	M	M	L	H	H	M
Training	L	M	M	H	H	H	H	L
Trade negotiations	H	M	L	L	L	M	M	H
Export financing	H	H	L	L	L	L	L	L
Free trade zones	L	M	M	L	M	M	L	L
Export credit insurance	L	H	L	L	L	L	M	L
Technical assistance (advisory services)								
Export procedures	H	H	M	M	M	H	M	M
Product adaptation	L	H	M	M	L	M	H	M
Quality control	L	M	L	L	L	M	L	L
Packaging	L	H	L	L	L	M	M	L
Design	L	M	L	L	L	H	H	L
Transport	L	H	L	L	L	L	L	L
Export development	M	M	M	L	L	M	M	L
Export marketing	H	H	L	M	L	M	M	L
Trading companies	H	H	L	L	H	H	L	L
Market profiles	H	H	M	M	M	H	H	M

Source: *Institutional Systems for Export Promotion in Latin America and the Caribbean: A Comparative Analysis*, International Trade Centre UNCTAD/GATT, Geneva, 1984, p. 80.

Note: Importance of service denoted as H = high, M = medium, L = low.

some power to control them by granting or refusing financial incentives.[32]

Regional export promotion in South-East Asia

In 1968 the United Nations agency Economic and Social Commission for Asia and the Pacific (ESCAP) established a Trade Promotion Centre (TPC) to serve the trade promotion needs of developing countries in South-East Asia. While ITC has a mandate of serving developing countries, the needs of this region – which includes some of the world's least developed countries as well as developing island countries – were seen to warrant ESCAP's separate efforts. The TPC co-operates closely with the ITC and other agencies, but has also independently developed some services and activities for the region. A brief summary of these services is provided.[33]

Market and product development service

This service is broadly referred to as the research arm of TPC. Among the activities, all of which aim to provide a better understanding of the complexities of international marketing and to support export marketing by countries of the region, are

1 preparation of market reports and supply surveys,
2 organization of seminars and workshops through which market research information is distributed and follow-up undertaken,
3 organization of buyer–seller contacts through trade fairs, trade missions,
4 assistance with international sub-contracting,
5 preparation of case studies on trading experiences of others and their use as learning tools.

Professional development service

The objective of this service is, first, to assist in training individual countries' trade promotion officials, and second, to offer training to the business community in order to improve their knowledge and skills needed for the international competitive environment. These training activities have a practical focus and range from trade development with socialist countries to training EPO staff in techniques and methods of export promotion.

Trade promotion advisory service

This service is particularly concerned with the institutional and structural aspects of trade promotion. Assistance provided includes on the one hand, the planning, organizing, or restructuring of national centres for export development (such as EPOs), and on the other, formulation and establishment of specific programmes or activities the organizations are to deliver. The latter are export incentive schemes, simplification of trade procedures, organization, and procedure for trade fairs and missions, assisting countries in using the generalized systems of preferences, and establishing duty-free export processing zones. Other specialized assistance deals with the drafting and review of commercial legislation and trade regulations.

Trade information service

Established in 1975, this service attempts to centralize the flow of trade-related information to improve both its dissemination and use. Three elements of the Trade Information Network (TISNET) are worth noting. First, the systematic collection of trade information; second, dissemination of information through regular publications of statistical data as well as a trade inquiry/reply service; and third, advisory and training services to assist others in setting up trade information services.

Overall, ESCAP seeks to address regional trade promotion needs primarily through regional expertise.

Export promotion in Thailand

Thailand can be described as a moderately outwardly oriented country and has pursued such a development strategy for the past twenty-five years.[34] Over the period 1965 to 1985 manufacturing's share of GDP increased from 14 to 20 per cent while agriculture dropped from 35 to 17 per cent. Exports of goods grew from 18 to 27 per cent of GDP over the same period,[35] and manufactured exports grew eighty-six times. Thailand's success at export market development is reflected in its shift in export destinations for manufactured goods, i.e. industrial market economies absorbed 39 per cent of such exports in 1965 and 63 per cent in 1985.[36]

Thailand manages its economy under the National Social and Economic Development Plan which runs in four-year cycles. The sixth plan covers 1987 to 1991. While the Department of Export Promotion is a department within the Ministry of Commerce and was founded in 1952, its functions and activity has been rapidly expanded in recent years and the government's strong emphasis on trade promotion has been particularly evident over the past five years.

Two additional committees play an important role in supporting export-related activities. These are the government–private joint consultative committee (chaired by the prime minister) and the export development committee established in 1977 (chaired by the minister of commerce). The former provides the vital private sector input to export strategy formulation. The latter is a policy-level committee established by the cabinet to direct and co-ordinate improvement in Thailand's export efficiency. It is responsible for the country's export promotion plan as well as matters related to exportation. Its members are also drawn from public and private sectors and represent all major commercial and government agencies involved in exporting. The Department of Export Promotion acts as the secretariat for the export development committee and has been described as the country's export manager.[37]

The Department of Export Promotion has four main duties:

1 Promote and encourage export of Thai products and expanding export markets.
2 Promote and encourage product substitution and reduce the number of imported products for balance of trade purpose.
3 Create and develop basic awareness and knowledge of international trade and increase Thai export business capability to compete effectively in world markets.
4 Minimize export obstacles and solve export-related problems.

The approach to export development and promotion consists of three main planning activities. First, the export development plan combines a number of export-related activities aimed at continuous and long-term impact. Second, the export promotion plan covers several main activities primarily for immediate impact. Third, the trade defence plan in developed to shield Thai products against trade protectionist measures encountered in international markets. Figure 3.3 provides detail on the individual activities.

The plans are implemented through a variety of programmes under the Department of Export Promotion. These are highlighted:[38]

1 *Organizing international trade fairs* Many international trade fairs are held annually in Bangkok. The DEP invites representatives from recognized corporations and foreign buyers around the world to visit and discuss directly with selected Thai manufacturers. The annual programme is continuously arranged in advance.
2 *Organizing trade missions* Incoming and outgoing trade missions are arranged annually.[39] Pre-planning involves the selection of countries and potential products suitable to particular target markets. The DEP encourages and provides opportunity for selected manufacturers and exporters to participate in the activity.

Figure 3.3 Export development and promotion in Thailand

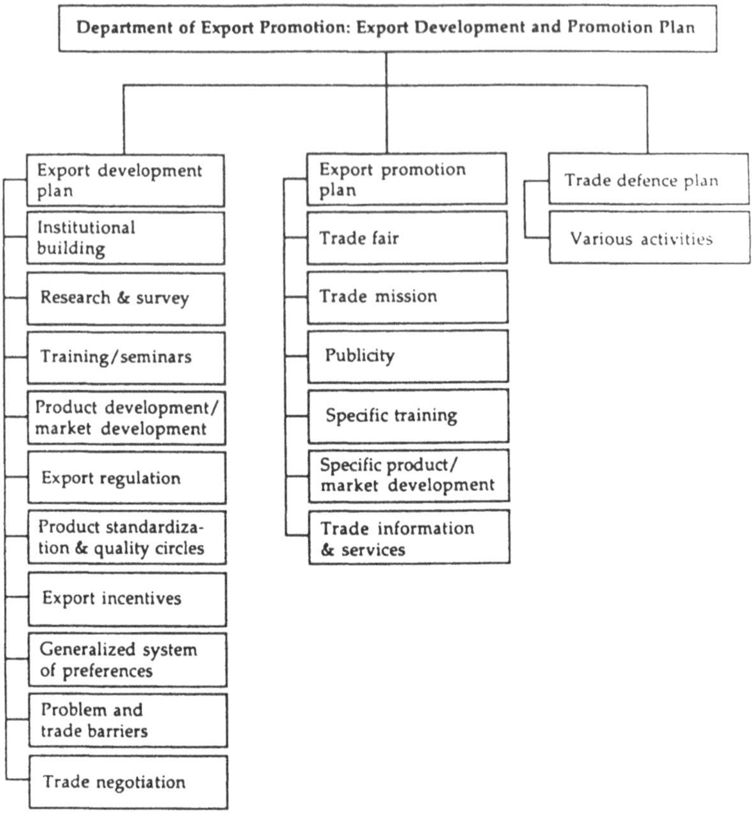

Source: *Export Promotion and Export Development Plan of the Department of Export Promotion*, Bangkok, Ministry of Commerce, undated, pp. 2–4.

3 *Information and publicity* One of the most important elements in facilitating export promotion is the preparation of 'the selected list of exporters' which contains all necessary information on Thai exporters. Many other publicity documents are also produced and disseminated around the world. They are also readily available at the Thai Centres and Office of Commercial Counsellors.

4 *Training and seminars on trade/product development* The DEP in co-operation with the ITC has conducted various training and seminar programmes in order to enhance related export

business knowledge and skill among Thai businessmen. The product development project is gradually developed with the co-operation of universities and other institutions.

5 *Specific product and market development* This draws on a variety of resources, including training and information services as well as contact programmes such as missions and fairs. Co-operation with the business community is vital to the successful creation and matching of export supply and demand. Clearly this activity involves many of the export development efforts shown in Figure 3.3.

6 *Trade and information services* The DEP provides various kinds of trade information services such as a library, official services on trade enquiries, and a computerized trade data system. The information network on trade data is being established and should be operational in the near future.

In addition to these export promotion activities, export development and promotion efforts often involve the close co-operation of government and business, as mentioned earlier, to minimize export obstacles and related problems. Funding for export promotion and trade-related activities comes from a special Export Promotion Fund (EPF) – established to administer programmes more effectively – as well as the general government budget.

There are also integrated projects on export promotion. These are joint projects between the DEP and international organizations from various countries such as United Nations Development Programme (UNDP), European Economic Community (EEC), Japan External Trade Organization (JETRO), and so on. The typical project starts from initial contact between the parties until the product reaches the final consumer. Apart from such joint projects, the DEP also initiates other new projects to be financed under the EPF. Products under the projects are canned seafood, garments, shoes, jewellery products, artificial flowers, rubber products, furniture, floor and wall tiles, plastic products, and printing materials.

At present the DEP is responsible for thirty-eight trade offices around the world. There are twenty-four offices of commercial counsellors attached to the Royal Thai Embassy and fourteen Thai trade centres, eight of which are now in service, and six other offices are currently being established. Their main functions may be described as market penetration, market survey/information, and product development.

Recognition that export promotion involves co-operative effort by the private and public sectors is evident in the Thai approach. Under the fifth and sixth National Social and Economic Development Plans, export promotion has been given highest priority. The government initiatives, as summarized, depend on such co-operation:[40]

1 The Ministry of Industry provides technical and financial assistance for export-oriented production in small and medium-sized firms.
2 The Board of Investment grants special rights and privilege to export-oriented industries.
3 The Ministry of Agriculture encourages the export of products from the agro-industry sector.
4 The Ministry of Finance provides supportive policy measures, export credit to encourage and promote exports, and endeavours to simplify export procedures.
5 The Ministry of Education is involved in the introduction of export business courses to school curricula.
6 The Ministry of Foreign Affairs acts as a catalyst and guardian of Thailand's foreign trade interests.
7 The national airline, Thai International, plays a supporting and facilitating role as far as contact with foreign markets is concerned.

Export promotion in Sri Lanka

Sri Lanka has had a strong inward orientation which has moderated over the past decade.[41] While this country cannot be described as outward-oriented at all, its government has recognized the importance of export development and has created an Export Development Board. After a well-thought-out start-up, followed by a reassessment of the export development strategy in May 1987, the board prepared its first corporate plan for 1988–90.[42]

The re-orientation of the Sri Lanka government is borne of necessity. Over the period 1965 to 1985 the already low share of manufacturing in the GDP dropped from 17 to 15 per cent, while the share of agriculture remained about the same (28 versus 27 per cent).[43] Exports of goods decreased from 38 to 26 per cent of GDP over the same period. Sri Lanka has had some success in shifting its exports from an almost total reliance on primary commodities (in 1965, 99 per cent of merchandise exports were commodities) to manufactured merchandise (in 1985, 27 per cent of merchandise exports were in machinery, transport equipment, and other manufactures). Sri Lanka has further increased its dependence on industrialized market economies, which accounted for 89 per cent of its manufactured exports in 1989 (up from 59 per cent in 1965), while developing economies accounted for only 10 per cent in 1985 (down from 36 per cent in 1965).[44]

The Export Development Board was created in August 1979 in recognition that exports were a priority area in the country's economic development. The board, whose composition includes members from government and industry, carries out its day-to-day operations and functions through a number of officers. Its mandate is described in three key objectives:[45]

1 to improve progressively the climate for exporting in Sri Lanka,
2 to induce the expansion of production of export-related products and professional services,
3 to provide specialized export services to producers and exporters.

Figure 3.4 provides an overview of the organizational set-up of the export development board and its working divisions. A brief review of the functions of five key divisions is in order.

Policy and planning division

This division's contribution lies in the area of policy formulation for the development of exports. This involves broader international trade policies, such as appropriate foreign exchange rates conducive to exports, a role in the development of land-use policies to strengthen farming units, strengthened linkages between suppliers and exporters with appropriate incentives, and closer work with, and co-ordination of public and private sector interaction in creating a national industrial policy supportive of promotion and development of export-oriented industries.[46]

Product management division

Its function is to develop the supply of exports in particular target sectors (such as tea, rubber, spices, gems, light engineering products) through integrated programmes. On the one hand, non-exporting enterprises in target product areas are encouraged to enter exporting. This may involve the setting up of new institutional arrangements, such as the export production village programme. Here the focus is on systematizing rural supply development at the village level. Improvements in entrepreneurship, production efficiency, and quality control are the main steps in developing new employment and income opportunities. Figure 3.5 shows the overall approach used to link villages into the export development and promotion system.

On the other hand, market development and promotion are also pursued by this division. Market opportunity information is provided to exporters, contacts are established with markets through incoming

Figure 3.4 Export Development Board – Sri Lanka

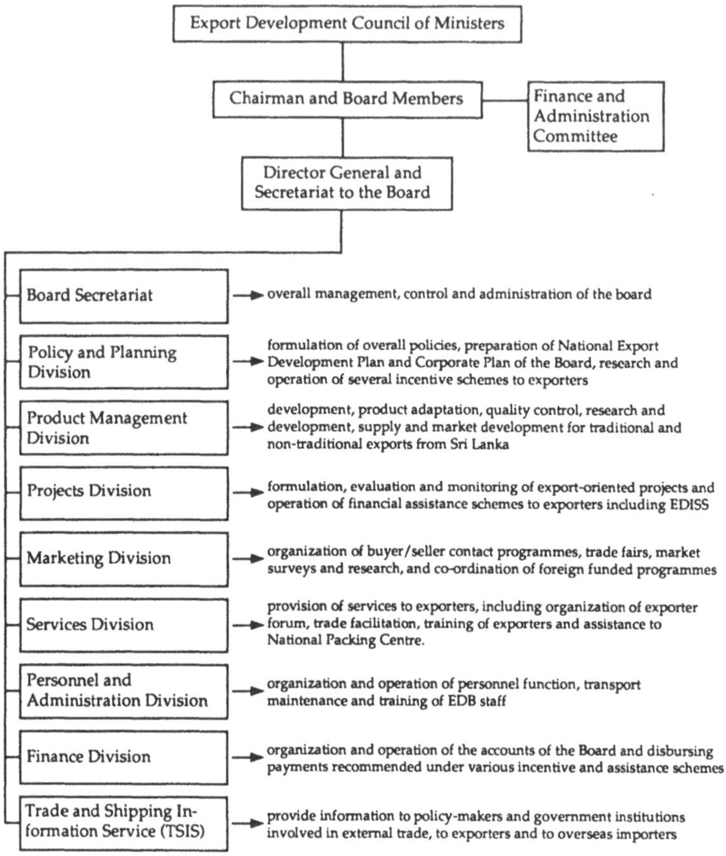

Source: Adapted from *Export Development Board and its Activities*, Sri Lanka, undated, pp. 3–4.

or outgoing missions as well as trade fairs. Product adaptation, quality improvement, and packaging development assistance are employed to make products more marketable to potential market segments abroad.

Projects division

The functions of this division relate primarily to the export development activity of the board. Measures to give financial support to export projects include short-, medium-, and long-term financing,

Figure 3.5 Concept of export production villages in export development and promotion

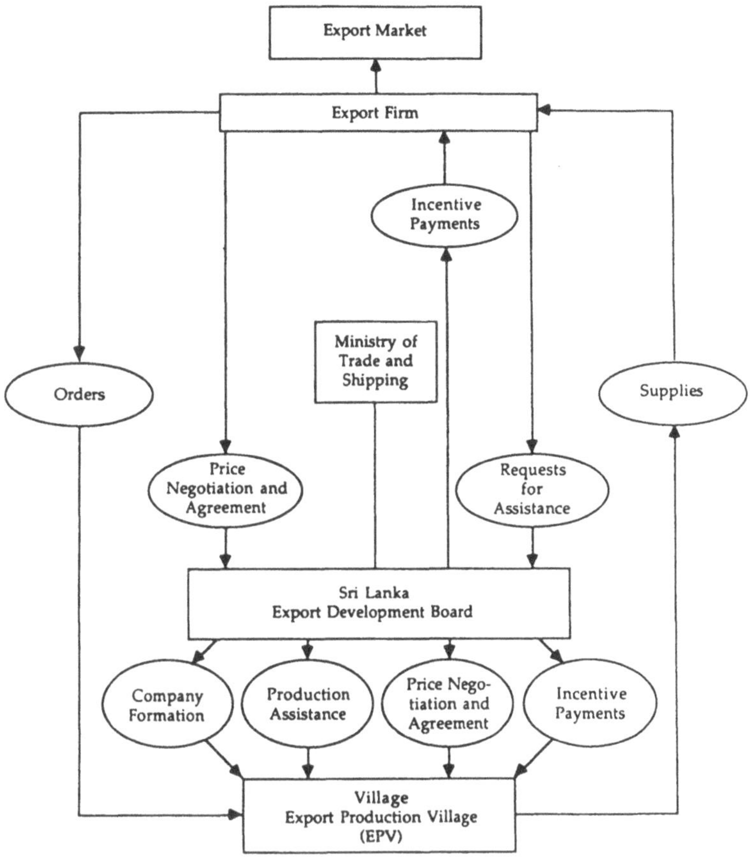

Source: *Export Development Board and its Activities*, Sri Lanka, undated, p. 13.

incentive schemes – ranging from coverage of certain expenses to equity participation – to pioneering export projects or those that require a company to restructure or reorganize. Particular attention is also given to small-scale enterprises currently exporting or those with export potential.

Marketing division

The key thrust of the marketing division is on market development.

Government export promotion

Market research programmes seek to identify priority products as well as priority markets, with a view to pursuing opportunities in existing markets as well as diversifying into new export markets. Emphasis is also placed on identifying non-traditional products that can be exported through counter-trade arrangements. Increasing Sri Lanka's foreign market presence as well as carrying out feasibility studies on establishing export houses and setting up bilateral co-operation arrangements with overseas trade promotion agencies form part of the division's efforts. Contact-facilitating programmes, such as incoming buying missions, outgoing trade missions, sample shows abroad, trade fair participation, and individual buyer–seller meet projects are available. The latter is a focused attempt at specific export expansion. About twenty-five exporters participate in such programmes which require one to one-and-a-half years to implement. First, potential products are selected; second, buyers' reaction is tested in target markets; third, products are adapted for production and export; fourth, buyer/seller meets in the form of a large Sri Lankan trade fair are held in the target market.[47] Building management competence through export marketing and promotion training programmes is an important part of the market development activity.

Services division

This division assists exporters in coping with barriers to trade. Its role is to simplify export procedures, liaise with regulatory bodies, and identify particular disincentives to export performance, specifically through:[48]

1 Exporters' forum – regular meetings of exporters and export regulating organizations.
2 Trade facilitation through a mixed private/public sector committee working closely with UNCTAD on export procedures.
3 Export packaging – integrating the packaging industry with exporters' specific needs for competitive packaging via the national packaging centre.
4 Registration of exporters – to maintain an up-to-date data bank on exporters and products as a tool in export policy formulation and as a resource to foreign buyers.
5 Exporter training – through internal and external seminars and workshops in export production, marketing, and management.
6 Advisory services – on practically all aspects of exporting.

Summary

This section dealt with export promotion organizations in operation. It was seen that some of the issues of economic development discussed earlier in this chapter indeed impact on export development and thus affect the export promotion organizations. The situation in the Latin American and Caribbean area was examined by considering countries' experiences as far as national export development strategies, export promotion policies, and the scope of services are concerned. Although one geographic region was examined, there is considerable diversity as far as characteristics and operation of export promotion organizations is concerned. Still on a regional focus, brief reference was made to the Economic and Social Commission for Asia and the Pacific. This organization serves the developing countries in the region. The focus is on understanding the complexities of international marketing, through both informational support and training as well as export development schemes. Finally, this section profiled two countries' export promotion efforts: Thailand as a country committed to export development, and Sri Lanka as a country with an emerging export orientation.

Conclusions

Export promotion in the developing world was reviewed against the backdrop of the particular economic and trade situation of these countries. It is apparent that these countries have made substantial progress towards both export development and diversification of their exports into more sophisticated manufactured products. At the same time, the ongoing challenge of narrowing the expectation and reality gap between developed and developing countries suggests that tremendous efforts lie ahead, in economic development, export development, and, in particular, export promotion.

It was shown that the International Trade Centre UNCTAD/GATT has a major role in this process. Its comprehensive programmes are becoming increasingly strategic in focus, namely assistance is provided at the institutional and individual business level integrating their respective efforts so that export supply and demand are developed in tandem. As with all assistance, however, it is only a means not an end in itself and the onus for successfully establishing structures and programmes rests largely with the developing countries themselves.

Export promotion organizations were discussed in the context of a framework which links the two main components of export development, namely export supply and export demand. The role and function of such organizations was seen to depend in no small measure on their position in the government hierarchy and the importance accorded to them by the authorities. Their involvement in policy formulation and implementation was also seen to be diverse. To develop a better appreciation for the actual operation of export promotion organizations, countries in the Latin American/Caribbean region were reviewed, as was the truly regional focus of ESCAP, which serves the trade promotion needs of developing countries in South-East Asia. Two examples of export promotion, namely Thailand and Sri Lanka, indicated that with strategic export development guidance and co-operation between public and private sectors, economic development is enhanced. Commitment and an outward orientation are critical to such a result.

Notes and references

1 *Economist*, 3 October 1987, p. 115.
2 *World Development Report 1987*, New York, Oxford University Press, 1987, p. 57.
3 'A survey of the world economy', *Economist*, 26 September 1987, p. 52.
4 The growth rates for 1965–85 are manufactured goods output – developing countries 7.2 per cent versus industrial countries 3.8 per cent; manufactured goods exports – 12.2 per cent versus 6.8 per cent: *World Development Report*, p. 47.
5 *World Development Report*, p. 48.
6 ibid., pp. 82–3.
7 *Economist*, 4 July 1987, p. 75.
8 *ITC Promoting Trade*, International Trade Centre, UNCTAD/GATT, Geneva, undated, p. ii.
9 *ITC Information*, International Trade Centre, UNCTAD/GATT, no. 23, 6 April 1987, p. 5; *ITC Promoting Trade*, pp. 6–23.
10 ibid., p. 3; *Annual Report on the Activities of the International Trade Centre UNCTAD/GATT 1985*, Joint Advisory Group on the International Trade Centre UNCTAD/GATT, Nineteenth Session Geneva 7–15 April 1986, p. 7.
11 *Annual Report on the Activities of the International Trade Centre UNCTAD/GATT 1986*, Joint Advisory Group on the International Trade Centre UNCTAD/GATT, Twentieth Session, Geneva, 6–10 April 1987, p. 14.
12 Personal interview with Mr G.M. Engblom, Executive Director, International Trade Centre, UNCTAD/GATT, Geneva, 8 December 1987.
13 'Report on enterprise-oriented approach in ITC's technical co-operation

for export development and promotion', International Trade Centre, UNCTAD/GATT, Geneva, November 1987, p. 1.

14 ibid., pp. 3–5.

15 W.J. Bilkey, 'An attempted integration of the literature on the export behaviour of firms', *Journal of International Business Studies*, 1978, vol. 9, no. 1, pp. 33–46; D.L. Brady and W.O. Bearden, 'The effect of managerial attitudes on alternative exporting methods', *Journal of International Business Studies*, 1979, vol. 10, no. 4, pp. 79–84; L.S. Welch and F. Wiedersheim-Paul, 'Export promotion policy – a new approach', *Australian Journal of Management*, 1979, vol. 4, no. 2, pp. 165–77, F.H. Rolf Seringhaus, 'Do experienced exporters have market entry problems?', *Finnish Journal of Business Economics*, 1987, vol. 36, no. 4, pp. 376–88.

16 *ITC Activities and Services in Trade Information*, International Trade Centre, UNCTAD/GATT, Geneva, 17 March 1987, pp. 1–12.

17 *Market News Service*, International Trade Centre, UNCTAD/GATT, Geneva, undated.

18 *Trade Data Analysis at Enterprise Level for Trade Promotion*, International Trade Centre, UNCTAD/GATT, Geneva, December 1986, p. 1.

19 ibid., pp. 2–3.

20 ibid., p. 1.

21 The following discussion of Export Promotion Organizations draws extensively on *Trade Promotion Institutions: Monograph on the Role and Organization of Trade Promotion*, International Trade Centre, UNCTAD/GATT, Geneva, 1986.

22 *Economist*, 26 December 1987, p. 88.

23 *Trade Promotion Institutions: Monograph*, pp. 18 ff.

24 ibid., pp. 20–2.

25 ibid., pp. 11–16.

26 *Trade Promotion Institutions: Monograph*, pp. 51–96.

27 *Selected Export Promotion Organizations: Structures, Functions and Activities*, International Trade Centre, UNCTAD/GATT, Geneva, 25 September 1986.

28 Personal interview with Mr Yasusuke Mori, Chief, Trade Information Service, and Mr Jaime Crespo-Blanco, Senior Trade Promotion Officer, Office for Latin America and the Caribbean, International Trade Centre, UNCTAD/GATT, Geneva, 9 December 1987.

29 *Institutional Systems for Export Promotion in Latin America and the Caribbean – A Comparative Analysis*, Document No. 1, International Trade Centre, UNCTAD/GATT, Geneva, 1984, p. 10.

30 ibid., pp. 16–17.

31 ibid., p. 20.

32 ibid., pp. 6–7.

33 *ESCAP Trade Promotion Centre*, Economic and Social Commission for Asia and the Pacific, United Nations, Bangkok, undated, pp. 2–4.

34 *World Development Report*, p. 83.

35 ibid., pp. 206, 210.

36 ibid., p. 228.
37 *Thailand's Department of Export Promotion: At Your Service Around the World*, undated, p. 4, written communication from Mr Pattana Siriphand, Export Service Division, Department of Export Promotion, 4 November 1987.
38 'Export promotion and export development plan of the Department of Export Promotion', Ministry of Commerce, Bangkok, undated, pp. 2–4.
39 Incoming trade missions are those bringing foreign buyers to visit companies in a domestic market; outgoing trade missions are those where domestic companies visit foreign markets.
40 'Export promotion', pp. 4–5.
41 *World Development Report*, p. 83.
42 'Annual work programme, budgeting and evaluation procedures, adopted by the Sri Lanka Export Development Board', Sri Lanka Export Development Board, 31 October 1987.
43 *World Development Report*, p. 206.
44 ibid., pp. 222, 228.
45 *Export Development Board and its Activities*, Sri Lanka, undated, p. 2.
46 'Annual work programme', p. 18.
47 ibid., pp. 20–1.
48 *Export Development Board*, pp. 26–9.

Chapter four

Legal barriers to government export promotion*

Introduction

Government export promotion includes 'all public policy measures that actually or potentially enhance exporting activity either from a firm, industry or national perspective'.[1] Clearly in today's fiercely competitive world the enhancement of one nation's exporting activity must be at the expense of other trading nations. Consequently the international community has developed rules, at the international, regional, and national level, to combat these practices where they distort trading patterns by giving a nation an unfair advantage over its competitors. This chapter will outline these rules and attempt to indicate which of the myriad of government export promotion measures are affected by them.

The first section addresses the issue of international barriers as they apply to government export promotion. This is accomplished by discussing, first, which export promotion measures fall under GATT, and second, which GATT rules apply. The second section considers barriers at the national level by discussing applicable national rules and specifically considering countervailing and anti-dumping duties. Regional barriers to export promotion are covered in the third section with particular attention to intra-area trade and trade with third countries. The chapter closes with conclusions from the discussion of legal barriers.

International barriers to government export promotion

Introduction

The main international agreement that regulates government export promotion is *The General Agreement on Tariffs and Trade*,[2] the rules of which are binding on contracting parties. The Organization

* This chapter was written by Philip Raworth, University of Alberta, Edmonton, Canada.

for Economic Co-operation and Development (OECD)[3] has drawn up certain additional non-binding undertakings, which are largely observed by the industrialized nations, and the Food and Agriculture Organization (FAO)[4] has drawn up principles that regulate the disposal of surplus agricultural output. These latter two sets of rules are considered in the context of GATT regulation.

At this stage we are concerned only with the direct regulation of government export promotion by GATT. Countervailing duties and anti-dumping duties are subject to Article VI of the General Agreement but are imposed under national legislation. They are considered separately. It should also be borne in mind that GATT almost exclusively covers trade in goods. Government measures relating to the export of services are by and large exempt from GATT or indeed most international regulation.[5]

Types of government export promotion measures covered by GATT

Government export promotion is regulated by the rules on subsidies contained in Article XVI of the General Agreement and the 1979 Subsidies Code.[6] The latter agreement resulted from the Tokyo Round[7] of multilateral trade negotiations and was intended to clarify the substantive provisions of Article XVI and to provide for more efficient remedial procedures. Not all contracting parties to the GATT have subscribed to the Subsidies Code,[8] but those that have included some of the most important trading nations – the USA, Japan, the European Community countries, Canada, and most member states of the European Free Trade Area. A signatory to the Subsidies Code has the option of proceeding under the Subsidies Code or the General Agreement, but the former is more beneficial. In this chapter we shall deal with the provisions of both the General Agreement and the Subsidies Code, but it should be borne in mind that, except where it is dealing with general principles, the Subsidies Code rules are applicable only to signatory nations.

In order to come within the GATT rules, a government export promotion measure must first constitute a subsidy. There is no definition of this term in the General Agreement or the Subsidies Code, but both clearly indicate that a subsidy connotes some form of financial support. Article XVI:1 mentions specifically 'any form of income or price support'; Ad Article XVI:3 singles out domestic agricultural price stabilization or support schemes that rely partially or wholly on government funds; and by prohibiting export subsidies that result in bi-level pricing – i.e. export sales at a price lower than the domestic price – Article XVI:4 is similarly taking aim at forms of price support. The Subsidies Code is even clearer. All the domestic subsidies mentioned in Article 11:3 as well as the various incentives and aids for exporters included in the appended *Illustrative List of Export Subsidies*[9] involve direct or indirect financial support by the state. GATT practice also regularly equates subsidization with pecuniary benefits.[10] One source combines these and describes subsidy as 'a measurable economic advantage afforded to an enterprise by or at the direction of a government'.[11] This is perhaps the best definition of a subsidy under the GATT rules.

It is not, however, the subsidy *per se* that is subject to GATT regulation; there must also be an effect on exports that distorts normal trading patterns. Thus Article XVI:1, which deals with subsidies in general, singles out those that operate directly or indirectly to increase[12] exports in a manner that causes or threatens to cause serious prejudice to the interests of other contracting parties. Article XVI:B sets out special rules for export subsidies because it is recognized that they are particularly prone to have this effect. The Subsidies Code is even clearer that the target is trade distortion by linking serious prejudice to *inter alia* (1) the effects of the subsidized imports in the domestic market of the importing signatory and (2) the effects of the subsidized exports in displacing the exports of like products of another signatory from a third country market.[13] In the tax cases, the GATT panels also relied on the trade-distorting effects of the various legislations, concluding that there was a subsidy under Article XVI:4 because of the impact on the export sector.[14]

GATT barriers to government export promotion operate, therefore, only against those measures that confer a measurable economic advantage on domestic exporters that distorts trading patterns by increasing exports to a higher level than would otherwise be the case.[15] The question is which government export promotion measures fall into this category.

Government export promotion takes two essential forms: institutional support and financial support. Institutional support exists where governments through various ministries and agencies provide general information, organizational help, and expertise to their exporters. General information covers such matters as developments and opportunities in various markets as well as the underlying economic situation, socio-cultural environment, business practices, and trade barriers. Organizational help consists in arranging trade fairs, exhibitions, trade missions, and foreign visits, finding agents in foreign countries, and specialized services such as those offered by the Canadian Commercial Corporation. The expertise offered can range over the whole area of international business transactions from specific marketing guidance to advice on the mechanics of exporting

– for example, financing, documentation, insurance, and transportation.

While institutional support provided by governments is clearly aimed at increasing exports and represents a degree of financial saving for domestic industry, it is doubtful whether such support comes under the GATT rules on subsidies. In the first place, although it may represent a financial saving for domestic industry, measurement of the economic advantage institutional support confers is very complex as the services provided can not readily be quantified in money terms. Chapter 6 addresses this issue in detail. It is difficult to imagine a company building these savings into its cost-accounting procedures. Second, institutional support cannot really be said to cause trade distortion. Its purpose is indeed to increase exports but it aims to do this by making exporters more effective; it does not reduce the price of exports, increase profits, or otherwise give firms a pecuniary incentive to increase their exports, all of which GATT practice has identified as the essential elements of a trade-distorting subsidy.[16] Moreover, the widespread provision of institutional support by governments, at least in the industrialized world, would tend to neutralize any discernible trade-distorting effect. Indeed it is partly because institutional support is such a common practice, in addition to the arguments advanced above, that it has never been challenged under the GATT rules on subsidies. We may safely assume, therefore, that it is not subject to GATT rule.

Government financial support for export falls into two categories, incentives and direct financial support. In the case of incentives normal rules are modified in order to encourage exports directly or to stimulate production with the incidental result that exports are increased. Some of the most common incentives are fiscal incentives, such as the full or partial exemption, remission, or deferral of direct and indirect taxes or social security payments, accelerated depreciation, tax-free reserve funds, and special allowances for marketing expenses; the reduction or exemption of import duties, either by drawback or waiver, on inputs used in exported goods; and the use of multiple exchange rates and other currency practices that either directly reduce the price of exported goods or otherwise financially benefit exporters. All these incentives confer a measurable economic advantage that has potential for trade distortion.

Direct financial support for export comes in various ways. First, there are the government agencies that provide buyer and supplier credit, insurance, and guarantees. Second, there is financial support for the process of exporting. Marketing may be supported through the full or partial payment of expenses involved in such matters as participation in trade fairs, market and feasibility studies, market identification and penetration, bidding on tenders, incoming buyer and hiring outside professionals. Distribution aid will often involve preferred internal transportation rates for goods destined for export. Third, production support in the form of low-interest loans and direct production grants, infrastructure investment, investment grants, wage subsidies, labour training programmes, government-sponsored research and development, and the delivery of goods or services by governments or their agencies on preferred terms. Finally there is tied aid, where a government makes a grant to another country, usually a developing country, that is to be used to buy goods and/or services from the donor country.

Direct financial support almost always confers a measurable economic advantage with potential for trade distortion. An exception would be government-provided credit, guarantees and insurance provided at commercial rates. Certain marketing support measures may also escape GATT regulation where their trade-distorting effect is negligible. Tied aid is a special case, for here the financial support is the pre-condition of the sale. In reality the transaction is little more than the purchase by a government of domestic goods or services for donating abroad. There may be competition between donor nations, but trade is distorted only where the donated goods supplant a commercial sale or where the aid is part of a commercial package. Tied aid has not been challenged under the GATT rules, but it is subject to some regulation by the OECD and the FAO.

Government export promotion and the GATT rules

Introduction

There are two basic types of subsidies: export subsidies and domestic or production subsidies. The difference between them has been summarized with admirable terseness.

> Export subsidies are those granted only on that portion of the goods destined for export. 'Domestic' or 'production' subsidies, on the other hand, are those granted for the manufacture or production of goods irrespective of their ultimate destination for consumption.[17]

The term 'government export promotion' can be taken to embrace both types of subsidies if it includes 'all public policy measures that actually or potentially enhance exporting activity'.[18] Clearly, however, most government export promotion will be directed openly towards export performance, and so this chapter will concentrate on the GATT rules on export subsidies. Some treatment of the regulation of domestic subsidies is still necessary, as many domestic programmes have export ramifications. Some may even in reality be export-oriented. This may be because a country has such a small domestic market that any increase in production must inevitably go abroad, or because the particular industry or firm that is being aided relies heavily on exports.

An issue that should be addressed before considering the GATT rules is what actually qualifies as a government measure under these rules. The US view, as illustrated by the practice of the International Trade Commission (ITA),[19] is that benefits provided by private bodies at the direction of a government should be included. The European Community (EC),[20] on the other hand, has always maintained that to qualify a measure must involve direct government funding. In support of its contention the EC has pointed to the catch-all final paragraph of the Illustrative List appended to the Subsidized Code, which refers to 'any other charge on the public account'.[21] The European position is further bolstered by paragraphs (j) and (k) of the List dealing with government export insurance, guarantees, and credits, which apply only to governments and special government institutions. Even paragraph (c), which includes transport subsidies 'mandated by governments', does not really support the American view; most national transport systems are either owned or subsidized by governments and hence any benefits they confer ultimately derive from public funds.

None the less the American position is not without logic. It is difficult to see why an exporter who receives a benefit from a private corporation under a government-sponsored programme should be treated more leniently than one who receives the very same benefit directly from the government. The issue has never been definitively resolved, although a GATT Working Party report on subsidies has indicated some support for the US view by declaring that when a government entrusts its function to a private body, 'the practice would in no real sense differ from those normally followed by governments'.[22]

Export subsidies

The General Agreement contains no definition of an export subsidy, and this has led to a fundamental disagreement between the EC and the USA over its nature.[23] The EC believes that only the definition of export subsidies given earlier in this section is appropriate. In support of its position the Community can point to paragraphs 2 and 4 of Article XVI, which refer to export subsidies as a 'subsidy on the export of any product'. The USA, on the other hand, has argued that any subsidy which operates to increase exports, whether that is its purpose or not, is an export subsidy. Support for the US position can be found in Article XVI:3, which includes among the special provisions on export subsidies 'any form of subsidy which operates to increase the export of any primary product'. The General Agreement is clearly ambiguous on this issue. On the other hand, although the Subsidies Code does not actually define an export subsidy, the examples of export subsidies given in the Illustrative List are all pure export subsidies. In addition, Article 11 explicitly separates out 'subsidies other than export subsidies'; and the examples it gives of the purposes of such subsidies and their nature indicate without doubt that these are what have been described earlier as domestic subsidies.[24] In fact the Subsidies Code would appear to be a compromise. The USA has implicitly accepted the narrower European definition of export subsidies in return for the explicit right to bring action against domestic subsidies that operate in practice to increase exports. This narrower definition of export subsidies also accords with GATT practice, which sees the essence of an export subsidy in its non-applicability to domestic activities.[25]

The GATT rules on export subsidies distinguish between exports of primary and non-primary products. The former, which are described by Ad Article XVI: Section B (2) as

> any product of farm, forest or fishery, or any mineral, in its natural form or which has undergone such processing as is customarily required to prepare it for marketing in substantial volume in international trade

are subject only to a conditional ban. Article XVI:3 requires that the subsidy not result in the subsidizing nation acquiring more than an equitable share of world trade, taking into account past export performance over a previous representative period and 'any special factors which may have affected or may be affecting . . . trade in the product'. These special factors have never been clearly identified, but they probably have to do with relative productive efficiency and export ability.[26] Ad Article XVI:3(1) confirms in principle the right of a contracting party which has not exported previously to obtain a share of world trade in a primary product.

The Subsidies Code clarifies and tightens up these provisions of the General Agreement. In the first place it excludes minerals from the definition of primary products. It also deals with certain problems that had arisen because of the vague wording of Article XVI. Article 10:2(a) aims at preventing contracting parties from using export subsidies to increase their exports to a particular market even though their overall share of world trade remains equitable. Article 10:2(b) attempts to safeguard the position of traditional suppliers to areas where new markets arise. Article 10:3 contains an agreement by signatories not to depress prices through the use of excessive subsidies. Finally, Article 10:2(c) defines the term 'previous representative period' as 'the three most recent calendar years in which normal market conditions existed'.

The efficacy of the GATT rules on export subsidies on primary products is in considerable doubt. Agricultural production in particular has long exceeded world demand. As a result, international competition is fierce, and the use of subsidies is widespread and largely uncontrolled. The EC's Common Agricultural Programme is widely perceived by outsiders as providing European producers with lavish export subsidies that have permitted them to obtain a more than equitable share of the world market, but despite this the EC has by and large succeeded in shielding it from GATT regulation. Recently the USA has retaliated by embarking upon its own subsidization programme for exports of primary products. The situation is particularly chaotic in the cereals market, but in general it is fair to say that much of the international trade in primary products is conducted outside the GATT subsidy rules.[27] It remains to be seen how far the Uruguay Round of multilateral trade negotiations will go in correcting this situation.

By contrast the GATT rules on subsidies on export of non-primary products are more widely followed. Indeed the rules have been strengthened since 1947. Originally Article XVI:4 provided only for a standstill on export subsidies that resulted in bi-level pricing. In 1960 a number of contracting parties, including the USA, Japan, Canada, and the European countries, signed a declaration giving effect to the first sentence of Article XVI:4, which prohibits such price-reducing subsidies.[28] In addition an illustrative list of export subsidies was appended to the declaration, in respect of which there was to be a rebuttable presumption of bi-level pricing. Certain other contracting parties agreed to extend the standstill,[29] but this undertaking lapsed in 1967.

The requirement of bi-level pricing in the application of Article XVI:4 has been criticized as too narrow,[30] and in fact GATT practice under that article was to downplay its status as the sole criterion of trade distortion. In the tax cases, for example, the panels based their findings of an illegal subsidy on increased profits and increased motivation to export as well as bi-level pricing.[31] This development culminated in Article 9:1 of the Subsidies Code, which prohibits export subsidies on non-primary products without any reference to bi-level pricing. This means that increased profits and increased export sales activity as a result of the subsidy can also now be considered, as the tax cases suggested. What may have become the rule for export subsidies on non-primary products under Article XVI:4 by virtue of GATT practice is thus implicitly adopted by the Subsidies Code. The Code retains the presumption of trade distortion for this type of export subsidy.[32]

There are special rules under the Subsidies Code for developing countries with respect to export subsidies on non-primary products.[33] The absolute prohibition contained in Article 9:1 does not apply to them, but they are not given *carte blanche*. They are not to use these subsidies in a manner that causes trade distortion, which, however, is not presumed as in the case of developed countries but must be proven by positive evidence. Should a developing country enter into a commitment to reduce or eliminate these subsidies when they become 'inconsistent with its competitive and development needs', no retaliatory action can be taken against a subsidy that conforms to the commitment.[34]

In order to determine which government measures constitute export subsidies and hence fall under the above rules, it is best to consult the Illustrative List contained in the Annex to the Subsidies Code (see Table 4.1).

The List is largely self-explanatory and covers most of the measures that were characterized earlier as government financial support for export. Paragraph (l), which is a catch-all provision, would cover some government measures that are not explicitly mentioned, such as financial support for marketing. The measure in question must, however, be subsidy 'in the sense of Article XVI', which means that it must confer a measurable economic advantage that distorts trading patterns. Not all government marketing support will qualify. For example, it is difficult to attribute significant trade-distorting effect to small contributions to the expenses of attending a trade fair or accompanying a trade mission, where the participant firm bears most of the cost.[35] On the other hand, the claim by the Canadian federal government that the PEMD programme is not a subsidy because the government contribution made under some parts of this programme must be repaid in the event of export sales is unconvincing.[36] As paragraphs (e) and (h) of the List make clear, deferral of payment can also bestow a benefit.[37] In addition, the subsidization of unsuccessful marketing efforts will clearly affect a firm's overall marketing costs.

Certain government export promotion measures are implicitly or explicitly declared by the List not to constitute export subsidies. One of these is the exemption, remission, or deferral of indirect taxes on the production and distribution of exported products, as long as the relief is not in excess of the taxes levied on like products when sold for domestic consumption.[38] Prior stage cumulative indirect taxes

Table 4.1 Illustrative list of export subsidies

(a) The provision by governments of direct subsidies to a firm or an industry contingent upon export performance.
(b) Currency retention schemes or any similar practices which involve a bonus on exports.
(c) Internal transport and freight charges on export shipments, provided or mandated by governments, on terms more favourable than for domestic shipments.
(d) The delivery by governments or their agencies of imported or domestic products or services for use in the production of exported goods, on terms or conditions more favourable than for delivery of like or directly competitive products or services for use on the production of goods for domestic consumption, if (in the case of products) such terms or conditions are more favourable than those commercially available on world markets to its exporters.
(e) The full or partial exemption, remission, or deferral[a] specifically related to exports, or direct taxes[b] or social welfare charges paid or payable by industrial or commercial enterprises.
(f) The allowance of special deductions directly related to exports or export performance, over and above those granted in respect to production for domestic consumption, in the calculation of the base on which direct taxes are charged.
(g) The exemption or remission in respect of the production and distribution of exported products, of indirect taxes[c] in excess of those levied in respect of the production and distribution of like products when sold for domestic consumption.
(h) The exemption, remission, or deferral of prior stage cumulative indirect taxes[d] on goods or services used in the production of exported products in excess of the exemption, remission, or deferral of like prior stage cumulative indirect taxes on goods or services used in the production of like products when sold for domestic consumption; provided, however, that prior stage cumulative indirect taxes may be exempted, remitted, or deferred on exported products even when not exempted, remitted or deferred on like products when sold for domestic consumption, if the prior stage cumulative indirect taxes are levied on goods that are physically incorporated (making normal allowance for waste) in the exported product.
(i) The remission or drawback of import charges[e] in excess of those levied on imported goods that are physically incorporated (making normal allowance for waste) in the exported product; provided, however, that in particular cases a firm may use a quantity of home market goods equal to, and having the same quality and characteristics as, the imported goods as a substitute for them in order to benefit from this provision if the import and the corresponding export operations both occur within a reasonable period, normally not to exceed two years.
(j) The provision by governments (or special institutions controlled by governments) of export credit guarantee or insurance programmes, of exported products or of exchange risk programmes, at premium rates, which are manifestly inadequate to cover the long-term operating costs and losses of the programmes.
(k) The grant by governments (or special institutions controlled by and/or acting under the authority of governments) or export credits at rates below those which they actually have to pay for the funds so employed (or would have to pay if they borrowed on international capital markets in order to obtain funds of the same maturity and denominated in the same currency as the export credit), or the payment by them of all or part of the costs incurred by exporters or

Table 4.1 contd.

financial institutions in obtaining credits, in so far as they are used to secure a material advantage in the field of export credit terms. Provided, however, that if a signatory is a party to an international undertaking on official export credits to which at least twelve original signatories to this Agreement are parties as of 1 January 1979 (or a successor undertaking which has been adopted by those original signatories), or if in practice a signatory applies the interest rate provisions of the relevant undertaking, an export credit practice which is in conformity with those provisions shall not be considered an export subsidy prohibited by this Agreement.
(l) Any other charge on the public account constituting an export subsidy in the sense of Article XVI of the General Agreement.

Source: *Subsidies and Countervailing Duties*, Appendix, 26 BISD 56 (1978–79) April 1979.

Notes:

[a] Deferral of taxes is not considered a subsidy where the appropriate interest charges are paid (paragraph [e]) is not intended to prohibit government measures to prevent the double taxation of foreign income.

[b] Direct taxes comprise taxes on wages, profits, interest, rents, royalties, and all other forms of income, and taxes on ownership of real property.

[c] Indirect taxes comprise sales, excise, turnover, value added, franchise, stamp, transfer, inventory and equipment taxes, border taxes, and all taxes other than direct taxes and import charges.

[d] Prior stage indirect taxes are those levied on goods or services used directly or indirectly in making the exported product. Cumulative indirect taxes are multi-staged taxes levied where there is no mechanism for subsequent crediting of the tax if the goods or services subject to tax at one stage of production are used in a succeeding stage of production.

[e] Import charges such as tariffs, duties, and other fiscal charges.

on goods and services used in the production of exported products may also be exempted, remitted, or deferred as long as the same relief is extended to the production of goods for domestic consumption, or in cases where the taxes are levied on goods that are physically incorporated into an exported product. These provisions would seem to go beyond Ad Article XVI, which provides only for the exemption of domestic consumption taxes, but it accords with General GATT practice.[39] They arise from the adoption by GATT of the 'destination' principle, whereby all indirect taxes are held to be borne by the consumer and hence will be imposed by the importing country.[40] The exception is thus necessary to prevent the double taxation of exports.[41] Similar reasoning applies to the remission or drawback of import duties on imported goods that are physically incorporated into exported goods, as any foreign tariff on these exports will normally take into consideration the inputs used to produce them. This type of relief is thus also not considered an export subsidy as long as it does not exceed the tariff payable on the intermediate goods.[42]

Paragraph (k) of the List deals with the problem of officially supported export credits. These are not to be considered export subsidies in two cases; first, where the credit is extended at rates that are not below those which the government would have to pay to obtain the funds on international capital markets, and second, where the credit is extended in conformity with the OECD *Arrangement on Guidelines for Officially Supported Export Credits* (the OECD Arrangement).[43]

The OECD Arrangement, which covers government credits for the export of both goods and services with a repayment term of two years or more,[44] was signed in 1978 and has been amended several times since then. It is an information arrangement but it has secured a high degree of compliance, in part no doubt because compliance exempts a signatory from the Subsidies Code provisions on export subsidies and probably from the provisions of Article XVI as well. The major provisions of the OECD Arrangement are given in Table 4.2.

There is some disagreement as to whether export credits that are granted in derogation from the substantive provisions of the Arrangement pursuant to paragraphs 11 and 14 are also excepted by paragraph (k) of the Illustrative List. The EC maintains, and the USA disagrees, that they are as the Arrangement specifically permits the derogation. The American position would seem to be the more logical. Even where the subsidizing country has followed the notification or matching provisions of paragraphs 11 and 14, it still cannot be said that the export credit conforms to the Arrangement. It is, in fact, a permitted exception, and as such it could well be argued that it falls outside paragraph (k).[45]

Another problem is whether the two exceptions in paragraph (k) are to operate separately. This issue would arise where a government extends an export credit that conforms to paragraph 5 of the Arrangement but which is provided at less than the government paid or would have had to pay commercially for the funds. The construction of paragraph (k) would indicate that such a credit is indeed still excepted, as the second sentence clearly states, that provided a credit conforms to the Arrangement, it is absolutely protected.

It was suggested earlier that tied aid, which is really the equivalent of donating goods or services to a developing country, can be considered a trade-distorting subsidy only where it displaces a commercial sale or is part of a commercial package. The OECD Arrangement treats all tied aid as a derogation that is subject to its notification and matching provisions, but the only limitation it contains is the requirement that tied aid in a commercial package must equal at least 25 per cent of the overall financing. Special guidelines have, however, been drawn up by the FAO to deal with the displacement of commercial sales by food aid. Under the FAO's

Table 4.2 Major provisions on government credits of the OECD arrangement

(a)	Purchasers must make cash payments amounting to at least 15 per cent of the export contract value. No official support except insurance and guarantees against pre-credit risks may extend to this down payment (Paragraph 3);[a]
(b)	Maximum repayment terms are set down, stretching from five years for relatively rich countries to ten years for relatively poor countries.[b] Payment of both principal and interest must be made in equal and regular instalments not more than six months apart (Paragraph 4);
(c)	Minimum interest rates are set down, depending on the recipient country and the term of the loan. These rates were initially fixed, but now they are automatically adjusted where there is a change within the last six months of at least fifty basis points in market rates as measured on a weighted basis by the yields in secondary markets for medium-term government bonds denominated in US dollars, sterling, deutschmarks, French francs, and yen. Special interest rates are set for low-interest currencies, such as the yen, deutschmark, and Swiss franc. These rates, which are called Commercial Interest Reference Rates, are set according to five-year government bond yields plus a mark-up of 0.2 per cent (Paragraph 5);
(d)	The OECD Arrangement incorporates the 1975 *Understanding on Local Cost Standard*, which provides that credit shall not be extended to cover the local costs of importers that are not payable to the exporter. This provision is particularly relevant to the export of services, in particular construction contracts. For relatively rich countries this support can be only in the form of insurance or guarantees (Paragraph 6);
(e)	Participants must notify all other participants whenever they finance a purchase through tied aid (Paragraph 8). In the case of associated financing, where outright aid is combined with export credit to achieve an effective interest rate below the level set pursuant to paragraph 5, the OECD Arrangement mandates a minimum aid component of 25 per cent (Paragraph 129b). All tied aid is subject to the matching provisions of paragraphs 11 (Paragraph 15[a] [3]);
(f)	Parties to the Arrangement are allowed to derogate from its provisions as long as they notify the other participants, which are then allowed to match the derogation (Paragraphs 11 and 14).
(g)	The Arrangement does not cover trade in military equipment and agricultural commodities (Paragraph 1[c]) and there are special arrangements for trade in ships, nuclear power plants, ground satellite communication stations, and aircraft (Paragraph 9);[c]

Source: OECD Arrangement on Guidelines for Officially Supported Export Credits, OECD DOC.TD/CONSENSUS/–86.33.

Notes:
[a] The downpayment may, however, be financed in the form of local cost support, see para. 6.
[b] For a list of the various countries in the three categories see Hufbauer and Erb, *Subsidies*, pp. 236–9.
[c] See Annexes II to V.

Principles of Surplus Disposal and Consultative Obligations of Member Nations, donor and recipient nations are supposed to come to a bilateral agreement under which the recipient nation agrees to maintain its normal levels of commercial imports (the Usual

Marketing Requirement). Notification and consultation procedures exist with respect to traditional exporters to the recipient country.[46] There is no similar regime for non-agricultural products, but recourse could probably be had to Article XXII:1(b) of the General Agreement in cases of trade distortion.[47]

One final point concerns the relationship between the Illustrative List and Article XVI. With respect to actionable export subsidies, it is understood that the List is merely restating accepted GATT practice and that these measures are also subject to the rules of Article XVI. Some of the exceptions in the List, such as the exemption of indirect taxes and import charges are also unobjectionable, but the exceptions dealing with concessionary financing are a clear departure from GATT practice under Article XVI.[48]

The USA seems to take the view that the Subsidies Code and Article XVI can be used separately and on one occasion referred an instance of concessionary financing by Canada's Export Development Corporation (EDC) to GATT.[49] Although in this case EDC had derogated form the OECD Arrangement in order to match a lower offer by France so that paragraph (k) might not have applied, none the less the American move could be seen as an attempt to circumvent the Subsidies Code by direct recourse to Article XVI of the General Agreement.[50] The matter was dropped before any GATT ruling could be given, but it is suggested that this circumvention should not be allowed. Bearing in mind that the Subsidies Code is an agreement on the interpretation and application of Article XVI, it surely binds the signatores to use Article XVI according to its provisions.[51]

Domestic subsidies

One source defines domestic subsidies as 'those granted for the manufacture or production of goods irrespective of their ultimate destination'.[52] As with export subsidies, however, there is no definition of domestic subsidies in the General Agreement or the Subsidies Code, but the Code does distinguish between export and other subsidies. The latter are dealt with specifically by Article 11, and from the examples given in paragraph 3 it is clear that these other subsidies are domestic subsidies. They cover a broad range of government aids: government financing of commercial enterprises, including grants, loans, or guarantees; government provision or government-financed provision of utility, supply distribution, and other operational or support services or facilities; government financing of research and development programmes; fiscal incentives (such as exemption or reduction of direct taxes and social security payments and accelerated depreciation); and government subscription to, or provision of, equity capital.

The GATT rules are only concerned with domestic subsidies that operate incidentally to increase exports, as otherwise they can have no trade-distorting effect.[53] The General Agreement specifically prohibits such subsidies only where their effect is to increase the exports of primary products beyond a contracting party's equitable share of the world export trade.[54] Ad Article XVI:3 sets out special rules of domestic price stabilization and support systems that result in bi-level pricing. They are subject to Article XVI:3 unless (1) they have also resulted or are designed to result in higher export prices and (2) they are operated or are designed to operate so as not to stimulate exports unduly or otherwise cause trade distortion. Wherever the system is wholly or partly financed out of government funds, it is always subject to Article XVI:3. All other domestic subsidies that cause trade distortion are subject only to Article XVI:1; which requires contracting parties to notify GATT of any they are maintaining and to consider the *possibility* of limiting them when requested to do so. This is a very mild provision; it does not prohibit the subsidy and imposes no obligation on a subsidizing nation to take action against it.

The Subsidies Code goes some way towards tightening up the general rules on domestic subsidies.[55] It recognizes that they are used by governments for genuine public policy reasons[56] and explicitly states that the signatories 'do not intend to restrict [this] right'.[57] Like Article XVI:1 it recognizes also that domestic subsidies can cause trade distortion,[58] but it goes a step further. Article 11:2 requires signatories to seek to avoid causing trade distortion through the use of domestic subsidies and obliges them, when setting their policies in this field, to 'weigh, as far as practicable, taking account of the nature of the particular case, possible adverse effects on trade' and to 'consider the conditions of world trade, production . . . and supply in the product concerned'. This does not amount to a prohibition, but it does contain a definite obligation to avoid trade distortion which can be enforced by way of Articles 12 and 13.

Government export promotion will be subject to the above rules where it involves financial support for the production or manufacture of goods that are in fact exported, even though increasing exports was not the primary aim of the aid. As Article 11:3 of the Subsidies Code indicates, the measures concerned will cover such matters as fiscal incentives, low-interest loans, guarantees, and direct production grants, infrastructure investment, investment grants, wage subsidies, labour training programmes, government-sponsored research and development, and the delivery of goods or services by governments or their agencies on preferred terms.

The enforcement of the GATT rules on subsidies

The General Agreement provides two ways for action to be taken against a trade-distorting subsidy maintained by a contracting party. Article XVI:1 requires all contracting parties which maintain subsidies that operate to increase exports to notify GATT of the extent and nature of the subsidization, the estimated effect of the subsidization on the quantity of the affected products exported from its territory, and of the circumstances making the subsidization necessary. Where, on the basis of this information, GATT determines that the subsidy is indeed distorting trade, it can request the subsidizing nation to discuss the possibility of limiting the subsidy either with GATT itself or with the contracting party that is affected by it. Alternatively, any other contracting party can request such discussions and invite GATT, if so desired, to become involved as a conciliator.[59]

Apart from the obvious fact that this procedure lacks any coercive force, it can be easily circumvented by a subsidizing party merely omitting to notify GATT of the subsidy in question. This may not be due to bad faith but to a genuine belief that the practice is not in fact a subsidy, or that it is not increasing exports. Article 7 of the Subsidies Code remedies this important defect. It gives signatories the right to request information on practices that they believe should be notified under Article XVI:1 and to bring any failure to provide this information to the attention of the Committee of Signatories. Furthermore, a signatory may request another signatory to notify GATT of any subsidies that are increasing exports and may inform the Committee if this is not done.[60] These additional provisions clearly improve the effectiveness of Article XVI:1, but they do not change the non-coercive nature of the procedure.

If a contracting party wishes to take more effective action under the General Agreement against another party's subsidy, it will have to use the general dispute settlement provisions of Article XXIII. The steps in the procedure are as follows. First there is consultation between the parties to the dispute. If this fails to yield a mutually satisfactory solution, GATT becomes involved as a conciliator. If the matter is still not resolved by conciliation, GATT will set up a panel or a working party to investigate the matter and report back. Working parties invariably include the disputants and tend to produce a general review of the problem without any definite recommendations. Panels, which are more commonly used, are comprised of disinterested third parties and normally rule on the merits of the case. Before the panel or working party report is officially accepted by GATT, a last chance is given for the parties to reach agreement. If the report does go to GATT, it will be used as the basis for any recommendation. Retaliatory action may be authorized by GATT if its recommendation is not followed.[61]

The basis for an action under Article XXIII is the nullification or impairment of benefits accruing to a contracting party under the General Agreement as a result of another contracting party either violating the General Agreement (XXIII:1[a]) or applying any measure whether it conflicts with the General Agreement or not (XXIII:1[b]). Subsidies that contravene Articles XVI:3 and XVI:4 would fall into the first category; other subsidies, in particular domestic subsidies, fall into the second. Nullification or impairment, which means that the subsidy is distorting trade to the detriment of the complainant, is presumed in the case of subsidies that contravene the General Agreement unless the subsidizing party can prove otherwise; for other subsidies it must be proven.[62]

Theoretically Article XXIII is a powerful weapon against all subsidies, but in practice this has not proved to be the case. Its procedures are long and retaliation is rarely authorized,[63] so that it is not particularly effective even against prohibited subsidies. Actions under Article XXIII:1(b) have been discouraged in favour of consultations under Article XXII, and the provision has fallen into disuse.[64] As a result there is no effective remedy against domestic subsidies and export subsidies that are not in contravention of Article XVI.

The dispute settlement procedures under the Subsidies Code follows the same basic structure as that prescribed by Article XXIII, namely consultation, conciliation by the Committee of Signatories, a panel report, recommendations by the Committee, and the authorization of countermeasure.[65] The procedure may be invoked both against prohibited export subsidies and against any other subsidy, in particular domestic subsidies, that is causing trade distortion.[66] In the case of prohibited export subsidies such distortion is presumed failing evidence to the contrary;[67] for other subsidies, which means all domestic subsidies and export subsidies on primary products that do not contravene Article 10, trade distortion must be proven.[68]

Disagreement exists over whether action can be taken under the Subsidies Code against practices that are deemed not to constitute export subsidies according to the Illustrative List, in particular export credits that conform to the OECD Arrangement and those that are extended at rates that are not below those which the government would have to pay to obtain the funds on international capital markets.[69] The EC takes the position that an export credit falling within these two exceptions is not a subsidy at all under the Subsidies Code. The USA tends to the view is that wherever an exporter obtains export credit from a government at rates below commercial level, there is still a subsidy, albeit not an export subsidy, and thus action can be taken. It is a moot point. Certainly the Subsidies Code permits action against 'any subsidy' that is causing trade distortion.[70] On the other hand, the Subsidies Code clearly distinguishes between two types of subsidies, export and domestic, and if export credits are not deemed export subsidies, they can hardly be assimilated to domestic subsidies. There would, however, be nothing to prevent a contracting party attempting to seek a remedy under Article XXIII:1(b) of the General Agreement. As Article 19 of the Subsidies Code provides, signatories are not deprived of any rights of action they may have under the General Agreement.[71]

The enforcement provisions of the Subsidies Code are a substantial improvement on Article XXIII. Strict time-limits are imposed, working parties are not used and clearer criteria are set down for taking action against offensive subsidies, whether they contravene the Subsidies Code or not. Above all, the Subsidies Code establishes the right to take action against domestic subsidies that distort trade.

National barriers to government export promotion

Introduction

Article VI of the General Agreement permits contracting parties to levy compensatory duties in the form of countervailing duties or anti-dumping duties on imported goods that benefit from a subsidy in the exporting country. Countervailing duties are levied directly against the subsidy, whereas anti-dumping duties may be levied only where the subsidy has resulted in bi-level pricing and are directed against the margin of price reduction. Contracting parties cannot levy both duties on the same goods,[72] and the general practice is to use countervailing duties; these have the additional advantage that they can be levied on the whole amount of the subsidy and not just on the amount that may be passed on in the form of price reduction.[73]

Compensatory duties, or 'contingent protection' as they are now widely called,[74] are levied according to national legislation, but this legislation must conform to Article VI and, in the case of signatories, to the Subsidies Code and the Anti-Dumping Code.[75] Non-members of the GATT are free to apply contingent protection as they see fit, but they do not include the world's major trading nations and their trade laws are not considered here. In fact we shall restrict ourselves, for the sake of practicality, to discussing the GATT rules in this area and looking briefly at how some major trading nations have applied them in their legislation. All of these nations – the USA, the members states of the EC,[76] Canada – are signatories to the codes.

Government export promotion measures covered by national rules

The definition of a subsidy under Article VI

Under Article XVI certain subsidies are specifically excepted, namely export subsidies on primary producers that do not give the subsidizing nation a more than equitable share of world trade and the exemption of indirect taxes and import duties[77] on exported goods. According to the strict wording of Article XVI:4, export subsidies on non-primary products are excepted unless they result in bi-level pricing, but GATT practice indicates that any trade-distorting effects will now render them actionable. Domestic subsidies are not specifically excepted under Article XVI; they are tolerated unless they are used in connection with primary products in contravention of Ad Article XVI:3. The Subsidies Code confirms the stricter treatment of export subsidies on non-primary products and gives an explicit right of action against domestic subsidies that distort trade. The Subsidies Code also, however, introduces two new exceptions in the area of concessionary financing: (1) the provision of export credits at interest rates that are not below those which the government would have had to pay on international capital markets to obtain the funds, and (2) exports credits that conform to the OECD Arrangement. As indicated earlier, the Subsidies Code should take precedence over Article XVI for signatory nations.

A crucial issue with respect to contingent protection is whether the definition of an actionable subsidy for the purposes of direct action under the GATT rules is the same as that for national action pursuant to Article VI. It is suggested that contingent protection is available 'irrespective of whether or not the subsidy falls within the parameters of Article XVI'.[78] Under this Article XVI and the Subsidies Code a subsidy is actionable if it causes trade distortion, which the Subsidies Code defines *inter alia* as displacing another signatory's exports to a third country market or affecting adversely the domestic market of a signatory.[79] The test for the availability of contingent protection under Article VI is stricter; the subsidized imports must cause or threaten material injury to an established domestic industry (or to the industry of a competing exporter) or materially retard the establishment of such an industry.[80] This greater strictness is recognized by the Subsidies Code, which, in order to make more lenient provision for developing countries, stipulates that direct action under the GATT rules can be taken against their domestic subsidies only where injury occurs in terms of Articles VI.[81]

It is suggested that the corollary of the stricter test is that any subsidy which meets it is actionable regardless of its status under the GATT rules against subsidies. Certainly Article VI and both the Subsidies and Anti-Dumping Codes can be read as requiring only that the injury test be met. Moreover, the difference in the way Articles XVI and VI treat domestic agricultural price stabilization and support systems would seem to confirm this view. Under Ad Article XVI:3 such schemes are not considered to constitute subsidies where they are *designed* to result also in higher export prices and not to increase exports or otherwise cause trade distortion. Article VI:7 is cast more narrowly; only systems that *result* in higher export prices or *actually operate* so as not to increase exports or otherwise cause trade distortion are exempted from contingent protection. There are two points to note here. First, the systems are exempted under Article VI:7 not because they are not considered a subsidy, but because they are deemed not to cause injury within the meaning of Article VI. This confirms the primacy of the injury test. Second, the effect of the difference between the two articles is that a measure that is not held to be a subsidy under Article XVI can none the less be subject to contingent protection under Article VI. This confirms that the primary of the injury test means in practice that Article VI is not bound by the exceptions under Article XVI or the provisions of the Subsidies Code.[82] Only exceptions that are expressly mentioned in Article VI still obtain, that is to say, the practice mentioned in Article VI:7 and the exemption of indirect taxes and import charges on exported goods.[83]

All three countries under discussion conform to Article VI, at least with respect to indirect taxes and import charges. Both the EC and the Canadian legislation specifically excepts their exemption from contingency protection measures,[84] and the USA does so in practice.[85] The exception under Article VI:7, discussed above, is not specifically dealt with in the EC or US legislation, but to reject it would represent a clear violation of the General Agreement. Under Canadian legislation this exception is probably covered by the provision that subsidies that are in accordance with the General Agreement should be exempted from contingency protection.[86]

The real issue, however, is whether the exception for subsidies affecting the export of primary products in Article XVI:3 and the two exceptions for concessionary financing added by paragraph (k) of the Illustrative List of the Subsidies Code are also protected from national contingency measures. As far as subsidies on the export of primary products are concerned, it is noteworthy that the EC and US legislation[87] incorporates only the Illustrative List and not the substantive provisions of the Code, which, like Article XVI:3, except these subsidies where they do not lead to the subsidizing nation obtaining more than an equitable share of world trade. Nor does the legislation incorporate Ad Article XVI:3, which excepts certain domestic schemes that lead to an increase in exports of primary products. There is reason to assume, therefore, that the EC and US legislation also conforms here to Article VI and that these subsidies are subject to contingency protection measures.

The situation under Canadian legislation may be different. Article 2(5) of the Special Import Measures Act (SIMA) directs the deputy-minister to take into account Article 9 of the Subsidies Code, which permits these subsidies and, in addition, Articles 38(1)(b)(iii) and 41(1)(b)(iv) enjoin him to except subsidies that are in accordance with the General Agreement when making a determination. It is not clear, however, what 'taking into account' means or whether the reference to the General Agreement means Article VI or XVI or both.

The status of concessionary financing under national legislation is somewhat controversial. Government export credits have long been a source of friction between the USA and some of its major trading partners. Traditionally the USA has taken the view that any financing for domestic or export purposes that is provided by governments at below normal commercial rates is a subsidy,[88] and it only reluctantly agreed to the legitimation of export credits by the OECD Arrangement as a step towards their eventual elimination. It has consistently taken a very narrow view of paragraph (k) of the Illustrative List. The EC, supported tacitly by Canada, views the OECD Arrangement as a validation of government export credits and regards paragraph (k) as excepting either type of concessionary financing that comes within its terms from all GATT regulation.

The EC and US legislation includes the Illustrative List along with paragraph (k) but both also provide that actionable export subsidies are not limited to those contained in the List.[89] This may mean that the national authorities are free to ignore paragraph (k), but the more acceptable interpretation is surely that they are not prevented from taking action against export promotion measures that are not included in the List, which is after all only illustrative.[90] The Canadian legislation does not incorporate the List but does direct the Deputy-Minister to take it into account when considering matters of subsidization.[91]

Given the attitude towards and more extensive use of official export credits by the EC and Canada, the form of their legislation is not surprising, and, even though the legislation stops short of an explicit exception, concessionary financing is unlikely to be subject to contingent protection in those countries.[92] The inclusion of the List in the US legislation is, however, surprising, and the ITA is clearly uncomfortable with paragraph (k). In its preliminary determination in the *Bombardier* case it refused to apply it, not because of a broad interpretation of the non-limitation provision but because, in the ITA's view, the List had no status under US law.[93] This view had been severely criticized,[94] and rightly so as the List is now an integral part of the Tariff Act, 1930. In its final determination the ITA drew back from this uncompromising position and based its finding of a countervailable subsidy on the fact that the financing by Canada's EDC derogated from the OECD Arrangement and was therefore not covered by paragraph (k).[95] But it did not expressly reverse its previous stand, and it rejected a plea that a subsidy should be calculated on the difference between the derogating interest rate and the conforming OECD rate. Instead the ITA took as its benchmark the higher commercial rates otherwise available to the purchaser.

From all this we may surmise that the ITA will probably come to accept paragraph (k) but will apply it very strictly. It will continue to find derogations from the Arrangement to be subsidies and will probably construe the two parts of paragraph (k) disjunctively, thus permitting a finding of subsidization where credits that conform to the Arrangement are none the less provided at above cost to the government according to the prevailing international rates available to it.

Contingent protection can be taken against any subsidy. Countervailing duties may be levied under Article VI:3 against a subsidy that is 'granted, directly or indirectly, on the manufacture, production or export' of any product. This wording clearly includes both export and domestic subsidies. During the negotiations on the Subsidies Code, the EC strove to have countervailing duties confined to export subsidies in the more narrow sense in which the term is used in the Subsidies Code. This was resisted by the USA and the Subsidies Code reiterates the wording of Article VI:3[96] As far as anti-dumping duties are concerned, the only criterion for their imposition is bi-level pricing that causes injury; the nature of the subsidy is irrelevant.[97]

All three of the countries under discussion provide for countervailing duties on domestic subsidies. The European provision is the most narrow and covers subsidies only on the manufacture and production of goods.[98] The Canadian provision is very wide and covers all aid to 'persons engaged in the production, manufacture, growth, processing, purchase, distribution, transportation, sale, export or import of goods'.[99] However, neither the Europeans nor the Canadians have as yet countervailed domestic subsidies in practice, and the Canadian legislation actually directs the deputy-minister to specify which are export subsidies.[100] The USA is the only one of the three countries to have acted against domestic subsidies,[101] but under its legislation only domestic subsidies that are granted to 'a specific enterprise or industry, or group of enterprises or industries' are actionable.[102] There has recently been a broadening in the US interpretation of specificity, as is illustrated by the ITA's differing rulings in the *Softwood Lumber* cases. In 1983 it ruled that Canadian stumpage fees were not countervailable as they were 'available regardless of the industry or enterprises of the recipient'.[103] Then followed the judgement of the Court of International Trade in *Cabot* that even generally available domestic subsidies were countervailable where 'the actual results or effects of assistance' were found to favour specific recipients.[104] The ITA applied this revised test in its 1986 decision and found that, although stumpage fees were still theoretically generally available, they were in fact used by only a specific group of industries.[105] Clearly the new US approach places more domestic subsidies in jeopardy. The US legislation also specifically singles out 'upstream subsidies', which are subsidies on inputs that are used in the manufacture of production of exported products.[106]

The implications of all this for government export promotion are that where there is injury to foreign domestic industry or (theoretically) to the industry of a competing exporter[107] that can be related to any promotional measure that bestows a benefit on an enterprise, the exports in question may be subject to contingent protection. This benefit may, depending on the national legislation, include most subsidies permitted under Article XVI as well as some of the exceptions contained in the Illustrative List appended to the Subsidies Code. The only practices that are definitely excepted under Article VI are the exemption, remission, or deferral of indirect taxes and import duties and domestic agricultural schemes that conform to Article VI:7.

National legislation tends to be somewhat vague on what type of measure may be subject to national import relief laws. US legislation includes 'subsidies . . . required by government action'.[108] Canadian legislation refers to a 'benefit . . . provided or implemented by [a foreign] government',[109] while Regulation 2176/84 talks of 'any subsidy bestowed, directly or indirectly, in the country of origin or export'.[110] In all three cases benefits conferred by private bodies at the direction of a government could fit within the terms of the legislation, but so far only the ITA has found such benefits to be subject to contingent protection.[111]

It is not certain whether or not the benefit must still constitute 'a measurable economic advantage', as it has been suggested it must under Article XVI and the Subsidies Code. Article VI:3 prohibits countervailing duties that are levied in excess of the amount of the subsidy, while Article 4:4 of the Subsidies Code directs that a signatory make a final determination of the amount of the subsidy. Both these provisions thus require the subsidy to be quantifiable. On the other hand, Article VI:3 does permit the subsidy to be estimated, which opens the door to attempts to quantify benefits that have no obvious pecuniary value, such as institutional support. Certainly the Canadian and US legislation could have this result. SIMA defines a subsidy very broadly as 'any financial or commercial benefit that has accrued or will accrue, directly or indirectly, to persons'; US law uses the all-inclusive term 'bounty or grant'.[112]

The imposition of countervailing and anti-dumping duties

Determination of the subsidy or dumping

Neither Article VI nor the Subsidies Code set down any firm rules for determining the existence of a subsidy beyond the requirement in the Code that there must be sufficient evidence of it.[113] The legislation of all three countries fulfil this requirement.[114]

The GATT rules for determining dumping are more detailed. Dumping is defined by Article VI:I as the selling of goods for export at a price that is below their normal value. Normal value is defined as the comparable domestic price for like goods, or, in the absence of such, either the highest comparable export price to any third country or the cost of production plus a reasonable amount for selling cost and profit. The Anti-Dumping Code reiterates this definition except that it stipulates that the export price to a third country must be representative.[115] The export price of imported goods will be the price at which the goods are sold to the importer, unless the price is suspect, in which case it will normally be based on the price at which the goods are resold to an independent buyer.[116] The legislation of all three countries follows these rules.[117]

Determination of material injury

Article VI:6(a) stipulates that countervailing and anti-dumping duties may be imposed only where a subsidy causes material injury.[118] No definition of material injury is given in the General Agreement or the Codes, but the latter do set out quite a detailed list of economic factors to be considered in determining whether material injury has been caused.[119] The legislation of all three countries faithfully reproduces this list,[120] but the application of US law by the International Trade Commission (ITComm) has been heavily criticized.[121]

Much of the problem with the ITC's approach derives from the definition of material injury in the US legislation as 'harm which is not inconsequential, immaterial, or unimportant'.[122] The ITComm has interpreted this to mean that any injury will qualify unless it is insignificant, and on many occasions this has caused it to find material injury where it could not really be said that US industry was hurting. In one case against Canadian hog products the injury was a decrease of less than 1 per cent in domestic US prices.[123] The ITComm has been criticized for superficial treatment of the available economic data.[124] The result of the ITComm approach is that it tends to find material injury wherever there is a significant increase in subsidized or dumped imports.

Neither the EC nor the Canadian legislation defines material injury, but by and large the responsible authorities have adopted the economic analysis prescribed by the GATT rules. In these jurisdictions material injury at least seems to require some significant harm to domestic industry;[125] an increase in imports alone is not sufficient.

Causality

Article VI:6(a) also requires the material injury be caused by the effect of the dumping or subsidy. The necessity for this causal connection is taken up and emphasized by the Codes, which stress that 'injuries caused by other factors must not be attributed to the subsidized [dumped] imports'.[126] In order to make this causal connection the Codes require that evidence of the subsidy or dumping be considered simultaneously with the question of injury.[127]

The treatment by the ITComm of this issue of causality has been even more criticized than its methods of determining material injury.[128] In part this is due to the vagueness of the Codes themselves, which do not specify what is required to establish the causal connection.[129] But the US legislation is also largely at fault. In the first place it contravenes the Codes by linking injury to the effect of the imports themselves rather than to the subsidy or dumping.[130] This had led the ITComm to concentrate on *whether* domestic products have been displaced by subsidized imports rather than on *why* this has happened. Evidence of exogenous factors such as the superiority of the imported product is often either ignored or disregarded.[131] This approach has led, on more than one occasion, the ITComm Vice-Chairman to stress in a separate opinion the necessity to relate the injury to the dumping or subsidization.[132]

The second problem with the US legislation is that it omits to include the Codes' directive that injury caused by other factors should not be attributed to the subsidized or dumped imports. In a decision which has set the tone for the ITComm's approach, the US Customs Court declared that this means that once a link between the subsidized imports and the injury is established – be it ever so insignificant – there is 'no reason to discuss the other causes which had contributed in the injury'.[133]

Given that a mere increase in subsidized imports is sufficient to justify a finding by the ITComm of material injury, the fact that the ITComm does not always attempt to relate this injury to the dumping or subsidization and ignores other, often much more important, factors causing that injury, means that US contingency protection law has strayed far from the terms and spirit of the GATT rules. The European and Canadian approach, on the other hand, is by and large more consistent with the GATT rules, due in large measure to the way the legislation is framed. In both cases the legislation emphasizes that the injury must be caused by the subsidy or dumping,[134] and Regulation 2176/84 actually incorporates the provision from the Codes that related injuries should not be attributed to subsidized products.[135] This has meant that in both Canada and the EC proof of the causal link requires at least that the subsidy or dumping be shown to be a significant and separate cause of the injury.[136]

The EC is the only one that fulfils the requirement in the Codes that questions of subsidy and dumping and injury be considered simultaneously. The Commission of the EC is responsible for both issues. In the USA the ITA is responsible for determining questions of subsidization and dumping, while the ITComm deals with the issue of injury. Canada has the same dual process as the USA, with the Deputy Minister of National Revenue for Customs and Excise and the Canadian Import Tribunal carrying out the functions of the ITA and ITComm respectively.

Other matters

Both Codes require that the injury must be to all domestic producers or at least to those who are responsible for a major proportion of domestic output.[137] All three legislations conform with this requirement, although the Canadian provision could be said to lack clarity.[138] Anti-dumping and countervail actions may be initiated by governments or the affected industry.[139] The Subsidies Code does not define 'affected industry', but it is suggested that the same number of producers are required as for showing injury. This is the meaning given to the term in the Anti-Dumping Code.[140] Unfortunately the legislation of all three countries has very lax rules on this point.[141] This is unfortunate as it encourages unrepresentative groups to bring actions that, even if they are ultimately unsuccessful, have a powerful protectionist effect.

Anti-dumping and countervailing duties may not exceed the margin of dumping or the amount of the subsidy.[142] The Codes declare it to be desirable that the imposition of duties be permissive.[143] This is the case under the Canadian and European legislation, but in the USA the imposition of duties is mandatory.[144]

Anti-dumping duties can be imposed even where there is no subsidy involved. In cases of subsidization, which is our concern, they are in fact rarely used. There are three reasons for this. First, they are restricted to the margin of dumping; second, they require that the subsidy actually result in bi-level pricing; and third, they would be available only against measurable economic benefits conferred under a government export promotion scheme, as only these could result in bi-level pricing. However, where the existence of the subsidy is difficult to ascertain or prove but there is bi-level pricing, anti-dumping duties are the preferred remedy.

Regional barriers to govermnent export promotion

Introduction

A great number of countries belong to regional trade arrangements.[145] These include all western European countries, which belong to either the EC or the European Free Trade Area, Australia, New Zealand, Israel, and the USA. Canada has joined this group of nations by entering into a Free Trade Agreement with the USA. This will leave Japan as the only major industrialized nation that is not a member of any regional trade arrangement.

A common aim of all these arrangements is the free flow of goods between member states through the abolition of tariffs and non-tariff barriers. In some cases this even involves the elimination of contingent protection measures,[146] but, even where it does not, the smooth functioning of the trade arrangement requires some common rules with respect to subsidies on intra-area trade. In some instances there is also an attempt to co-ordinate subsidies on trade with third countries.

What follows is a brief survey of some of the rules that apply to subsidies, and hence to government export promotion, in a selected group of these trade arrangements.

Rules with respect to intra-area trade

Most or all export subsidies on intra-area exports that benefit from area treatment are specifically prohibited or scheduled to be phased out in all of the agreements under discussion,[147] with the exception of the Canada–USA Free Trade Agreement, which applies the prohibition only to export subsidies on agricultural goods.[148] Certain common practices may be excepted from this general rule against export subsidies.

The exemption of indirect taxes on exported goods is specifically allowed in several agreements.[149] Where an agreement is silent on the matter, the availability of this exception may be implied from explicit references to the parties' continuing rights under GATT,[150] which permits the exception. The exemption of import charges on exported goods is not permitted in four of the agreements under discussion;[151] the other two are silent, but here too the exception is probably covered by continuing GATT rights. Concessionary financing is dealt with only in the US–Israeli agreement, pursuant to which Israel is to observe the provision of the OECD Arrangements.[152] This is, however, unlikely to prevent action being taken under US law against Israeli products as Section 406 of the 1984 Trade and Tariff Act states that the agreement does not affect the application to Israel of US import relief laws.[153] It is probably that the member states of the other trade arrangements will either follow their usual internal practice with respect to concessionary financing by foreign countries or use the dispute settlement procedures in the relevant agreement. Between the member states of the EC there is an informal understanding that only export guarantees will be used in intra-area trade. Some of the agreements extend the prohibition against subsidies to all measures that distort trade, which would include domestic subsidies.[154]

Rules with respect to trade with third countries

The Canada–USA agreement provides for consultation on the use of subsidies on exports to third countries and obliges the parties to take into account each other's export interests in their third-country trading.[155] The EC treaty goes much further. Article 112(1) calls for the progressive harmonization of such subsidies in order to 'ensure that competition between undertakings of the Community is not distorted'. Some common rules have been laid down for export credits and insurance,[156] but as yet the Commission's goal to a common policy in this whole area has not been realized.

Conclusions

Government export promotion, whether actively pursued through export subsidies or incidentally through domestic subsidies, is a common occurrence in many countries. Whatever its effectiveness, a large number of companies throughout the world take advantage of it. This chapter has attempted to point out the possible downside to such aid, namely the possibility that a government may find itself brought before GATT for distorting international trading patterns or that a company may find its products made the subject of compensatory duties in the importing country. Where a nation belongs to a regional grouping, a government must also bear in mind any additional limitations that this entails on its freedom to promote exports. Exporters have most to fear from countervailing and anti-dumping duties, which affect them directly; at the same time they should also be aware that certain government programmes on which they rely may eventually have to be altered or eliminated where they contravene GATT or regional rules.

By and large institutional support is unlikely to cause many problems. It is not subject to the GATT rules on subsidies and probably does not come under any prohibition on export subsidies in regional arrangements. There is the danger that it could fall foul of national contingency protection rules, but as yet this has not happened. The reasons for this are that institutional support is such a common practice and the financial benefits it confers are normally minimal. Financial support to domestic industry, however given, that has an affect on exports is much more likely to provoke a response form the international trading community. This is particularly so in the case of overt export subsidies, most of which are prohibited under GATT and regional rules and, even where not, are likely to call forth contingency protection measures in the importing nations. Financial support in the form of domestic subsidies is also becoming a riskier proposition. The Subsidies Code now gives a clear right of action against domestic subsidies where they distort trade, and it may only be a matter of time before other nations follow the US lead in subjecting them to countervail action. They are also prohibited in many regional arrangements where they distort trade.

Despite these barriers governments will continue to attempt to help their industry in the export market. The very ubiquitousness of the practice bestows upon government export promotion some sort of acceptability. In many instances government help is needed to even out the conditions of competition. But the fact remains that in a competitive world governments and companies, particularly in the

USA, are becoming ever more willing to use international, regional, or national rules to challenge export promotion by foreign governments. *Caveat exportator*!

Notes and references

1 F.H. Rolf Seringhaus, 'The impact of government export marketing assistance', *International Marketing Review*, 1986, vol. 3, no. 2, summer, p. 55.

2 October 1947, 55 UNTS 187. The document has been modified in several respects since 1947; the current version is contained in *General Agreement on Tariffs and Trade, Basic Instruments and Selected Documents*, vols I–IV, supps 1–34. The term 'General Agreement' is used in the text to refer to the main 1947 agreement as amended; the term 'GATT' refers to the General Agreement and the various ancillary agreements on its interpretation and application.

Ninety-four countries are contracting parties to the General Agreement; they account for approximately 80 per cent of world trade. Thirty other countries apply the Agreement on a *de facto* basis and Tunisia is a provisional contracting party. China and the Soviet Union are the two prominent non-members.

3 The OECD is the direct successor of the Organization for European Economic Cooperation (OEEC) and was established pursuant to the *Convention on the Organization for Economic Cooperation and Development*, December 1960, 888 UNTS 179. It consists of twenty-four member countries; the countries of western and southern Europe, the USA, Canada, Australia, New Zealand, and Japan.

4 The FAO is a specialized agency of the United Nations created in June 1943. Its constitution is reprinted in *Yearbook of the United Nations*, 1946, pp. 693ff. One of the FAO's activities is to promote consultation and co-operation amongst countries dependent on the production and export of agricultural commodities.

5 Export promotion of services is not mentioned in the 1973 *OECD Code of Liberalization of Current Invisible Operations*, Paris, OECD, 1973, which is the only major international agreement dealing with services. It is, however, covered by the OECD *Arrangement on Guidelines for Officially Supported Export Credits*, but no action can of course be taken under the GATT rules against subsidies if the Arrangement is disregarded.

6 *Subsidies and Countervailing Duties. Agreement on Interpretation and Application of Articles VI, XVI and XXIII of the General Agreement on Tariffs and Trade*, April 1979, 26 BISD 56 (1978–9).

7 The Tokyo Round (1973–9) was the seventh round of negotiations between the contracting parties to the General Agreement. It not only dealt with the usual issue of tariff reductions but also resulted in a number of agreements on non-tariff barriers, of which the Subsidies and Anti-Dumping Codes are two examples. At present the contracting parties are engaged in the eighth (Uruguay) round.

8 Only thirty contracting parties to the General Agreement have subscribed to the Subsidies Code.
9 *Illustrative List of Export Subsidies*, Appendix in *Subsidies and Countervailing Duties*, Agreement on Interpretation and Application of Articles VI, XVI, and XXIII of the General Agreement on Tariffs and Trade, 26 BISD (Basic Instruments and Selected Documents) 56 (1978–9), April 1979.
10 *Tax Legislation: United States Tax Legislation (DISC)*, 23 BISD 98 (1975–6), para. 76; *Income Tax Practices Maintained by France, 23* BIDS 114 (1975–6), para. 47; *Income Tax Practices Maintained by Belgium*, 23 BISD 127 (1975–6), para. 34; *Income Tax Practices Maintained by the Netherlands*, 23 BISD 156 (1975–76), para. 34.
11 E. McGovern, *International Trade Regulation*, 2nd edn, Exeter, Globefield Press, 1986, S11.12.
12 It is agreed that this includes subsidies that maintain exports at a higher level than would otherwise be the case – 2 BISD 44 (1952), para. 29(a); 9 BISD 191 (1961), para. 10.
13 *Subsidies and Countervailing Duties*, Art. 8:4(a), (c).
14 *Disc*, para. 73; *French Income Tax Practices*, para. 52; *Belgian Income Tax Practices*, para. 39; *Dutch Income Tax Practices*, para. 39.
15 See note 12.
16 *Disc*, para. 73; *French Income Tax Practices*, para. 52; *Belgian Income Tax Practices*, para. 39; *Dutch Income Tax Practices*, para. 39.
17 R.K. Paterson, *Canadian Regulation of International Trade and Investment*, Toronto, Carswell, 1986, p. 138.
18 Seringhaus, 'The impact of government', p. 55.
19 *Certain Nails from the Republic of Korea*, ITA 47 FR 27397 (1982); *Certain Steel Products from Spain*, ITA 47 FR 51438 (1982).
20 The European Community consists of Belgium, Denmark, France, Germany, Greece, Ireland, Italy, Luxemburg, the Netherlands, Portugal, Spain, and the United Kingdom. The Community is responsible for foreign commercial policy of the member states.
21 *Subsidies and Countervailing Duties, Annex (1).*
22 9 BISD 192 (1961), para. 12. McGovern indicated qualified support for the American position, McGovern, *International Trade*, S11.12.
23 McGovern, *International Trade*, S11.41.
24 *Subsidies and Countervailing Duties*, Art. 11:1, 3.
25 *French Income Tax Practices*, para. 48; *Belgian Income Tax Practices*, para. 35; *Dutch Income Tax Practices*, para. 35.
26 J.H. Jackson, *World Trade and the Law of GATT*, New York, Bobbs Merril, 1969, SS13.5 and 15.7.
27 See the comments on world trade in agriculture in 28 BISD 77 (1982), paras 26, 33–5; 29 BISD 81 (1983), paras 18–21; 33 BISD 24 (1987), G.C. Hufbauer and J.S. Erb, *Subsidies in International Trade*, Cambridge, Mass., Institute for International Economics, 1984, p. 5.
28 *Declaration Giving Effect to the Provisions of Article XVI:4 of the General Agreement on Tariffs and Trade*, November 1960, 9 BISD 32 (1961).

29 9 BISD 33 (1961).
30 Hufbauer and Erb, *Subsidies*, p. 46.
31 *Disc*, para. 73; *French Income Tax Practices*, para. 52; *Belgian Income Tax Practices*, para. 39; *Dutch Income Tax Practices*, para. 39. It should be noted that bi-level pricing has never been required in the case of subsidies that operate to increase the export of primary products.
32 *Subsidies and Countervailing Duties*, Art. 8.
33 ibid., Art. 10. Developing countries are subject to the same rules with respect to export subsidies on primary products, Art. 14:10. Few developing countries signed the Subsidies Code or the 1960 Declaration. Article 14 is an attempt to encourage them to sign the Code.
34 ibid., Art. 14:2, 14:3,4, 14:5,6.
35 The ITA held such a benefit to be too insignificant to attract countervailing duties (*de minimis*) in *Certain Fresh Atlantic Groundfish from Canada*, ITA 51 FR 1010 (1986).
36 The ITA held PEMD programmes to constitute a *de minimis* subsidy in *Atlantic Groundfish* and *Softwood Lumber Products from Canada*, ITA 48 FR 10395 (1983) (*First Softwood Case*) and ITA 51 FR 37453 (1986) (*Second Softwood Case*).
37 *Disc*, para. 71.
38 *Subsidies and Countervailing Duties*, Annex, paras (g), (h). Article XVI.
39 GATT, *Working Party Report on Border Tax Adjustments*, 18 BISD 97 (1970–71), *Working Party Report on Suspension of Customs Liquidation by the United States*, 24 BISD 134 (1976).
40 Article 111:2 of the General Agreement specifically permits the levying of indirect taxes on imported goods as long as they do not exceed the taxes on like domestic goods.
41 Illustrative List, para. (e), also the attitude of the US Supreme Court in *Zenith Radio Corporation v. United States*, 437 US 443 (1978), p. 455.
42 *Subsidies and Countervailing Duties*, Annex, para. (i). Although the wording may be a little ambiguous, Ad Article XVI probably also excepts the exemption of import charges.
43 The text of the OECD Arrangement is confidential, but the writer was able to obtain a copy of the 1986 version – OECD Doc. TD/CONSENSUS/ – 86.33. The following discussion is based on this version, which has not been significantly amended. The participants in the Arrangement are Australia, Austria, Canada, the EC, Finland, Japan, New Zealand, Norway, Sweden, Switzerland, and the USA.
44 *OECD Arrangement*, para. 1(a).
45 The ITA took this view in its final determination in *Railcars from Canada*, ITA, 49 FR 6569 (1983) (*The Bombardier Case*). This view is supported by Hufbauer and Erb, *Subsidies*, p. 72. *Contra*, see O. Frenkel and C.G.B. Fontheim, 'Export credits; an international and domestic legal analyses', *Law and Policy in International Business*, 1981 vol. 13, p. 1,078, and D. Simon, 'Can GATT export subsidy standards be ignored by the United States in imposing countervailing duties?', *Northwest Journal of International Law and Business*, 1983–4, vol. 5, p. 201.

46 The Principles are not binding, but the parties to the Wheat Trade Convention have obligated themselves to follow them.
47 It should be noted, however, that actions under Article XXIII:1(b) are rarely successful.
48 This is particularly the case where such financing is provided at below the cost to the government – see 26 BISD 333 (1980), para. 14.
49 This was in relation to the *Bombardier Case*.
50 Of course, even if concessionary financing is also to be considered an exception under Article XVI, this does not prevent the USA from seeking a remedy under Article XXIII:1(b).
51 Paterson, *Canadian Regulation*, p. 172, Frenkel and Fontheim, 'Export credits: an international and domestic legal analysis', pp. 1,078–9.
52 Paterson, *Canadian Regulation*, p. 138.
53 By accepting the Code the USA can be taken to have abandoned its attempt to have this type of domestic subsidy treated as an export subsidy.
54 Article XVI:3. In this instance a domestic subsidy is subject to the same rules as an export subsidy.
55 McGovern doubts whether the Subsidies Code really strengthens the rules (McGovern, *International Trade*, S11.312), but this view fails to take into account that for the first time definite and enforceable obligations are placed on signatories that grant domestic subsidies.
56 *Subsidies and Countervailing Duties*, Arts 8:1, 11:1. The social and economic policy objectives that domestic subsidies may promote include, according to Article 11:1; the elimination of industrial, economic, and social disadvantages of specific regions; the restructuring, under socially acceptable conditions, of certain sectors; sustaining employment and encouraging re-training; encouraging research and development; economic programmes and policies to promote the economic and social development of developing countries; and redeployment of industry in order to avoid congestion and environmental problems.
57 ibid., Art. 11:1.
58 ibid., Arts 8:1, 11:2.
59 Article XVI:1 does not explicitly give this right of initiation to other contracting parties, but it has been confirmed as GATT practice – 2 BISC 39 (1952), 10 BISD 207 (1962). Action could also be taken under the general consultation and conciliation provisions of Article XXII, but this procedure is essentially the same as that under Article XVI:1. The US did, however, use Article XXII in the *Bombardier Case*.
60 *Subsidies and Countervailing Duties*, Art. 7:1, 2, 7:3.
61 A detailed account of the procedure is contained in the *Understanding Regarding Notification, Consultation, Dispute Settlement and Surveillance*, GATT, BISD 26th Supp. 210 (1978–9).
62 *Understanding*, Annex, para. 5.
63 In fact retaliation has been authorized only once.
64 *Uruguayan Recourse to Article XXIII*, 11 BISD 95 (1963), 105, 111, 113 and 116, K.W. Dam, *The GATT: Law and International Economic*

Organization, Chicago, University of Chicago Press, 1970, pp. 359–63.
65 *Subsidies and Countervailing Duties*, Arts 12, 13, 17, 18. Countermeasures may not be taken against export subsidies on non-primary products maintained by developing country signatories that conform to a commitment to reduce or eliminate such subsidies – Art. 14:5–6. Countermeasure against domestic subsidies maintained by developing country signatories will be authorized only where the subsidy is causing injury to the domestic injury of the importing signatory in terms of Article VI of the General Agreement – 14:7.
66 ibid., Arts 12:1, 3; 13.
67 ibid., Art. 8, fn. 26.
68 ibid., Arts 12:3; 13:4. Trade distortion must always be proved in the case of developing country signatories, Art. 14:4.
69 These two practices are excepted by paragraph (k) of the *Illustrative List*.
70 *Subsidies and Countervailing Duties*, Arts 12:3; 13:2–4.
71 Paterson, *Canadian Regulation*, p. 172; Frenkel and Fontheim, 'Export credits: an international and domestic legal analysis', pp. 1,078–9, Article XXIII:1(b).
72 Article VI:5. This stipulation is followed in the national legislations – 19 USCS S1677; Special Import Measures Art, S.C. 1984, c25 (SIMA), Art. 2(7); Co. Reg. 2176/84, (1984 O.J. L201, p. 1), Art. 13(9).
73 *Subsidies and Countervailing Duties*, Art. 4:1 US and Canadian legislation provides for levying a countervailing duty equal to the amount of the subsidy – 19 USCS S167(a); SIMA, Art. 3(b). The European Community legislation, on the other hand, stipulates that the countervailing duty should be levied only in an amount necessary to remove the injury – Co. Reg. 2176.84, Art. 13(3).
74 R. de C. Grey, *United States Trade Policy. A Canadian View*, Montreal, Institute for Research on Public Policy, 1982, p. 7.
75 *Agreement on Implementation of Article VI of the General Agreement on Tariffs and Trade*, 26 BISD 171 (1978–9).
76 Contingent protection is regulated at the Community level as part of the Common Commercial Policy; for the sake of convenience the terms 'national' and 'country' are also applied to the EC.
77 *Subsidies and Countervailing Duties*, Annex para. (i).
78 Paterson, *Canadian Regulation*, p. 139; Dam, *The GATT*, p. 43. For a contrary view, see McGovern, *International Trade*, p. 263; Simon, 'Can GATT export subsidy standards by ignored by the United States in imposing countervailing duties?', p. 200.
79 *Subsidies and Countervailing Duties*, Art. 8:4(a), (c).
80 Article VI:6.
81 *Subsidies and Countervailing Duties*, Art. 14:7, Hufbauer and Erb, *Subsidies*, pp. 22–3.
82 Note too that multiple currency practice authorized by the International Monetary Fund are excepted by Ad Article XVI, Section B, para. 1 but may still be subjected to contingency protection pursuant to Ad Article

VI:2–3, para. 2.
83 Article VI:4.
84 SIMA, S.2(1); Co. Reg. 2176/84, Art. 3(3).
85 See *Leather Wearing from Uruguay*, ITA 46 FR 19288 (1981); *Certain Nails from the Republic of Korea*, ITA 47 FR 27397 (1982).
86 SIMA, Arts 38(1)(b)(iii) and 41(1)(b)(iv).
87 19 USCS S1677(5); Co. Reg. 2176/84, Art. (2).
88 See *Certain Pig Iron from Brazil*, ITA 44 FR 67554 (1979); *Ferroalloys from Spain*, ITA 45 FR 25 (1980); *Certain Steel Products from Belgium*, ITA 47 FR 39304 (1982).
89 19 USCS S1677(5); Co. Reg. 2176/84, Art. 3(2).
90 Simon, 'Can GATT export subsidy', p. 205.
91 SIMA, Art. 2(5).
92 Paterson, *Canadian Regulation*, p. 175.
93 *Railcars from Canada*, ITA 47 FR 53760 (1982).
94 Simon, 'Can GATT export subsidy', pp. 200ff.
95 *Railcars from Canada*, ITA 48 FR 6569 (1983).
96 *Subsidies and Countervailing Duties*, Art. 12, fn 2.
97 Article VI; 1, 2, 6. See, too, 19 USCS S1673; SIMA, Art. 2; Co. Reg. 2176/84, Art. 2A(2).
98 Co. Reg. 2176/84, Art. 3(1).
99 SIMA, Art. 2(1).
100 SIMA, Arts 38(1)(b)(iii) and 41(1)(b)(iv). The EC Commission has, however, envisaged the possibility of countervailing domestic subsidies in Comm. Rec. 2129.83.ECSC, 1983 O.J. L205, p. 30.
101 The first case where this was done was the *Steel Belted Tires from Canada*, ITA 39 FR 1018 (1973), also *Certain Steel Products from Belgium*, ITA 47 FR 39204 (1982) and the *Softwood Lumber* cases below.
102 19 USCS S1677 (5)B.
103 *Softwood Lumber Products from Canada*, ITA 48 FR 10395 (1983).
104 *Cabot Corporation v. United States*, 620 F. Supp. 722 (1985) at p. 730.
105 *Softwood Lumber Products from Canada*, ITA 51 FR 37453 (1986).
106 19 USCS S1677–1.
107 Although Article VI:6(b) permits a contracting party to levy anti-dumping and countervailing duties against subsidized imports that are injuring a third country, this has never been done in practice. None of the countries under discussion provides for this situation in her legislation.
108 19 USCS S1677(5)(B).
109 SIMA, Art. 2(1).
110 Article 3(1).
111 See *Certain Steel Wire Nails from Korea*, ITA 47 FR 27397 (1982); *Certain Steel Products from Spain*, ITA 47 FR 51438 (1982).
112 19 USCS S1677(5); SIMA, Art. 2(1). In *G.S. Nichols & Co. v. United States* (249 US 34, 1919), the US Supreme Court observed that while 'bounty' may have a limited connotation, a 'grant' can mean almost any benefit.

113 *Subsidies and Countervailing Duties*, Art. 2(1), 4(1), 5(1).
114 19 USCS S1671a(a), (b), 1671b(b); SIMA, ss. 31(1)(a), 35(a)(ii), 41(1)(a); Co. Reg. 2176/84, Arts 7(1), 11(1), 12(1).
115 *Anti-Dumping Code*, Art. 2:3.
116 Ad Article VI:V; *Anti-Dumping Code*, Art. 2:3.
117 19 USCS S1677a, b; SIMA, ss. 15–30; Co. Reg. 2176/84, Art. 2.
118 Injury is required according to all three countries' legislation – 19 USCS S1671(a); SIMA, Art. 3; Co. Reg. 2176/84, Art. 4(1). However, the United States requires injury in countervail cases only for signatories to the Subsidies Code and for some other countries with which it has a bilateral understanding. This may well be a breach of the General Agreement, for, although the original US legislation not requiring injury in countervail cases was grandfathered by Article 1(b) of the *Protocol of Provisional Acceptance* (October 1947, 55 UNTS 308), the new discriminatory provision contravenes Article 1, which is not covered by the Protocol. On the other hand it has been argued that this is not so as the Subsidies Code only applies to signatories; Paterson, *Canadian Regulation*, p. 15; McGovern, *International Trade*, S8.32.
119 *Subsidies and Countervailing Duties*, Art. 6:1–3; *Anti-Dumping Code*, Art. 3:1–3.
120 19 USCS S1677(7)(B), (C); Co. Reg. 2176/84, Art. 4(2). SIMA does not incorporate the GATT provisions, but they are contained in the Rules of the Canadian Import Tribunal, SOR/85-1068, s. 36(a)–(c).
121 A.M. Rugman and A.D.M. Anderson, *Administered Protectionism in America*, London, Croom Helm, 1987.
122 19 USCS S1677(7)(A).
123 *Live Swine and Pork from Canada*, ITC 701-TA-224 (GOP, Jan. 86-1403). See too *Moulded Pulp Egg Filler Flats from Canada*, ITC 731-TA-201 (GOP, Jan. 86-1410) and *Oil County Tubular Goods from Argentina and Spain*, ITC 731-TA-191 (GOP, Jan. 86-1407).
124 This is in relation to *Certain Fresh Atlantic Groundfish from Canada*, ITC 701-TA-257 (GOP, July 86-13123); Rugman and Anderson, *Administered Protectionism*, pp. 43–7 and 61–70.
125 For Canada see *Surgical Adhesive Tapes and Plasters from Japan*, 10 CER 174 (1986) at p. 183 and *Moldex Limited v. Anti-Dumping Tribunal*, 7 CER 323 (1985) at p. 324. For the EC see Co. Regs. 228/85 and 1698/85.
126 *Subsidies and Countervailing Duties*, Art. 6:4; *Anti-Dumping Code*, Art. 3:4. According to a footnote to article 6(4) of the Subsidies Code (3[4] of the Anti-Dumping Code), these factors include the volume and prices of non-subsidized imports of the product in question, contraction in demand or changes in the pattern of consumption, trade restrictive practices of and competition between the foreign and domestic producers, developments in technology, and the export performance and productivity of the domestic industry. Some of these factors were indeed considered by the Canadian Anti-Dumping Tribunal in *Colour Television* (Anti-Dumping Inquiry No. ADT-4-75) and led to a

dismissal of the request for anti-dumping duties.

127 *Subsidies and Countervailing Duties*, Art. 2:4; *Anti-Dumping Code*, 5:2.

128 McGovern, *International Trade*, S12.131; Rugman and Anderson, *Administered Protectionism, 5th Report of Committee on Anti-Dumping Practices*, 20 BISD 43 (1973).

129 It must be noted, however, that this vagueness was due to US pressure. Most of the other signatories wanted to include in both Codes the requirement of Article 3(4) of the 1967 Anti-Dumping Code that the dumping or subsidy by the principal cause of injury.

130 19 USCS SS1671(a), 1673.

131 *Oil County Tubular Goods from Argentina and Spain*, ITC 731-TA-191 (GOP, Jan. 86-1407); *Fabric and Expanded Neoprene Laminate from Japan*, ITC 731-Ta-206 (GOP, Jan. 86-1412).

132 See the *Oil County* case above and *Certain Red Raspberries from Canada*, ITC 731-TA-196 (GOP, Jan. 86-1408).

133 *Pasco Terminals, Inc. v. United States*, 477 F. Supp. 201 (1979).

134 SIMA, ss. 3(1), 31(1)(b), 42(1)(a); Co. Reg. 2176/84, Arts 4(1), 11(1), 12(1).

135 Co. Reg. 2176.84, Art. 4(1)(b).

136 For Canada see *Colour Television Receiving Sets from Japan, Taiwan and Singapore*, 1 CER 262 (1980) and *Industrial Wood Cutting Band Saw Blades from the US*, 5 CER 207 (1984). For the EC see Co. Regs. 228.85 and 1698/85.

137 *Subsidies and Countervailing Duties*, Art. 6:5; *Anti-Dumping Code*, Art. 4(1).

138 19 USCS S1677(4)(A); Co. Reg. 2176/84, Art. 4(5). The Canadian legislation only requires the Canadian Import Tribunal to 'take fully into account' the provisions of the Codes - SIMA, s. 42(3). In *Japan Electrical Manufacturers' Association v. Anti-Dumping Tribunal*, 12 CER 260 (198) at p. 267 the Federal Court of Appeal considered it sufficient under SIMA if a significant number of producers are affected. This, it is submitted, is not in conformity with the Codes.

139 *Subsidies and Countervailing Duties*, Art. 2:1; *Anti-Dumping Code*, Art. 5:1.

140 *Anti-Dumping Code*, Art. 5:1 fn.

141 19 USCS S1677(9); SIMA, Art. 31(1); Co. Reg. 2176/84, Art. 5(1).

142 *Subsidies and Countervailing Duties*, Art. 4:2; *Anti-Dumping Code*, Art. 8:3. This rule is followed in the national legislations - 19 USCS SS 1671(a), 1673; SIMA, Art. 3(a); Co. Reg. 2176/84, Art. 13(3).

143 *Subsidies and Countervailing Duties*, Art. 4:1; *Anti-Dumping Code*, Art. 8:1.

144 19 USCS SS 1671(a), 1673; SIMA, Art. 14; Co. Reg. 2176/84, Art. 12, which leaves the question of the imposition of duties to be decided by a majority vote in the Council.

145 The ones that are reviewed here are: *Convention Establishing the European Free Trade Association*, 4 January 1960, 370 UNTS 3 (hereinafter EFTA); *Treaty Establishing the European Economic*

Community, 25 March 1957, 298 UNTS 4 (hereinafter EEC); *Australia–New Zealand: Closer Economic Relations – Trade Agreement*, 28 March 1983, 22 I.L.M. 945 (hereinafter ANZCERT); *Israel–United States: Free Trade Area Agreement*, 22 April 1985, 241 I.L.M. 653 (hereinafter Israel); *Agreement Between the European Economic Community and the Republic of Austria*, 22 July 1972, Encyclopedia of European Community Law, vol. BIII, K.R. Simmonds (ed.), London, Sweet & Maxwell, 1974, pt. B12 at B12369 (hereinafter EEC); *Canada–United States Free Trade Area Agreement* (hereinafter Canada). the EEC–Austrian agreement is practically identical to all the other free trade agreements between the EEC and EFTA countries.

146 Countervailing and anti-dumping duties can be authorized in intra-Community trade by the Community authorities, but in practice this is rarely done. Where a subsidy causes trade distortion within the Community, it is normally dealt with by the Commission or the Court of Justice pursuant to EEC, Art. 93(2). No countervailing duties are provided for in the treaty between Austria and the E.C.

147 *Israel*, Art. 2(4), Annex 4; *EEC*, Art. 92; *ANZCERT*, Art. 0; *EFTA*, Arts 13(1)(a), 24; *Austria*, Art. 23(1)(iii). The *EEC* and *Austria* provisions apply generally to any trade-distorting subsidy, which obviously includes export subsidies.

148 *Canada*, Art. 701(2). The prohibition also applies to the Western Grain Transportation subsidies for shipments via west coast ports – Art. 701(5).

149 *Austria*, Art. 18; *EEC*, Art. 96; *EFTA*, 24(3) with respect to agricultural goods.

150 *ANZCERT*, Arts 15, 16; *Israel*, Art. 3; *Canada*, Art. 104(1). Treaty rights can be taken away at international law only by an explicit provision.

151 *EEC*, Art. 98; *EFTA*, Art. 7(1); *Canada*, 404(1); *ANZCERT*, Art. 14 where the exemption leads to trade distortion.

152 *Israel*, Annex 4.

153 98 STAT 3018. See too 19 USCS S2112.

154 *EEC*, Arts 92, 93; *EFTA*, Art. 13(1)(b); *Austria*, Art. 23(1)(iii). *ANZCERT*, Art. 10 requires consultations where domestic agricultural programmes cause trade distortion. Action can also be taken against trade-distorting domestic subsidies under the other agreements by way of the dispute settlement procedures – *Israel*, Art. 19(1)(a); *Canada*, Arts 1804–6; *ANZCERT*, Art. 22.

155 *Canada*, Art. 701(4).

156 See, for example, Co. Dir. 70/509, 1970 O.J.L. 254; Co. Dir. 70/510, 19700 J.L. 254; Co. Dir. 71/86, 1971 O.J.L. 36; Co. Dec. 73/391, 1973 O.J.L. 346.

Part III

Impact of government export promotion

Chapter five

Company needs and government export promotion assistance

Introduction

We have seen that government export promotion programmes have been developed to assist companies in overcoming the export barriers they face and, it is hoped, go on to achieve success in foreign markets. The argument developed here is a simple one, namely that these programmes will have their greatest impact when the assistance provided corresponds with the needs of companies served. Clearly a customized approach to assistance should produce the best results. Given the large number of companies seeking assistance and the restricted nature of government budgets, however, such a approach is obviously not practicable. At the other extreme, a very small number of programmes may make for administrative ease but will not satisfy specific exporter needs. As Chapters 2 and 3 indicate, most governments have opted for the middle-ground, where the challenge is to establish enough different export promotion programmes to satisfy the varied needs of companies, but not so many as to stretch budgets too thinly or make programme administration and delivery too burdensome.

Given this situation, Chapter 5 explores how companies' export promotion needs might best be met through thoughtful design and delivery of government programmes. It begins with the basic matter of the export barriers companies face, some of which seem generic to most exporters, while others vary from one company situation to another. One widely recognized framework for understanding export barriers – and so, company needs – considers the stage that a company has reached in its export development. Recognizing this, three types of export process models are examined in the second section. The link between export stage and the assistance needs of companies is explicitly made in the third section, and two attempts to map out the connections are reviewed. These show that it is possible to define systematically groups of companies with particular export assistance needs. However, there is a shortcoming in these approaches which leads to an alternative proposal. This is described in the fourth section, and illustrated in the context of trade fair and trade mission programmes.

Barriers to exporting

Categories of export barriers

In Chapter 1 three main categories of export barrier were briefly described: barriers that are (1) motivational; (2) informational; and (3) operational/resource-based. Because they prevent many companies from seriously considering exporting, motivational barriers mostly affect non-exporters. However, they may also stand in the way of further market or product expansion among current exporters. Examples of motivational barriers include: a buoyant large home market; the perceived higher cost and risk of doing business overseas; and the burden of export documentation requirements.

Informational and operational/resource barriers are a reality for both exporters and non-exporters. These also prevent export potential from being realized. For instance, information on foreign markets for specific products is seldom readily available to companies. Yet at the same time, analysis of just this information is important to new and existing exporters. Similarly many companies are uncertain about how to operate in the foreign market – whether to deal directly with customers or use an intermediary. In the latter case, the task of finding an agent or distributor scares away numerous would-be exporters. Expansion into foreign markets also requires additional resources – whether for working capital or extra staff – and marshalling these is a further problem faced. A fourth barrier should be added for completeness at this point. While motivational, informational, operational/resource-based barriers are quite distinctive from each other, knowledge barriers are less so. *Knowledge* may be thought of as a stock of capabilities a person (or company) possesses. The company that is knowledgeable about exporting will be able to determine what information to collect and how to use it, to a greater extent than their less knowledgeable counterparts. While based on information then, knowledge is clearly a much broader concept, guiding the company in all its endeavours. In a sense, knowledge is a special resource that is present to varying degrees in companies. Like other resources, we should recognize that, without husbanding and replenishment, export knowledge will be depleted over time. Thus knowledge is a fourth export barrier for

Table 5.1 The five most important export impediments

	German managers	*Japanese managers*
1	price	personnel
2	competition	distribution
3	distribution	price
4	personnel	language
5	marketing costs	market research

Source: E. Dichtl, H.-G. Köglmayr, and S. Müller, 'Identifying export potential: a comparative analysis of German and Japanese firms', in S.T. Cavusgil (ed.) *Advances in International Marketing*, Greenwich, Conn., JAI Press, 1986, pp. 233–54.

companies. These categories of export barrier are, of course, used as a convenient means for summarizing the numerous, more specific, barriers that exist. We now discuss export barriers more fully, referring to a number of recent studies.

Export situations and barriers

The studies described below were carried out in a variety of settings, for different reasons, and using contrasting methods. This necessitates a certain caution when making comparisons. However, the studies and their findings suit our purposes well, because we simply wish to highlight the kinds of barriers that companies face, as well as point to differences in a broad and suggestive sense.

Germany and Japan are in the front rank of exporting nations. A comparative study[1] in these two nations shows that German and Japanese managers rate three of the same barriers to be among the top five, specifically competition, personnel, and price (see Table 5.1). However, some differences are also suggested: German managers see their degree of competitiveness (1, 2, and 5) as the biggest problem, whereas Japanese managers stress knowledge barriers more (1, 4, and 5).

Sharp contrasts are seen when results from a less developed country study of export barriers are viewed. The most common barriers for Turkish food and textile exporters[2] relate to the high cost of producing and financing exports, poor transportation, inadequate information, and inconsistent government export incentives. The barriers cited are largely external to the companies involved. This may reflect real inadequacies in infrastructure and institutions or simply mean that managers blame their problems on others! Whatever the case, the listing of barriers for Turkey is dramatically different from those in the developed countries of Germany and Japan (see Table 5.2).

Table 5.2 Barriers for Turkish exporters

Problems experienced

Often encountered
- High costs associated with producing and financing exported products
- Poor scheduling and lack of good programming in public as well as private transportation
- Obstacles and delays in preparing the necessary documents
- Lack of an organized information centre at the public level

Often/sometimes encountered
- Instability and insufficiency of export incentives provided by government export promotion programmes
- Lack of cost-effective and protective transportation
- Promotion and packaging of exported product
- Production planning
- Specific information on foreign markets and on domestic and foreign competitors

Source: M. Bodur, 'A study on the nature and intensity of problems experienced by Turkish exporting firms', in S.T. Cavusgil (ed.) *Advances in International Marketing*, Greenwich, Conn., JAI Press, 1986, pp. 205–32.

Table 5.3 Barriers for Australian companies

Austrialian managers' perceived problems in exporting (rank order of top five problems)

	Small exporters (20–99 emps)	*Medium exporters* (100–499)	*Large exporters* (500+)
Freight costs	1	1	1
Competitive prices	2	2	2
Locating good agents	3	—	—
Lack of information about markets	4	—	—
Lack of order continuity	5	4	4
Competitive credit	—	3	5
Exchange rate fluctuations	—	5	3

Source: I. Wilkinson and N. Barrett, 'Australian management's attitudes to exporting – past and present', unpublished paper presented to the Market Research Society of Australia's Annual Conference, Canberra, 1986.

Another characteristic of companies that is often held to affect export activity is size. This is partly borne out in an Australian survey.[3] Small companies report that export basics such as locating good agents and finding out about markets are problem areas. Medium-sized and large companies cite problems of a more operational nature – keeping orders flowing, access to competitive credit, and dealing with exchange rate movements. However, the two most

Figure 5.4 Barriers for high-technology companies

Perceived barriers to exporting for high technology companies (top five)

	USA	*Canada*
1	Paperwork	Inadequate representation
2	Selecting a reliable distributor	Locating potential markets and determining demand
3	Comparative disadvantages	Tariff and non-tariff barriers
4	Honouring letters of credit	Lack of trained and experienced international marketing staff
5	Communication with foreign customers	Currency fluctuations and restrictions

Source: S. Rabino, 'An examination of barriers to exporting encountered by small manufacturing companies', *International Management Review*, 1980/1, vol. 20, pp. 67–73, and E.J. Kleinschmidt and R.E. Ross, 'Export performance and foreign market information: relationships for small high-technology firms', *Canadian Journal of Small Business and Entrepreneurship*, 1984, vol. 2, no. 2, pp. 8–23.

significant barriers for companies of all sizes are exactly the same, and these relate to their price competitiveness in world markets. The freight cost barrier clearly has to do with Australia's relative remoteness from major markets, especially those of North America and Europe (see Table 5.3).

For developed nations, high-technology products are important sources of export earnings. Two studies provide an idea of the barriers high-technology companies experience. With the exception of distribution partner problems though, the list of barriers for USA[4] and Canadian[5] companies show little similarity (see Table 5.4).

A final characteristic of companies that may be considered important, in terms of barriers faced, is the stage of export development. At the most basic level, we might expect export barriers to differ between companies that have yet to begin exporting and those that do export. This is seen in Canadian research.[6] The list of non-exporters includes competitive, knowledge, resource, and motivational barriers and, collectively, 'explain' well their lack of involvement in foreign markets. In contrast, exporters cite barriers that have to do with the consummation of foreign sales, including regulations, business practices, and distribution (see Table 5.5).

Having contrasted non-exporters and exporters, next we consider companies engaged to varying degrees in exporting.[7] Three categories of US exporter are shown in Table 5.6, and some similarities and differences in barriers are evident. Exchange rate risks are a concern for all three types of exporters, but especially among more committed companies. Another major barrier for beginning

Table 5.5 Barriers for non-exporters and exporters

Major problems perceived in exporting (top five)

	Non-exporters	*Exporters*
1	Foreign competition	Governmental barriers (customs/tariffs)
2	Lack of information on foreign markets	Different competitive practices
3	Lack of staff time	Selecting a reliable distributor
4	Service difficult in foreign markets	Inadequate transportation systems
5	Large domestic market	Existence of non-tariff barriers

Source: E. Kaynak and L. Stevenson, 'Profile analysis of Nova Scotia exporters', *Proceedings*, Administrative Sciences Association of Canada-Marketing Division, University of Ottawa, 1982, pp. 98–108.

Table 5.6 Barriers at various export stages

The most troublesome problem in exporting for US managers (rank of five most frequent responses)

	Experimental exporters	*Active exporters*	*Committed exporters*
Working with foreign distributors	1	4	2
Exchange rate risks	2	1	1
Cultural and economic differences	3	—	3
Other	4	2	—
Red tape; regulatory restrictions, etc.	5	4	—
Political instability	—	3	3

Source: S.T. Cavusgil, 'Differences among exporting firms based on their degree of internationalization', unpublished paper, University of Wisconsin-Whitewater, undated.

('experimental') exporters is achieving effective distribution overseas. Finally, cultural and regulatory differences, and political instability in foreign markets, are other significant barriers for companies.

Another study reports the barriers Swedish companies face at two different stages in their penetration of foreign markets: prior to and after the establishment of a subsidiary.[8] Before a subsidiary is set up, the most important barriers are those of 'transfer' and 'problem definition', or receiving orders and information on customer needs. Direct customer communication is, thus, a major problem. After a subsidiary has been established, these two barriers remain relatively high in the listing, whereas others – cultural, language, and problem definition – are reduced (see Table 5.7). This suggests that subsidiaries are able largely to 'translate' the foreign characteristics and needs of overseas markets for their companies.

Table 5.7 Barriers at two stages of foreign market penetration

Importance of various types of barrier (frequency of response)	*Prior to subsidiary (%)*	*After subsidiary (%)*
Market barriers		
- Geographic (distribution costs)	38	28
- Institutional (administrative and structural characteristics of the market)	41	51
- Cultural (social patterns and relations)	23	8
- Language (effective communication)	50	30
- Value system (relevance of business idea)	57	42
Customer barriers		
- Problem definition (specification of customer needs)	81	47
- Problem solution (degree of customer adaptation)	48	50
- Transfer (receiving orders and implementing contracts)	82	74
- Follow-up (customer loyalty)	60	56

Source: J. Mattson, 'Initial penetration of European continental markets by small and medium-sized firms', in S.T. Cavusgil (ed.) *Advances in International Marketing*, Greenwich, Conn., JAI Press, 1986, vol. 1, pp. 93–114.

Summary

It is difficult to summarize neatly the findings from the above studies. Some similarities can be discerned but many points of difference are also evident. The fact that there are similarities across such divergent samples suggests that the barriers in question (lack of market/customer information, difficulty in finding distributors, concerns about competitiveness, etc.) are significant and generic in nature. Other barriers should probably be seen as relating to the particular situation being reported. Good examples are provided by the infrastructure/institutional concerns expressed by Turkish exporters, and the questions about price competitiveness among Australian companies. Quite striking in the studies is the fact that the barriers cited may relate to the company, to exporting in general, or to an export market in particular. Clearly with time and the right assistance, company barriers can often be overcome. The same cannot be said for general exporting barriers. Tariff and non-tariff barriers, for example, are a fact of life to be dealt with. Greater levels of cost and risk are also endemic to export markets, and these must be factored into a company's export decisions. Some assistance can be provided by government, but the company has to make the fundamental decision of whether to commit to expanding its operations through exporting and so deal with these matters. Government can also assist in overcoming the barriers associated with a company's move into a specific export market. Trade missions, market visits, and trade fairs, for example, are a part of most government assistance programmes, and help the first-time or existing exporter to become that much more familiar with the vagaries of a particular foreign market. Sometimes, particular markets are hard for individual companies to penetrate. Japan is a good example. Again, government can play a role through high-level representations as well as taking a stronger lead with assistance programmes than might otherwise be expected.

In conclusion, it is apparent that export barriers can be either generic or situational. Both types of barriers indicate certain company needs that can potentially be addressed by government programmes. The aspect considered in the final studies above is the extent to which barriers are related to a company's stage of export development. Since we believe this to be a particularly useful framework for analyzing company needs, we now turn to this topic in more detail.

The export development process in companies

Export stages – involvement and strategies

Numerous models of the company export development process (often referred to as the internationalization process of the firm) have been proposed, and four of these are shown in Figure 5.1. Models A–C result from studies of exporting in developed, western, industrial nations (Australia and the USA), whereas Model D is based on research into companies in newly industrializing (NICs) and less developed countries (LDCs).

Taking the developed nations models first, five or six export stages are seen and, although the nomenclature varies, many points of similarity are evident. Model A[9] summarizes the stages that firms go though in general terms, their focus moving from solely that of the domestic market (stage 1), through assessment of the feasibility of exporting, to limited involvement, followed by expanded export activities, and finally, more substantial resource commitment to international operations (stage 5). Model B[10] introduces two additional important points for consideration. First, among companies that currently do not export, are some that may well have sold in foreign markets in the past (stage 3). For these companies, then, initial exports may have been less-than-rewarding, but they are possible candidates for renewed exporting activities. Second, stage 5 indicates that the process will lead some companies beyond exporting to more intensive forms of activity through, for example, foreign

Figure 5.1 Models of the company export development process

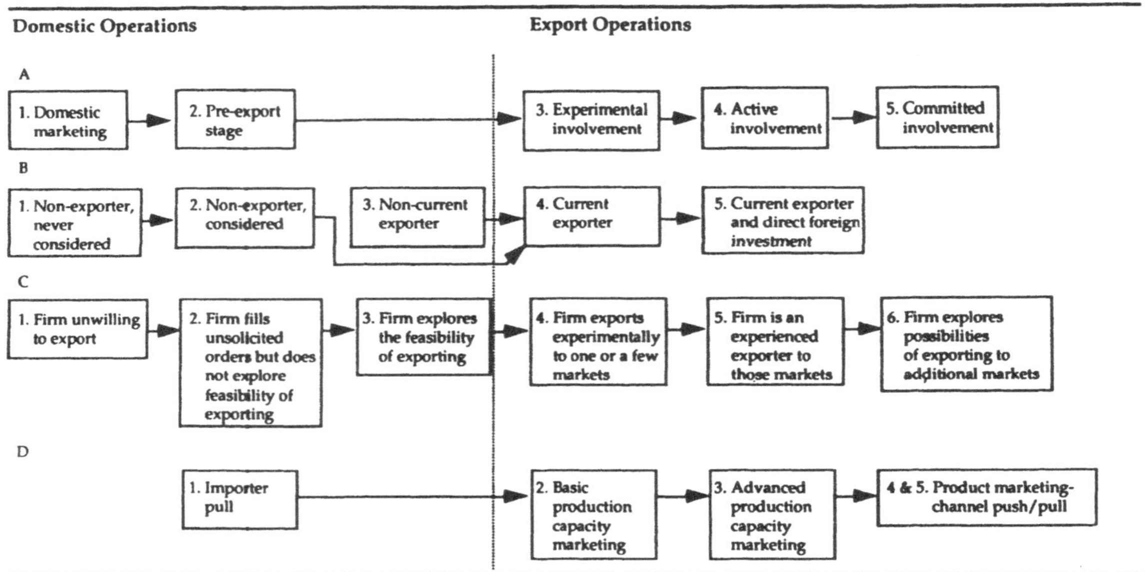

Notes: Drawn from:
A: S.T. Cavusgil, 'On the internationalization process of firms', *European Research*, November 1980, pp. 273–81;
B: N.J. Barrett and I.F. Wilkinson, 'Internationalization behaviour: management characteristics of Australian manufacturing firms by level of international development', in P.W. Turnbull and S.J. Paliwoda (eds) *Research in International Marketing*, Beckenham, Croom Helm, 1986, pp. 213–33;
C: W.J. Bilkey, 'An attempted integration of the literature on the export behaviour of firms', *Journal of International Business Studies*, 1978, vol. 9, no. 1, Spring/Summer, pp. 33–46;
D: L.H. Wortzell and H.V. Wortzell, 'Export marketing strategies for NIC and LDC-based firms', *Columbia Journal of World Business*, 1981, Spring, pp. 51–60.

direct investment. Model C[11] also provides two additional insights. First, this model explicitly recognizes that many companies' export interests are piqued by an unsolicited exporter order rather than through their own purposeful search for foreign opportunities (stage 2). In other words, some companies begin exporting without any deliberate plan to do so. Second, stages 4–6 elaborate the fact that many exporters extend their operations into new geographic markets as experience, knowledge, and skills develop,

These three models essentially describe the stages of company export involvement. Depending on the policy of a particular company, it may be at any one of the five or six stages portrayed in Models A–C. Movement from one stage to another is possible; indeed, many companies will secure an increasing portion of their total sales from foreign markets over time. Such greater involvement is, however, not inevitable: numerous companies will choose to concentrate on the domestic market, either completely or to a major degree.

Model D provides a contrasting approach, emphasizing that the export process of NIC and LDC companies requires considerable internal adjustment. Each succeeding stage is 'marked by the internalization of production and marketing decisions and functions that had been performed by the firms' customers'.[12] A brief description expands this point. Stage 1 and 2 companies essentially are sellers of production capacity. Stage 1 companies simply produce to a foreign importer's specification, whereas stage 2 companies possess some product design skills and a limited domestic marketing capability. Stage 3 companies still fill orders to foreign customer specifications and are self-sufficient in product terms; they also exhibit some marketing activity outside their own domestic market through, for example, trade fair attendance, advertising and, perhaps, a small overseas sales office. A deliberate low-cost or differentiation strategy often begins to emerge in this stage. Because it involves the production and selling of its own branded products, the transition to stage 4 requires that companies make significant operational, financial, and personnel changes. Foreign marketing is principally achieved through 'channel push' with the products in question often employed as promotional items in retail stores. Thus, low price is still the dominant strategy for these companies. Few, if any, NIC and LDC companies have reached stage 5. Little would distinguish a company at this stage from local producers in each export market, for competitive strategy will have shifted from price to product features, and from channel push to 'consumer pull'.

This model describes the internal adjustments made by companies as they engage more fully in export marketing. As such, it is qualitatively different from the models above. Although it is true that movement from stage 1 onwards brings a deepening export *involvement*, model D focuses more on the *strategy* changes that take place within companies as they secure more of their sales from foreign markets.

An earlier reference was made to the fact that the first three models result from research in developed nations while the fourth is based on companies in LDCs and NICs. It is tempting to explain these differing descriptions of the export process in terms of technology level. Most western companies that have a exportable product are likely to display a reasonable proficiency in production and marketing. For the most part then, the preoccupation for these companies – given an interest in exporting – is learning more about foreign markets and customers prior to possible market entry. Arguably NIC and LDC exporters will need to improve their production and marketing technologies more substantially than companies from developed economies in order to export effectively. This implies more internal change – in production methods, capacity development, marketing organization – so as to achieve a greater export proficiency.

Such an argument could explain why one modelling approach simply looks at the levels of export involvement, while the other examines internal changes necessary to exploit more fully demand in foreign markets. To associate the latter only with LDC and NIC companies, however, is a gross oversimplification. It is not difficult to think of commodity-based western companies, for example, that export through 'importer pull' (stage 1, Model B). Neither is there a shortage of developed nation companies whose strategies are described by stages 2 to 4. Our view then is that the export involvement and strategy models offer somewhat different but complementary perspectives on the general process of company export development.

Export stages – management decisions

Another stagewise approach to exporting considers the decisions that companies typically must make.[13] Clearly while export *involvement*, *strategies*, and *decisions* will always be interrelated, they are also somewhat different. A decision model was presented in Chapter 1 and is shown again below. Figure 5.2 presents four sets of decisions regarding exporting, the most fundamental of which naturally is whether the company chooses to expand its operations through exporting or in the home market. If exporting is chosen, the second decision involves which market(s) to target. With market(s) selected,

Figure 5.2 An export decision model

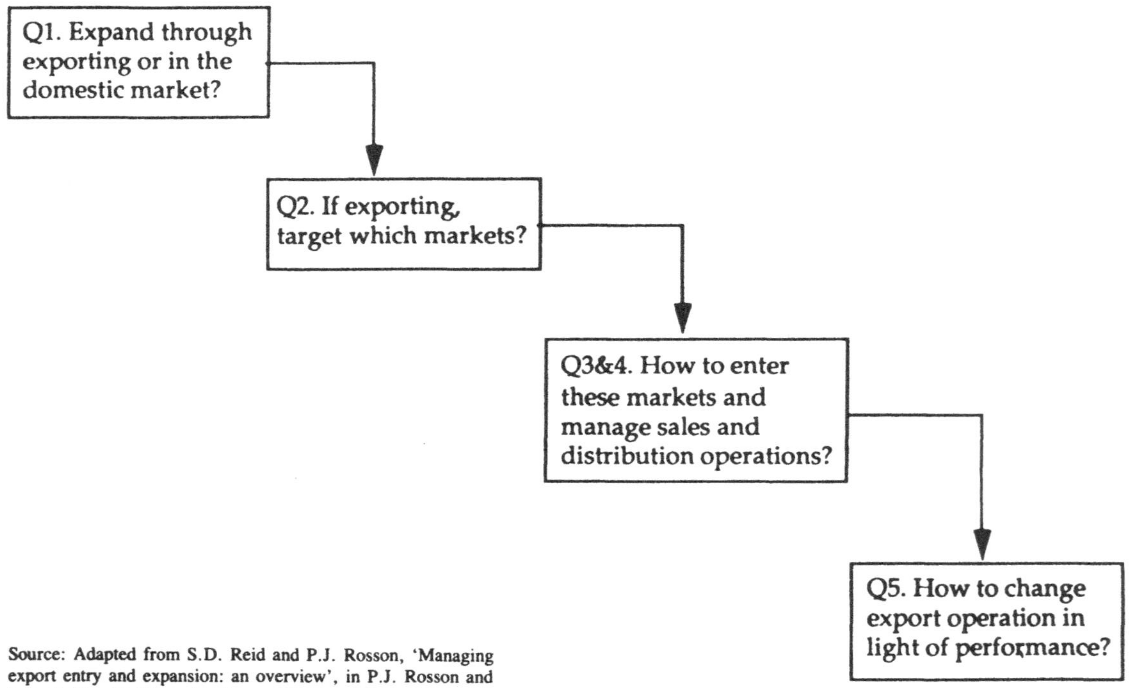

Source: Adapted from S.D. Reid and P.J. Rosson, 'Managing export entry and expansion: an overview', in P.J. Rosson and S.D. Reid (eds) *Managing Export Entry and Expansion: Concepts and Practice*, New York, Praeger, 1987, p. 6.

the next question for resolution is what entry method should be used. The entry method largely determines the way that the company's product will be sold and distributed, and this explains the grouping of these decisions. These first three sets of decisions are sequential and have to be resolved prior to any business beginning to flow from foreign customers. In small and medium-sized companies these three decisions are often made within a relatively short period of time. The fourth decision is faced periodically as the company assesses whether changes are required in light of its export experience and, more important, its performance. Needless to say, these are generic decisions, that is ones that all companies must make first as they look at the growth prospects export markets offer, and second, as attempts are made to realize such potential.

Before company export decision-making seems too simple, however, some elaboration is in order. Many companies pursue business in more than one foreign market, not necessarily with exactly the same product or product range.[14] This means that at any one point in time, a given company could be facing quite different decision situations in the various markets covered. Before it is assumed that experience gained in one market or with one product will make later entries straightforward, note should be taken of evidence to the contrary. Findings from a recent study of experienced exporters indicated that 'learning and adaptation to the challenges of new markets must be recognized as ongoing activities',[15] lending support to earlier assertions along the same lines.[16] The key point to be made regarding the present discussion is that where companies' strategies involve a portfolio of export markets and products, it is quite likely that they will exhibit contrasting export promotion support needs. In many situations, then, it is a mistake to think about 'Company X' as having one export assistance need. Rather it should be viewed as having a set of needs which reflect the exporting context it finds itself in.

Summary

The discussion above made the case that company export needs are best understood in relation to the stage of international development the organization has reached. Three ways of viewing export stages were presented, which emphasize either company export involvement, strategies, or decisions.

The needs of companies and government export assistance

Whether the export process of companies is viewed from an

involvement, strategy, or decision standpoint, it is clear that at specific stages, different problems have to be addressed. These problems create distinctive needs and a small number of studies have systematically examined the linkage between export stage and company needs. Two are reviewed here.

The study which most closely analyzes the stage-need linkage is based on data collected from small and medium-sized companies in the USA.[17] Six stages of export involvement were established and the 237 companies assigned to one of these based on their scores on the following variables: per cent of sales exported (past, present, and future); export sales volume; length of time exporting; number of persons committed to exporting; types of countries exported to; and the number of export customers and transactions.[18] A number of tabulations were then made by export stage. Those most relevant to this discussion include: difficulty of export problems; main export problems; problems most easily resolved by company; assessment of helpfulness of the Department of Commerce. The results are too extensive to describe here. However, the author concludes that 'the [export] assistance given must be more effective, which can be done by the differentiation of firms into the international stages and a targeting of assistance on the specific needs of each stage'.[19] The six export stages identified in the study, as well as the appropriate emphasis suggested for assistance programmes are:

1 *The completely uninterested firm* Raise awareness level of exporting.
2 *The partially interested firm* Raise awareness levels of export benefits; assist with information about mechanics of exporting.
3 *The exploring firm* Make exporting more profitable; provide general information and practical assistance.
4 *The experimental exporter* Encourage the active exploration of exporting; provide general assistance and help with product adaptation.
5 *The experienced small exporter* Make exporting more profitable, provide general assistance, and help with financing.
6 *The experienced large exporter* Facilitate customer service and provide general assistance.

A second large-scale study of the stage-need linkage is Australian.[20] Data were collected from a national sample of 314 companies of all sizes and cluster analysis performed on responses to 19 questions concerning export problems. This produced five distinct groupings; within all but the first group, both exporting and non-exporting companies are apparent. The labels shown below are descriptive of the companies found in each group and sub-group.

1 *Foreign parent controlled firms*
2 *No problem firms*
   - Successful exporters
   - Indifferent firms (non-exporters)
3 *Firms with price, cost and order problems*
   - Marginal exporters
   - Incompetent firms (non-exporters)
4 *Price and freight cost-conscious firms*
   - Developing exporters
   - Domestic market-oriented firms (non-exporters)
5 *Multiple problem firms*
   - Latent exporters
   - Small businesses (non-exporters)

This Australian approach is almost the reverse of the one above, working from export problems to the identification of company types (and, indirectly, export stage), whereas the US approach first determines export stage and then moves on to consider the related export problems (and needs). Neither approach is necessarily better; they are simply different.[21]

The Australian study describes each group and sub-group of companies in detail. Of most relevance here is the discussion about the targeting of sub-groups for assistance. The authors argue that public funds should be applied differentially across sub-groups, specifically so that group 2 and 5 non-exporters become the prime targets and group 5 exporters are treated as a secondary target.

These two studies are interesting in that they are able to identify groups of companies that face different export barriers and so have varied export assistance needs. While interesting, however, there is an important point that requires discussion. This concerns the extent to which the results of field studies such as those above can be used by government export assistance personnel. The US and Australian researchers, with data on numerous relevant variables, are able to differentiate between the types of companies and, consequently, recommend specific targets for attention. However, government programme officials seldom have access to such comprehensive data. This means that although research can lead to the development of profiles of companies with different needs (and priorities for assistance), the task of identifying companies that have such profiles is next to impossible. Our experience suggests that the data used to profile companies in the US study (see p. 166), although seemingly straightforward and accessible, in fact are not so.

In conclusion, 'segmentation' of the market for export promotion assistance is sensible and even essential in most nations.

Government programmes recognize that companies face different export barriers and, thus, have varied needs. How many of these distinctive needs to cater to, and what emphasis to place on each, are questions that continually need to be addressed. The studies reviewed show that groups of companies with distinguishable needs can be described. Although these approaches are interesting, owing to identification problems a more robust and usable segmentation scheme is necessary.

A practical approach for targeting export promotion

The approach

We propose a scheme for targeting export promotion assistance which recognizes that companies are at different export stages and accordingly face different decision situations. This is depicted in Figure 5.3, where five types of exporting company are evident: (1) non-exporter; (2) failed exporter; (3) first-time exporter; (4) expanding exporter; and (5) continuing exporter. These five company types are keyed to the export decision model described earlier (see Figure 5.2), so that three major clusters of activity become evident.

First, we find three types of companies that presently do not export. 'Non-exporters' are companies that have never exported and currently are not considering the same. 'First-time exporters' are companies that have decided to export in the near future. The latter companies have moved from having a simple awareness that foreign market opportunities exist, to a feeling that these could satisfy their aspirations for growth. With this realization made, the first-timer must then attend to the question of which market(s) to target (question 2), and how to enter and operate in the selected market (questions 3 and 4). Another type of company must address these same questions. The 'failed exporter' is a company that has some experience of foreign marketing but, for one reason or another, has chosen to withdraw from these activities and focus on domestic market operations. We comment on failed exporters again, later, but at this stage merely note that their decision to embark once again into export markets is likely to proceed in a different fashion from the first-timer, and that this is explained by its prior experience.

'Expanding exporters' are those that wish to move their products into one or more new foreign markets. For these companies, the question of prime concern is the second one: which market(s) offer the best prospects for the next phase in its foreign operations? With this decision made, the entry and operational mode questions (3 and 4) must again be resolved.

Figure 5.3 A practical export promotion targeting scheme

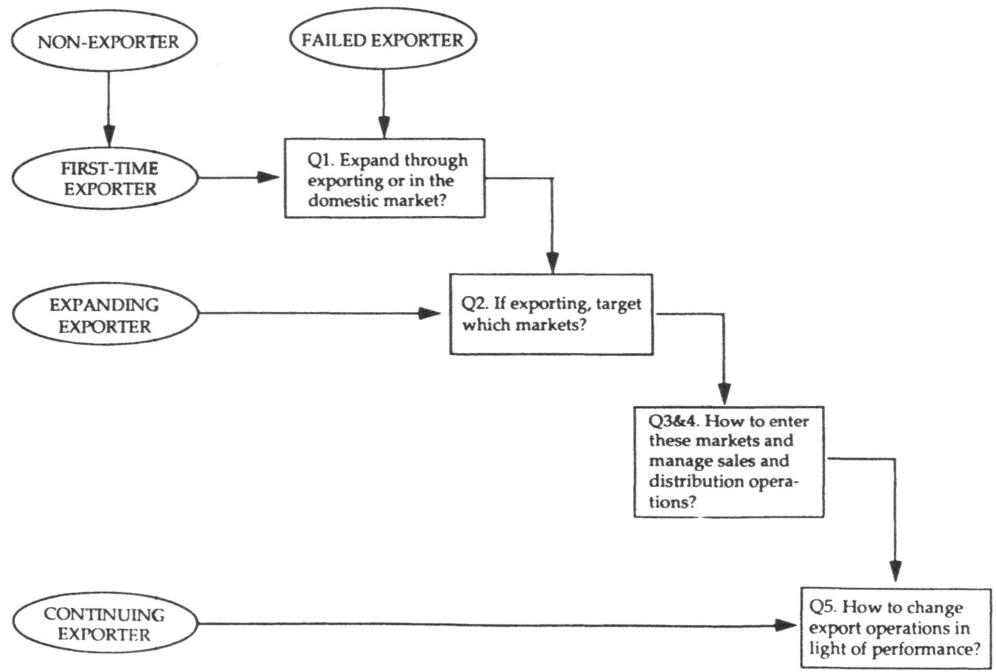

Source: Prepared by the authors.

'Continuing exporters' plan no major changes, but are concerned to fine-tune their present export operations as a result of current and projected performance levels. They may, for example, plan to launch a new product in an existing market, or desire to improve their existing foreign market operations. Their decisions are not unimportant; because of their accumulated experience, knowledge, and skills, however, they are of a less fundamental nature than first-time, failed or expanding exporters.

Four major types of initiative for government export promotion programmes flow from this approach.

1 Encouraging 'non-exporters' with competitive products to consider foreign market expansion.
2 (a) Helping 'first-time exporters' through the early, difficult phases of international marketing.
2 (b) Promoting the idea of renewed exporting to 'failed exporters' that could sustain such activities. Then helping these companies as in 2(a).
3 Assisting 'expanding exporters' to select the most promising foreign markets for entry and the best entry and operating modes.
4 Supporting 'continuing exporters' as they attempt to improve performance by adjusting their methods of foreign market operations.

These activities, decisions, and initiatives capture what is involved in the export development process and, thus, provide a guide for government export promotion programme design and delivery. (Indeed, many of these facets of export promotion programming were seen to be present in the government efforts described in Chapter 2.) Furthermore, the company targets we identify – 'non-exporters', 'first-time exporters', 'failed exporters', 'expanding exporters', and 'continuing exporters' – are believed to provide a workable tool for government officials in their export promotion efforts. We criticized earlier segmentation schemes because they depend on quantitative or attitude measures which are not available to those responsible for programme execution. This calls into question the usefulness of these schemes. Our scheme is a practical one: membership of one of the five categories is easily established from published information in the case of non-exporters, and from one simple question for the other four categories. This simplicity, coupled with the fact that the full range of export decision-making is represented by the five categories, suggests it as a potentially useful framework (see Figure 5.4).

Figure 5.4 Company targets for government export assistance

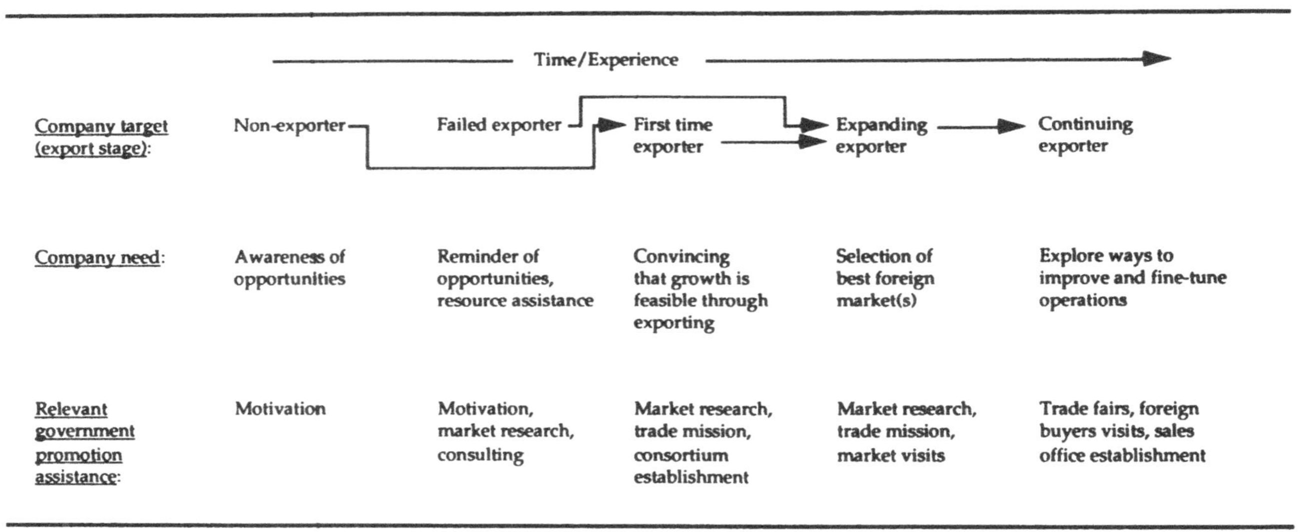

Source: Prepared by the authors.

Targeting companies

Careful targeting of companies is required if assistance is to be effectively managed. This is best illustrated by examining companies that have, in a sense, failed at exporting. Two studies are helpful. In the first of these, withdrawal from foreign market operations was found to be due not to higher levels of risk, greater costs or lower profits, nor to some adverse event.[22] Rather it reflected the fact that management somehow did not consider exporting worthwhile. Comments associated with such an attitude or behaviour include: 'We lack real motivation to market internationally and we really don't have the expertise'; and 'I have enough business to do in the USA'.

A second study of companies' initial exporting efforts highlights just how experimental this can be, and the failure that looms as a possibility for many. Business was very slow to develop among the fourteen failed Australian exporters surveyed: twelve companies achieved minor and/or sporadic sales, with six of these filling only one export order.[23] Interestingly, compared to the twenty-one continuing exporters also surveyed, the failed companies were twice as likely to have begun exporting in response to an unsolicited as opposed to a solicited order. The exporters' experience regarding their first order was exactly the reverse. Consequently, failed exporters entered foreign markets at an earlier stage in their development than companies that were continuing exporters. In addition, failed exporters had developed business across Australia to a much lesser extent. These results indicate a lack of pre-export preparation and help to explain the poor results which led to the termination of export activity.

Three points follow from this discussion. First, it is clear that some companies (the two studies suggest a fairly high proportion) begin exporting before they should, and not surprisingly fail. In some cases this export involvement is in response to an external stimulus (an order or a government programme), whereas in others a (new) manager may advocate exporting. Obviously companies should not start exporting unless they can sustain such operations and so have a reasonable chance of success. Government export promotion programmes often recognize this fact now and use 'export readiness' as one criterion for assistance. (What 'export readiness' is, of course, remains open to many interpretations.) Second, the initial exporting phase is one of great fragility, since it is a completely new experience for the company and one that can easily go wrong,[24] either because of uncontrollable external events or decisions made by management. This shows that companies just beginning exporting have very special needs and thus merit extra attention. Third, as touched on earlier, despite being labelled 'failed exporters', some companies in this category may be good targets for renewed foreign market involvement. Although they have prior export experience, however, their negative attitudes must be overcome before a new assault can be expected. As the US researchers note, 'a call to export because it is in "the national interest" is unlikely to have much effect on individual business decisions'.[25] Rather, the prospect of greater profits is likely to change attitudes, and so it is initiatives that convince companies that their export costs can be reduced and/or revenues increased that will likely tempt these companies to be drawn into exporting once again. This should be seen as the goal for government export assistance programmes.

Targeting companies: an elaboration

In this section the argument that government export promotion programmes should target companies quite carefully is developed further. So as to make the discussion a manageable one, rather than deal with export promotion programmes *en masse*, we choose two to illustrate our thinking. These are trade mission and trade fair activities, which are among the most important vehicles for export trade promotion in most countries.[26] We show how the practical targeting approach described above can be used in the context of trade missions and trade fairs.

The five types of target companies for export promotion assistance – 'non-exporters', 'first-time exporters', 'failed exporters', 'expanding exporters', and 'continuing exporters' – are shown in Figure 5.5, with the key export questions each must resolve, the associated decisions their managers face, and finally, the role that trade missions and trade fairs can play in making these decisions.

Trade missions and trade fairs are inappropriate export promotion vehicles for 'non-exporters' because these companies either have never considered marketing their products or services overseas, or have yet to be convinced of the merit of the idea. The goal for government programmes for this group then is to motivate non-exporters that have competitive products or services to consider venturing into the international market-place for the first time. Motivational methods include: promotional campaigns to create a general awareness of export potential (advertisements, export months, export success stories), industrial sector-specific meetings and circulars ('opportunities in telecommunications', 'how to sell into military markets', 'development bank projects and construction contracts'), working with and through established networks (chambers of commerce, boards of trade, world trade centres).

Figure 5.5 The role played by trade missions and trade fairs for various target companies

Target company	Key questions to resolve	Decisions to be made	Role played by trade mission for company	Role played by trade fair for company
Non-Exporter	Should exporting be considered as a vehicle for growth?	• Notional interest in exporting; • Exportability of product or service; • Resources that could be available for exporting.	• Trade mission not appropriate for these companies.	• Trade fair not appropriate for these companies.
First-Time Exporter	Should exporting be initiated?	• Growth potential from exports vs. domestic market; • Problems to be overcome to tap export potential; • Likely cost/benefit of export involvement.	• Potential to investigate market, buyers, competitors, distributors at first-hand; opportunity to discuss exporting with other, more experienced mission participants; make initial contacts; • Chance to better define what is involved in exporting - resources, commitments.	• Trade fair not appropriate for these companies.
Failed Exporter	Should exporting be reactivated?	• Determine if situation has changed enough to make exporting a better proposition; • Critical re-examination of factors leading to past failure.	• As for first-time exporters but recognizing that failed exporters have prior (and negative) experience. Thus, need to assess competitiveness and capability very carefully.	• Trade fair normally not appropriate for these companies.

Target company	Key questions to resolve	Decisions to be made	Role played by trade mission for company	Role played by trade fair for company
Expanding exporter	Which market(s) should be entered next? What market entry method is best?	• Determine market potential and barriers to entry; • Choose between feasible market entry alternatives; • Selection of foreign market partner (where applicable).	• Opportunity to meet buyers, members of trade, and government officials; do market size-up; check on competition; • Advice from mission participants experienced in market and/or own government officials covering market; • Chance to meet prospective agents/distributors and/or other trading partners.	• Chance to present product/service to the market and test response prior to entry decision; • Since key competitors are likely to be exhibiting, able to check out rivals in an efficient manner; • Opportunity to make useful future contacts with buyers and prospective trading partners.
Continuing exporters	How can performance be maintained/improved?	• Need to adjust/change existing operations for the market in question; • Decide what new initiatives look best.	• Trade mission normally not appropriate for these companies.	• Provides a vehicle to renew contacts with buyers, trading partners and to solidify company position in market; • If necessary, presents chance to test out new ideas for product features, price, promotion, etc., prior to final decisions being made • Opportunity to scout out new trading partners if changes viewed as necessary.

Source: Draws from framework developed by F.H. Rolf Seringhaus, 'Trade missions in exporting: state of the art', Working Paper Series 5.87, School of Business and Economics, Wilfrid Laurier University, Ontario, 1987.

'First-time exporters' are those companies whose interest has somehow been sparked in exporting. The key decision for these companies is whether to move from interest to action (that is to get involved overseas), and this requires that a go or no go decision be made. Trade missions can be very useful in this decision process because by actually visiting a likely foreign market, first-hand investigations can be made of how business is conducted overseas, what products/services are already available, how receptive buyers would be to the company's product/service, and so on. As well, other trade mission participants can provide a semi-captive audience for the prospective exporter and the various questions that loom large in its manager's mind. Finally, a good idea of the resources and commitment necessary to sell effectively can really be gained only from on-site visits of this kind. A well-planned trade mission that has been properly used by a company can accordingly provide a good sense of the costs and benefits of exporting. This will invariably have to be developed further. It could well be that the market visited on the mission may not be the one finally chosen for entry but, at the very least, the company in question will have moved beyond a general interest in exporting to having a more concrete idea about whether the idea should be pursued further. In this respect trade missions are much more appropriate for first-time exporters than trade fairs. Clearly taking space to exhibit at a trade fair is premature for the company that is still toying with the idea of foreign marketing. Attending a trade fair to investigate the market is another matter, but usually government programmes for exhibiting and attending are separate from one another, and here we consider the major thrust of exhibiting at trade fairs.

What of 'failed exporters'? As indicated earlier, to a large degree this group is similar to the previous one. Both failed and first-time exporters must resolve whether to get involved in exporting, so they may share many of the same concerns. There is the difference, however, that failed exporters do have some previous experience, and this will shape the thinking of their managers. Specifically the chief matter to be resolved by failed exporters is whether circumstances have changed sufficiently for the company to re-enter international markets. This can be answered only through close examination of the degree to which the company is now competitive and of its resource capacity – in other words, what chance does it have of success in the future and how prepared is it to seize the opportunity presented? These answers can be aided again by trade mission participation. Trade fairs will normally not be helpful to failed exporters for the reasons noted for first-time exporters. Trade fairs could conceivably be of use to failed exporters that have withdrawn only briefly from a market. In this situation, exhibiting at a trade fair could enable the company to re-establish contacts and test or announce changes in its approach. This will usually typify only a small minority of companies.

'Expanding exporters' are those that have been successful enough in foreign markets to consider further expansion. Trade missions and fairs can both be very beneficial for these companies because they are (somewhat different) approaches for assessing: market potential, barriers to entry, alternative entry methods, and prospective trading partners. While trade missions and fairs help to address the same issues, the fact that they are different kinds of events means that one may be preferable to the other. For example, because trade fairs take place in a fixed location, to be effective, a majority of the key players in the market should be in attendance. If this is the case, fairs can be a very efficient way to generate information and contacts – in the space of a few days, much useful work can be accomplished. Trade missions perhaps require better organization by government and more endurance of the participants if an equivalent amount of investigation and number of meetings (to trade fairs) is planned. On the other hand, missions can do their work without the distraction of participants being tied to an exhibit, and having to cope with the general hurly-burly of the trade fair. As well, a mission allows companies to see the market situation as it truly is, rather than through the somewhat artificial microcosm of a trade fair. While trade missions and fairs have their own advantages and disadvantages, for the expanding exporter, to some extent they are substitutes for one another. This is particularly important to note for companies wishing to examine new markets in certain parts of the world. Very few trade fairs are held in Africa, for example, so that for the company that saw potential on that continent, a trade mission might be the best way to approach a market expansion decision. Given the dearth of trade fairs in Africa, another approach is to exhibit in, say, Europe, at a fair that draws important African attendees. This removes the physical assessment process from the market(s) in question though, a decided disadvantage.

The final 'continuing exporter' group is one concerned with how it might maintain or improve its present position and operations in a foreign market. As noted earlier, from an export promotion support point of view, these companies face less fundamental decisions, because they are already tapping the potential overseas markets provide. This will often mean that these exporters have moved beyond the stage where they need government assistance. This is not always the case, however, and so we consider them briefly here, and discuss the role of trade missions and fairs. As far as missions are concerned, we view these companies to have mostly achieved for themselves the benefits that missions can confer; in other words, market potentials and barriers have been determined, and contacts and operating methods established. For the majority of continuing exporters, then, a trade mission will offer little that is new. Occasionally, however, the prestige of a mission can 'open doors' that might otherwise be closed, so a company selling to a foreign government, for example, may well benefit from the leverage that a mission organized by its own government provides. Generally, though, trade fairs are more useful to this category of company. With an established export operation in the country in question, the trade fair is a very useful venue for renewing contracts, solidifying relationships, and broaching ideas about ways to improve the existing strategy. Where the need for more radical change is recognized by the exporter, the trade fair again provides an arena in which to check out this notion, and to initiate the changes that seem necessary. For example, declining performance could indicate a problem with the local distributor. This idea can be examined further before a trade fair, with confirmation of the suspicion leading to agreements about correcting the problem or, in a worst case, termination of the distributorship and initiation of a search for a replacement at the fair itself.

These comments lead to some general conclusions. Trade missions are seen to be promotional methods of greater relevance to companies at earlier stages in their export decision-making. Figure 5.6 shows that the primary purpose of trade missions is to help companies to decide whether they should indeed attempt to grow through exporting, and if so, which market(s) to select. Trade mission participation should thus be targeted to 'first-time exporters', 'failed exporters', and 'expanding exporters'. Because they help companies to select markets for entry, and modify existing operations, trade fairs are of more benefit to companies that are further down the export decisions process. These company targets are the 'expanding exporters' and 'continuing exporters'. Since they serve somewhat varying purposes, the above analysis indicates that trade missions and fairs should be targeted to different types of company. Whether this is actually the case is unclear, but some interesting Canadian data are presented in Chapter 7.

Summary

We have presented a simple scheme for segmenting the market for government export promotion programmes in this section and shown how trade fairs and missions, for example, might best be targeted to the five company types described. In Chapter 7 we explore this

Figure 5.6 Trade fairs and trade missions as government export promotion assistance

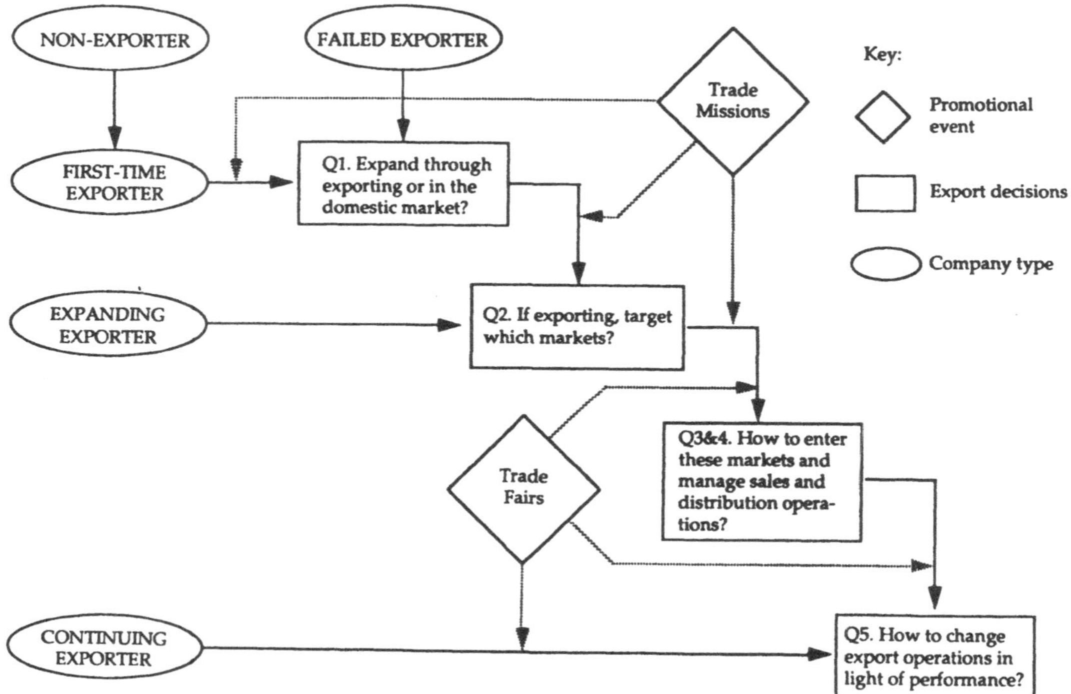

Source: Prepared by the authors.

matter further, this time in the context of data collected in an evaluation study of companies using government export programmes.

Conclusions

This chapter has been concerned with a dilemma experienced in most countries. An increasing number of companies are being drawn into foreign markets, usually as a means to grow, but sometimes simply to survive. In the process, trading barriers are experienced and governments around the world have responded by developing numerous export promotion programmes to assist companies deal with these problems. The dilemma is that there often exists a poor match between the assistance needs of companies and the programmes provided. Where the match is poor, it is likely that export performances will be compromised – obviously a result neither company or government finds satisfactory.

The chapter has explored this matter with a view to showing how government programmes might be better targeted to companies. Given shortcomings in previous schemes that have attempted to show the different groups (or segments) export promotion support serves, a practical scheme was presented. The five company groups in question – 'non-exporters', 'first-time exporters', 'failed exporters', 'expanding exporters', and 'continuing exporters' – span the export development process, are distinctive in their needs, and are easily identified by government officials. In the final section of the chapter, the usefulness of this scheme as a matching or targeting device was illustrated by considering trade missions and trade fairs. These significant export promotion vehicles were shown to be appropriate for different company targets. Thus it appears that the five-group scheme is a potentially useful device for the practical matching of company needs and export promotion support programmes by government officials. This is explored further in Chapter 7.

Notes and references

1 E. Dichtl, H.-G. Koglmayr, and S. Muller, 'Identifying export potential: a comparative analysis of German and Japanese firms', in S.T. Cavusgil (ed.) *Advances in International Marketing*, Greenwich, Conn., JAI Press, 1986, pp. 233–54.

2 M. Bodur, 'A study on the nature and intensity of problems experienced by Turkish exporting firms', in S.T. Cavusgil (ed.) *Advances in International Marketing*, Greenwich, Conn., JAI Press, 1986, pp. 205–32.

3 I. Wilkinson and N. Barrett, 'Australian management's attitudes to exporting – past and present', unpublished paper presented to the Market

Research Society of Australia's Annual Conference, Canberra, 1986.

4 S. Rabino, 'An examination of barriers to exporting encountered by small manufacturing companies', *International Management Review*, 1980/1, vol. 20, pp. 67–73.

5 E.J. Kleinschmidt and R.E. Ross, 'Export performance and foreign market information: relationships for small high-technology firms', *Canadian Journal of Small Business and Entrepreneurship*, 1984, vol. 2, no. 2, pp. 8–23.

6 E. Kaynak and L. Stevenson, 'Profile analysis of Nova Scotia exporters', *Proceedings*, Administrative Sciences Association of Canada-Marketing Division, University of Ottawa, 1982, pp. 98–108.

7 S.T. Cavusgil, 'Differences among exporting firms based on their degree of internationalization', unpublished paper, University of Wisconsin-Whitewater, undated. The classification of companies was carried out judgmentally, after consideration of a large number of factors.

8 J. Mattson, 'Initial penetration of European continental markets by small and medium-sized firms', in S.T. Cavusgil (ed.) *Advances in International Marketing*, Greenwich, Conn., vol. 1, 1986, pp. 93–114.

9 S.T. Cavusgil, 'On the internationalization process of firms', *European Research*, 1980, vol. 8, November, pp. 273–81.

10 N.J. Barrett and I.F. Wilkinson, 'Internationalization behavior: management characteristics of Australian manufacturing firms by level of international development', in P.W. Turnbull and S.J. Paliwoda, (eds) *Research in International Marketing*, Beckenham, Croom Helm, 1986, pp. 213–33.

11 W.J. Bilkey, 'An attempted integration of the literature on the export behavior of firms', *Journal of International Business Studies*, 1978, vol. 9, no. 1, spring/summer, pp. 33–46.

12 L.H. Wortzell and H.V. Wortzell, 'Export marketing strategies for NIC and LDC-based firms', *Columbia Journal of World Business*, 1981, spring, pp. 51–60. While developed through a study of consumer products companies, this model is claimed to be useful in the industrial products context as well. See D. Ford *et al.*, 'Managing export development between industrialized and developing countries', in P.J. Rosson and S.D. Reid (eds) *Managing Export Entry and Expansion: Concepts and Practice*, New York, Praeger, 1987, pp. 71–90.

13 S.D. Reid and P.J. Rosson, 'Managing export entry and expansion: an overview', in P.J. Rosson and S.D. Reid, (eds) *Managing Export Entry and Expansion: Concepts and Practice*, New York, Praeger, 1987, pp. 3–18.

14 A recent Canadian study reveals that, among the 271 manufacturing companies surveyed, 97 per cent planned to go on exporting current products to existing markets, 79 per cent planned to export new products to existing markets, 71 per cent planned to export current products to new markets, and 56 per cent planned to export new products to new markets. These data demonstrate clearly that companies pursue multiple exporting strategies: F.H. Rolf Seringhaus, 'The

relationship of knowledge and firm behaviour in exporting: test of a conceptual model', Working Paper Series 5.88, School of Business and Economics, Wilfrid Laurier University, Ontario, 1988.

15 R.H. Rolf Seringhaus, 'Do experienced exporters have market entry problems?', *Finnish Journal of Business Economics*, 1987, no. 4, pp. 376–88.

16 J. Johanson and J.-E. Vahlne, 'The internationalization of the firm: a model of knowledge development and increasing foreign market commitments', *Journal of International Business Studies*, 1977, vol. 8, no. 1, spring/summer, pp. 23–32.

17 M.R. Czinkota, *Export Development Strategies: US Promotion Policy*, New York, Praeger, 1982.

18 M.R. Czinkota and W.J. Johnston, 'Segmenting US firms for export development', *Journal of Business Research*, 1981, no. 9, pp. 353–65. This contains somewhat different stage labels but derives from the same study referred to in note 17.

19 Czinkota, *Export Development Strategies*, p. 110.

20 N.J. Barrett and I.F. Wilkinson, 'Export stimulation: a segmentation study of the exporting problems of Australian manufacturing firms', *European Journal of Marketing*, 1985, vol. 19, no. 2, pp. 53–72. In addition to data on export problems, information on the following was collected: organization and management characteristics, exporting attitudes and practices, and domestic marketing policies.

21 A point of similarity between these studies is that the researchers consider company export operations only in a global sense. Thus neither views exporting activity from a multiple strategies framework. This, again, makes for easier exposition but may conceal important variations. For example, Australian exporters presumably face different problems in the (relatively) nearby markets of Asia to those in Europe and North America, yet this issue (as well as others) cannot be addressed given the approach adopted.

22 D.A. Roy and C.L. Simpson, 'The decision to discontinue exporting: the experience of the smaller manufacturing firm in the Southeast United States', *Proceedings*, Academy of Marketing Science Conference, 1981, pp. 101–4.

23 L.S. Welch and F. Wiedersheim-Paul, 'Initial exports – a marketing failure?, *Journal of Management Studies*, October 1980, pp. 333–44.

24 A number of writers have argued that exporting is innovative behaviour. See, for example, K. Simmonds and H. Smith, 'The first export order: a marketing innovation', *British Journal of Marketing*, 1968, summer, pp. 93–100; W.-Y. Lee and J.J. Brasch, 'The adoption of export as an innovative strategy', *Journal of International Business Studies*, 1978, vol. 9, no. 1, pp. 85–93; and S.D. Reid, 'The decision maker and export entry and expansion', *Journal of International Business Studies*, 1981, vol. 12, no. 2, fall, pp. 101–12.

25 Roy and Simpson, 'The decision to discontinue exporting', p. 104.

26 These initiatives usually absorb a sizeable share of government export promotion budgets and also enable large numbers of companies to visit, investigate, select, and operate in foreign markets.

Chapter six

Measuring the impact of export promotion

Introduction

This chapter concerns the results and effects of government export promotion programmes. Up to this point our discussion has mostly concerned the role and purpose of export promotion, with less attention paid to the impact of such activity on companies or the economy. Knowing something about the impact of such programmes is clearly of interest and importance to both export promotion organizations and user companies. The former must periodically demonstrate that public funds are being properly used, while the 'bottom line' orientation of the latter is bound to generate an interest in the return of an investment from programme participation.

This chapter deals with the issue of impact measurement. It does this by examining available evidence from government and academic research. In the first section, the need for programme evaluation is reviewed and a number of differing levels of impact identified. In the second section, impact measurement is shown to be a complex and difficult exercise. The discussion points to the interactive nature of export promotion activities and highlights various definitional and methodological questions associated with measuring impact. Having set the scene, the third section goes on to consider impact at the export promotion programme level. It does this by drawing from evaluation studies that have been carried out in a number of developing and developed countries. The fourth section looks at impact from the user company standpoint. Here the main factors considered are companies' views about programme awareness, usage, helpfulness, and criticalness. The complex nature of measuring programme effects at the user level is illustrated by a recent trade mission study. The main issues surrounding impact measurement are summarized on pp. 213–14, and guidelines suggested for improving this difficult but important activity. In addition, a framework is developed showing that both public and private sector perspectives should be built into future attempts to measure government export promotion programme impact. The final section summarizes the discussion and brings the chapter to an end.

Impact assessment

Impact assessment and programme evaluation

Although we concentrate on impact assessment in this chapter, we should recognize that this is only one (albeit very important) facet in the evaluation of government export promotion programmes. Regular, periodic evaluations of such programmes are conducted in many countries, with a view to providing direct feedback to those charged with running them.[1] Four key issues are relevant in programme evaluation:[2]

1 Programme rationale – does the programme make sense?
2 Impacts and effects – what happen as a result of the programme?
3 Objectives – has a programme achieved what was expected?
4 Alternatives – are there better ways of achieving the results?

Turning more specifically to export promotion programmes, ITC states the following reasons as underlying their evaluation:[3]

1 To examine activities carried out under a given programme, in order to ascertain the magnitude of the result achieved and the effectiveness of the programme.
2 To uncover implementation problems and identify possible solutions.
3 To accumulate experience from the implementation of particular activities and of programmes as a whole.
4 To measure the impact of programme (or activity) and ascertain whether the results justify the implementation of the programme.
5 To help in defining activities that will contribute more positively to the effectiveness of programmes.

Having noted the part played by impact assessment in evaluation studies, we now focus our attention exclusively on the matter of impact.

Levels of impact

Two broad goals underlie government efforts in providing export promotion support: first, at the macro level, generating a favourable trade balance or reducing a trade deficit, and second, at the micro level, enhancing the international competitive competence of domestic companies and industries. These goals are clearly interrelated, as the following example demonstrates. The trade balance influences a country's foreign exchange rate, and hence affects the domestic and foreign market price of products (the former through imported goods and services that are inputs to the manufacturing process). Thus the foreign exchange rate is a factor for companies as they compete with imports domestically and with competitors in export markets.

Macro and micro levels, therefore, are interwoven as far as export promotion by government is concerned. However, impact assessment tends to be carried out using the macro/micro division. Within these two levels, a variety of further assessment options exist when looking at impact, for example:[4]

1 Country's foreign trade position
2 Overall government export promotion programme
3 Sectoral programmes, such as
   - Foreign trade fairs
   - Trade missions
   - Trade information services
4 Events or activities, such as
   - Foreign trade fair A or B
   - Trade mission A or B
   - Market feasibility study A or B
5 Exporters participating in
   - Foreign trade fair A
   - Trade mission of type A to country B
   - Market study tour to market A

Little agreement exists on how impact is best measured, the levels at which it should be assessed, or the indicators to be applied in such an exercise. There is broad agreement, however, on the need for and benefit to be derived from impact measurement.

Summary

The impact of government export promotion on targeted companies, as well as the economy generally, has become an issue of concern within the past decade. Two recent publications reflect the growing interest in evaluating these programmes and the recognition that present methods need to be improved.[5] The impact of government export promotion is seen to occur at several different levels, ranging from the broadest possible effect on a country's trade position to the highly specific results an exporter may realize using a particular export programme. This creates a real challenge in assessing programme impacts, and this matter is addressed in the remainder of this chapter.

Difficulty of measuring impact

In this section we explain why measuring the impact of government export promotion programmes is such a difficult undertaking. Three topics are covered and in each we identify some of the problems facing those undertaking impact assessment.

Relationship of programme and company

The first difficulty associated with impact assessment is suggested in Figure 6.1, adapted from pioneering Swedish research in this area. Note that government export promotion programmes are shown on the left of the diagram, company actual or future export sales on the right, and three intervening variables in between. 'Decision base in the company' refers to information the senior manager(s) has about the consequences or the alternatives being considered. The process portrayed in Figure 6.1 may be seen in these terms, then: following use of a government export promotion programme, a company is able to judge the merit of embarking on a related course of export action, decides to act accordingly, sets in motion appropriate activities, and makes export sales.[6] The critical research question here is: what was the impact of the programme in the company achieving the export sales it did? In the same way that advertising is not the sole cause of sales, so too government export promotion programme use cannot be shown as the only determinant of export sales. While programme use may have helped generate the sales, many other factors may have come into play. Consider, for example, that a substantial time-lag may have occurred between programme use and the achievement of the sales in question. During this period, the demand or competitive situation in the foreign market may well have changed dramatically, thus boosting sales to more than meet expectations.

Consider also that as a consequence of using the export promotion programme, another company selected the right market to enter but, in fact, went about foreign marketing in an inappropriate manner and achieved low sales. Consider a final company which used a programme to look at opportunities in a foreign market but, because of problems in finding an agent, decided not to proceed. With its interest in exporting piqued it then transferred its attention to another

Figure 6.1 Export promotional support and firm behaviour

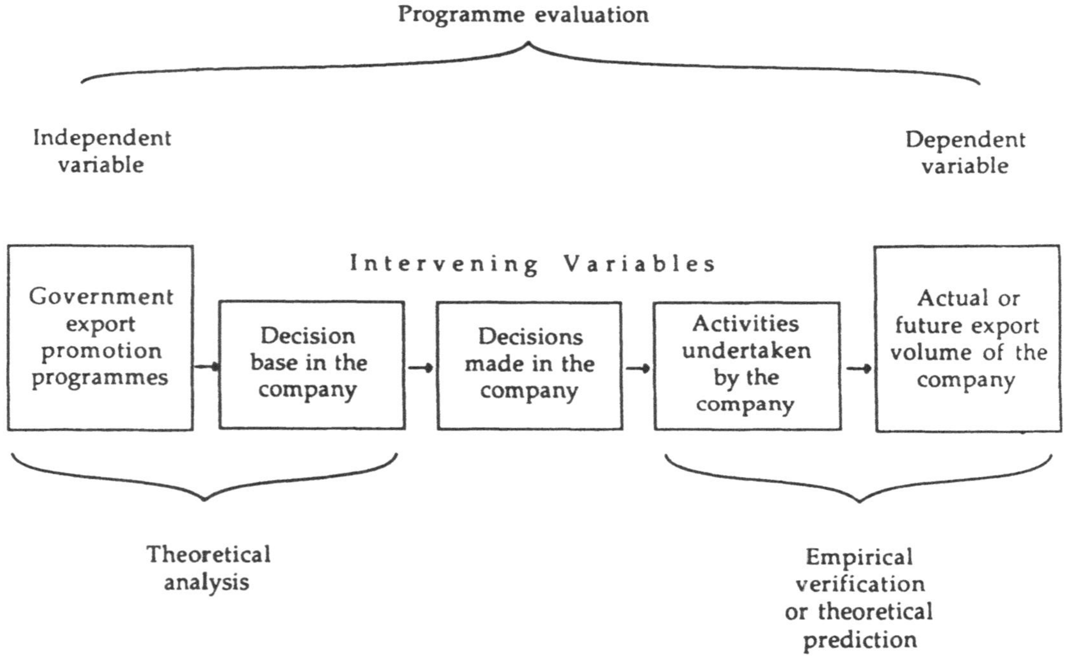

Source: Adapted from H.C. Olson, *Studies in Export Promotion*, Stockholm, Almqvist & Wiksell International, 1975, p. 31.

market and was able to make satisfactory representation arrangements and sales. In all three instances we can justifiably ask: What impact should be attributed to the government export promotion programme?

Clearly there is no easy answer to this question. In the evaluation studies presently carried out, impact is best addressed through examining company activities and related export sales.[7] The impact of government programmes is then looked at by trying to understand the decisions that led to the given activities, and how programme use may have shaped company decision-making. This is no easy task but, as we shall see in the next chapter, approximations of impact can be made.

The two areas of concern in measuring the effect of export promotion programmes are the methodology and measurement and the impact dimensions, which are discussed in the next two sections.

Methodology and measurement

A second difficulty in impact assessment concerns methodology and measurement practices. A brief discussion of this seems in order so as to understand the attempts at interpretation of programme results presented later in this chapter. Evaluations of programme impact have generally been carried out with emphasis either on quantitative or qualitative approaches.

Quantitative techniques tend to use very narrow and specific indicators of outcome, such as cost-benefit ratios of incremental export sales. (Other more complex decision-theoretic methods, such as multi-attribute utility techniques, have not greatly improved the measurement of impact largely because some variables that need to be measured are not directly observable.) What does it mean to say that in the UK, each pound sterling of export promotion expenditures generates £21 of export sales, or that in Canada a higher ratio of export sales to promotional expenditures (35:1) and in Ireland a lower ratio (8:1) has been determined?[8] Such numbers falsely suggest unequivocal and direct causality between programme expenditures and sales results. The principal difficulty with such indicators is that, as noted above, many other factors influence company export behaviour and results, and therefore the aggregate export performance of an industry of a country.

Qualitative methods, such as survey techniques, take a broad approach and collect profile, experience and performance characteristics of users of export promotion programmes. Survey research can provide large amounts of data but usually also suffers from drawbacks such a incomplete questionnaires, partial representation of the target group of companies and therefore questionable representativeness of results. Recently, efforts have been made to use more sophisticated research techniques (such as multiple measures of programme impact, and quasi-experimental research designs) to overcome some of these concerns.[9]

While some may find quantitative methods conceptually more appealing, others prefer qualitative approaches. Methodologically neither is flawless and both leave considerable uncertainty about programme outcomes and impact.[10] Whatever the method of programme impact evaluation, it is most probable that export support contributes incrementally to export sales.

A related issue in determining programme impact concerns the yardsticks used in assessment. Often the definition of effectiveness is vague or unspecific and clear objectives of a programme are lacking. It is common for goals of export promotion to be stated in qualitative terms.[11] Consequently adequate measures of programme impact on users are difficult to establish and very little can be said conclusively about the effectiveness of export promotion. A frequent contributor to the vagueness of such goals is the limited knowledge EPOs have of the characteristics of target user companies. Clearly it would benefit programme management to know where potential user companies are lacking export capabilities, at which stage of the export involvement process they are, what their resources are (management, financial, market-related), what long-term export plans they have, and so on. To be sure, companies should and need to determine their own destiny and manage their own affairs. Export promotion programmes, however, can assist better if they draw their focus, design as well as goals, from actual company situations and needs.

Dimensions of impact

The third difficulty in assessing impact relates to the absence of agreed-upon parameters against which export promotion programmes can be regularly and consistently measured. An awareness exists that impact may occur at various levels and in numerous forms, but attempts to define and describe these are quite recent. The challenge then is one of determining dimensions of impact that are appropriate and meaningful for different export promotion activities. This involves finding answers to questions such as: is the impact major or minor, is it positive or negative, immediate or lagged, intended or unintended, is it behavioural, financial, or structural as far as the user company is concerned?[12]

Before discussing these dimensions we should concern ourselves briefly with two assumptions that underlie impact measurement. First, that programmes have clear, specific, and measurable outcome goals and objectives, and second, that programmes are properly implemented, that their critical elements have in fact been delivered to the appropriate target group. These may be erroneous assumptions. Two examples illustrate this view.

On the first assumption, programme agencies may have an objective for a particular event, for example *x* dollar export sales for a trade mission to specific markets, not, however, for the programme. Mission participants may already have good contacts and sales prospects in the market prior to the visit with a mission. Thus sales realized by a company after such a visit may truly stem from earlier efforts in the market. The agency then may falsely attribute such sales as a mission result, when in fact the latter had little or no impact. Not only may there be no yardstick for the aggregate results from events but also individual reported outcomes from participants may be misleading.

On the second assumption, programmes are made available to established exporters, and consequently deprive the first-time exporter who more acutely needs assistance. The unassisted company may then opt not to export, or enter export markets ill-prepared. Another poor targeting situation is where programmes encourage companies to export before they are really ready. Clearly this not only wastes programme and company resources, but also may significantly retard subsequent export efforts because of an initial bad experience.

We now turn to the dimensions of impact. Our primary concern is with the size of impact, although the other dimensions listed above will also be briefly discussed. One can distinguish between major and minor effects of programmes. Neither is clearly defined. If the major effect sought is one of improving the competitive position of exporters then certain questions emerge. Does such improvement mean more profits or sales volume, entry into additional markets, or organizing a larger market share? What constitutes a major effect? Export promotion evaluations often fail to find a major effect which is attributable to the programme. The objectives must be pragmatic and the expectation for change realistic.

Minor effect, on the other hand, appears far more relevant than major effect in the assessment of impact. Two arguments can be made in support of this view. In a generic sense, there is a similarity in companies' export activities. However, companies pursue export-related goals through somewhat different means. Figure 6.2 shows how alternative or multiple paths may be involved in the pursuit of incremental export sales. When two groups of companies are compared, one using an export promotion programme, the other not,

Figure 6.2 Achieving incremental results through alternative/multiple paths

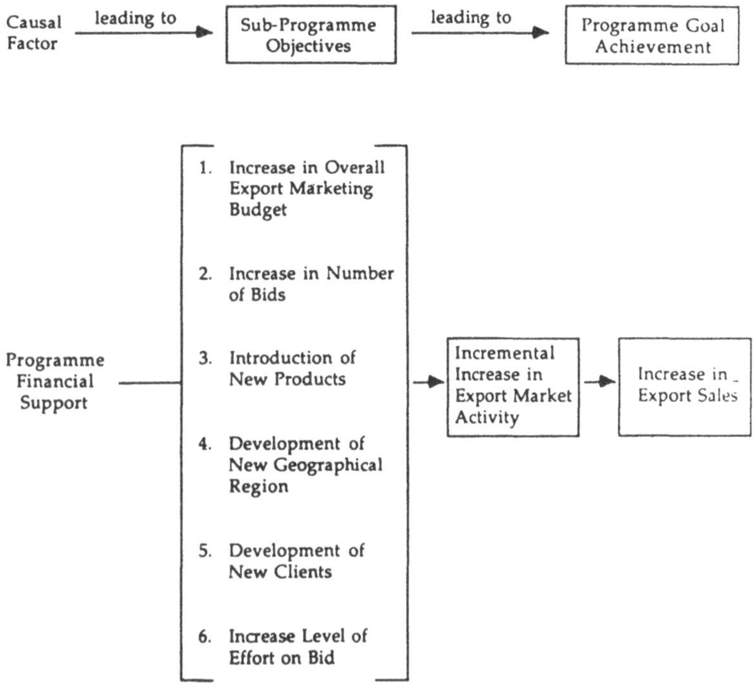

Source: Adapted from DPA Consulting Ltd, *Program for Export Market Development: A Company Level Approach*, Ottawa, January 1981, used with permission.

then the latter is likely to employ some other (substitute) activities in place of the programme. For example, a company is likely to visit a market on its own while the user may go on a trade mission. The net effect of the contrast may show only a minor difference in the impact measure (e.g. export sales, speed of negotiation, etc.). Another point has already been made, namely that export promotion programmes are but one factor in companies operations. The expectation that a programme will have a dominant effect on export impact is, then, unrealistic. A more reasonable view of the effect of export promotion programmes is that under the best circumstances only marginal or incremental impact will result. This should not be surprising as companies typically mount broad-scale, integrated efforts in pursuit of new or expanded markets.

The aim of programmes is for desirable, positive effects. It is possible that programme use can result in an undesirable, negative impact. The poor targeting situation mentioned above is one such example. Companies may become casual about assistance and fail to prepare adequately, say, for a trade fair or mission or do not follow up on leads. This can substantially reduce sales or result in lost contracts altogether. The company thus would damage its market position or prospects and the programme would see no evidence of a return on promotion expenditures. Impact can be immediate as in sales made at a fair, or lagged, as is likely when a company uses the event to establish customer contact as a basis for the gradual and often lengthy building of a business relationship. In the latter case, programme follow-up time periods may be too short to register sales results flowing from this activity. Impact may also be unintended with behavioural, financial, or structural consequences for the company. Thus numerous indirect, invisible, and yet desirable effects may emanate from programme use. For instance, (1) companies may learn about other forms of export support through the use of one programme, (2) awareness of a programme and understanding its workings may provide useful other sources of information to the exporter, (3) programmes may spur the company to rethink its exporting approach and activity, and (4) export support may strengthen a company's commitment to foreign markets.[13] Many of these different impacts are interrelated which complicates their measurement. In general, while government export promotion efforts are well structured (that is a policy leads to programmes, which in turn organize activities leading to specific events), the assumed direct relationship between export promotion and results at the user level is doubtful.

Summary

This section was concerned with three areas of difficulty in measuring export promotion programme impact. The relationship of programme and company is not only important but also needs to be clearly understood. First, particularly relevant is the linkage between programme and result through intervening variables. Understanding of programme impact is seen to be complicated, second, by methodological and measurement difficulties, and third, by the multiple facets of impacts programmes can have.

Impact from a programme perspective

Conceptual issues

Despite the problem of impact measurement, evaluation of export promotion programmes is increasingly viewed as important. Before we discuss the impact of government export promotion from a programme perspective, several conceptual issues are considered.

Experience with evaluation of export promotion programmes shows five main areas of difficulty:[14]

1 absence of precise targets,
2 statistics not available or lacking detail,
3 programme results flow from numerous actions,
4 information used comes from variety of sources,
5 results of general nature often cannot be measured.

It is obvious that programme impact and effectiveness are difficult to measure when no precise objectives are set for a programme. Results cannot be compared against targets and so a proper evaluation is impossible. Relevant and timely statistical data are required to go beyond highly qualitative measurements of programme effects. As was mentioned earlier, programmes function in a complex situation (one where multiple influences are at play), and this makes it impossible to show direct causal linkages. Furthermore, the sources of information play a significant role, which depends on their involvement in the programme as well as their motivation for giving information, and their credibility. Last but not least is the difficulty created by quantification; the narrowness of quantitative measures often fails to register broader effects, as well as being incomplete or biased and thereby potentially misrepresenting programme impact.

From a programme management point of view the critical evaluation question is: what evidence, measures, or indicators will demonstrate that a programme's intended results have been or are being achieved? In other words, what impact criteria can yield the information? Clearly we need to be more specific by what we mean by impact criteria. Considerable effort is required to spell out, for example, what the immediate objective, expected output or particular activities of an export promotion programme are. Several characteristics for such impact criteria can be suggested. It is necessary that they be: (1) pre-established, (2) specific and explicit, (3) relevant and pertinent, (4) objectively verifiable, (5) obtainable, and (6) quantitative and qualitative. In addition, the criteria must suit the type or kind of thing being measured, must be able to register the magnitude or quantity of the object being measured, and be able to record the necessary or desired quality of the change being produced or attained.[15]

Figure 6.3 develops a general framework for the concept of programme impact and the different criteria involved. The immediate objective refers to a change which is to be achieved by an export

Figure 6.3 The concept of programme impact

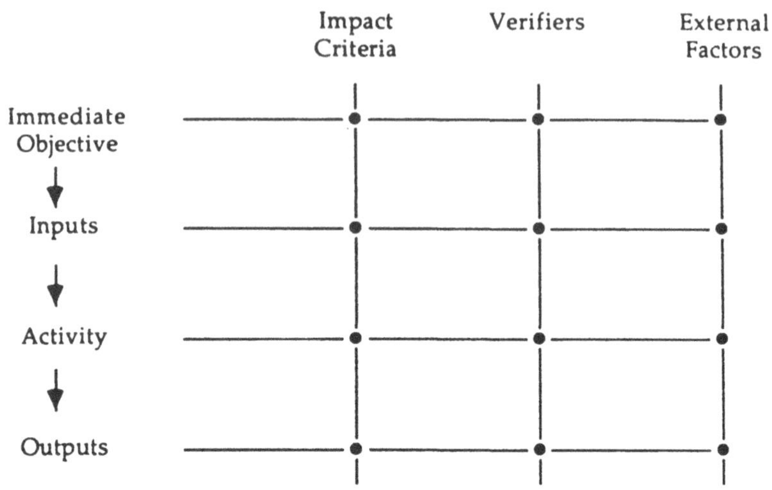

Source: Prepared by the authors.

promotion programme. This change then is the result the programme is designed to accomplish if completed or carried out successfully within the specified time frame, given the environment within which the programme–company interaction takes place. As we mentioned earlier, even if the programme delivers all intended activities it is not certain that the desired changes (as stated in the objective) will occur.

Immediate objectives should be:[16]

1 stated in terms of 'ends' not 'means', for example penetration into a given market, not carrying out a trade mission,
2 consistent with a reasonable expectation that they are achievable,
3 achievable through the actions of the programme and activities of the user company.

Inputs are programme resources. These consist of funding to carry on the programme, management expertise, planning, and organizational support, all organized in a relevant time-frame laid out in the objective statement. Activities are the processes through which inputs are transformed into programme results or outputs. Activities undertaken should be comprehensively listed and be verifiable in content, quantity, and time.[17] Outputs referred to, as in Figure 6.3, are results ensuing from the completed activities. Activities need to be distinguished from outputs. To illustrate:

1 business contacts established in the target market with potential buyers is an output, while undertaking a trade mission to that market is an activity;
2 assisting a group of exporters to gain greater knowledge and expertise in market research is an output, while conducting the workshops and training seminars for this purpose is an activity.

The relationship of the immediate objective to output is given in Table 6.1.

This shows that the programme elements are sequential and that at each level account needs to be taken of impact, verification, and of the possible external influences that may have some bearing on this process. The principal challenge here, however, is the creation of impact criteria and verifiers. An example of this basic framework applied to a product and market development programme in a developing country conveys the usefulness of this approach (Table 6.2). Two objectives – the adaptation of product to target market criteria and market entry into the target market – are specified. Several results of the programme are expected and specific impact criteria and verifiers are developed to measure the results.[18]

Evaluations of programmes

Any country with an export promotion organization, whether formally integrated or loosely organized, whether primarily government-run or carried on by the private sector, is concerned about the impact of its actions. The International Trade Centre recognized the need for evaluating its technical assistance projects in export promotion many years ago.[19] ITC's work consists of assisting developing countries in export development and its programmes are of a specific nature with stated objectives and goals. These are evaluated internally as well as through the use of independent consultants. The results of these evaluation activities are formally documented and issued in the form of a summary report annually, which in turn is placed on the agenda of the annual session of the Joint Advisory Group of the International Trade Centre UNCTAD/GATT. While these evaluations are concerned with how well ITC carries out its mandate and thus differ in focus from those carried out on behalf of specific government programmes, they show both the difficulty and usefulness of such work. Examples drawn from evaluations conducted in 1987 by ITC with the co-operation of the respective governments in three underdeveloped countries underline this point.

Table 6.1 Basic programme elements framework

Programme elements	*Impact criteria*	*Verifiers*	*External factors*
Immediate objectives(s) Describe the specific aim which the programme itself, with its own resources and activities, is expected to achieve in a given period of time.	Describe the qualititative and/or quantitative standards which will enable us to measure or demonstrate that the programme's objective(s) has/have been achieved. The impact criteria should be: – pre-established – specific and explicit – pertinent – objectively verifiable. They should be quantitative whenever possible. If they are qualitative, they should be formulated in such a way that they can be verified by a *yes* or *no* answer. Make sure that baseline and final data are collected to show the programme's contribution to moving from point 'A' to point 'B', that is from an initial situation to end of project status.	Describe the concrete evidence or source of information required to demonstrate that the programme objective's impact criteria have materialized. The evidence or source of information can be external to the project (for example: public or private statistics) or can be generated by the project itself (for example: publications, reports, statistics, surveys, etc.).	Describe the major conditions, assumptions, events, decisions, etc. which are beyond the programme's control and which nevertheless can influence the achievement of the programme objective(s). External factors should be reviewed for relevance and probability of occurrence.

Table 6.1 contd

Programme elements	*Impact criteria*	*Verifiers*	*External factors*
Inputs Describe the specialists, consultants, subcontracts, fellowships, equipment, and miscellaneous components required to carry out the activities contemplated in the work plan. Make sure that the type, quantity, quality, and timing of the inputs are consistent with activities to be carried out.	Identify suitable impact criteria which will enable us to demonstrate that the inputs will be adequate for implementing the work plan as specified.	Identify suitable verifiers to demonstrate that the inputs impact criteria have materialized.	Identify the main external factors outside the control of the programme which can influence the delivery and utilization of the inputs.
Outputs Describe these concrete and tangible 'products' that are needed to achieve the programme's objective(s). Make sure that the type, quality, quantity, and timing of the output are consistent with the programme's objective(s).	Identify suitable impact criteria which will enable us to demonstrate that the outputs will produce the desired effects.	Identify suitable verifiers to demonstrate that the output impact criteria have materialized.	Identify the main external factors outside the control of the programme which can influence the production of the outputs.

Source: Adapted from *ITC Manual on Programming, Project Design, Monitoring and Evaluation*, International Trade Centre UNCTAD/GATT, Geneva, August 1987, pp. 68–9.

Table 6.2 Example of basic project elements framework for a developing country

Project elements	*Impact criteria*	*Verifiers*	*External factors*
Product and market development			
Immediate objectives 1 Adapting the wood products of Ghana, including furniture, according to the quality, design, and finishing specifications of the United Kingdom markets.	– Application by the selected companies of the new design and finishing standards.	– Consultant's sketches included in his report.	– Allocation of foreign exchange by the Central Bank to import chemicals and some new machinery. – Decision by the selected companies to apply the new finishing technology.
2 Actual penetration into the United Kingdom market by obtaining trial orders in 1986, and firm orders by 1988.	– Trial orders obtained by at least five furniture-producing/exporting companies during 1986. – Actual exports of $1 million worth of furniture to the United Kingdom by 1988.	– Data to be collected by the Ghana Export Promotion Council from the selected producing/ exporting companies and from the Customs Department. – Abolishment of minimum price control system by the Ministry of Trade.	– Positive response by the United Kingdom importers to the offers to be made by the Ghanaian exporters. – Expansion of the existing incentives by the Ministry of Finance to include the furniture industry.
Inputs – Furniture design – Production technology – Furniture marketing – Study tours for six participants	– Not applicable.	– Not applicable.	– Timely clearance of consultancies by the government.

Table 6.2 contd.

Project elements	*Impact criteria*	*Verifiers*	*External factors*
Outputs In reference to immediate objective 1.			
– New modern furniture design provided to the five selected companies.	– Modern furniture designs and drawings included in the consultant's report.	– Consultant's report, companies' production of furniture using new designs.	– Companies' willingness and capability.
– Improved finishing technology described and the know-how transferred to the five companies selected.	– Description of the application of the improved finishing technology, workshops or on-the-job training provided.	– Companies' production using improved finishing technology.	– Companies willingness and capability.
In reference to immediate objective 2.			
– Business contacts established in the target markets with potential buyers.	– Negotiations during business contacts to cover points such as preferred designs and quality specifications, prices, delivery conditions, terms of payments, etc., initially for trial orders, and subsequently for company tacted abroad and the orders.	– Records of the business negotiations conducted as included in the report of the sales missions, and the subsequent correspondence with the United Kingdom importing companies.	– Attitude of the United Kingdom companies.
– A catalogue produced providing illustrations of various modern furniture produced by the selected companies in Ghana.	– Distribution of the catalogue to interested importing companies of modern furniture.		

Source: Adapted from: *ITC Manual on Programming, Project Design, Monitoring and Evaluation*, International Trade Centre UNCTAD/GATT, Geneva, August 1987, p. 81.

Developing country evaluations

Country A – Africa A programme to establish an autonomous trade information service was evaluated. The original plan called for a trade information centre to be set up within state enterprises; however, it was actually created within the Ministry of Foreign Trade. Commercial information needs had been identified and a system for collecting information established. Although some information was being distributed the trade information centre has not been able to undertake market studies or use some of the information at its disposal because of a lack of qualified staff. While some of the personnel had been trained abroad in the past, staff training was now mostly conducted in-house on the job. The importance of a trade information centre to the export development effort has been recognized; however, the implementation of all necessary elements misjudged and the goal of providing effective trade and market information to the export sector not realized. The lesson is clear. Without the appropriate organizational, administrative, and training support a trade information centre is not likely to achieve its goals. The example shows that such a centre requires both independence from government bureaucracy and continuing foreign market contact, for the purpose of staff training and assessing foreign market opportunities, if it is to play a useful role in the broader efforts of export development in the business community.[20]

Country B – Mediterranean A programme focused on improving the export promotion activities and orientation in a number of institutions including the EPO, chamber of commerce, development bank, and a training institution, was evaluated. The programme consisted of training and advisory activities aiming at enhancing the exporting mentality of the business sector. Sectoral analyses, seminars, and trade missions to foreign markets helped demonstrate that a larger export potential than previously realized existed. To convert such opportunities into company-specific plans for action was less successful for three main reasons. First, increasing company exports was found to require more time and tailored assistance than anticipated. Second, low budgets constrained the EPO's ability to provide follow-up on market contacts and exporting companies. Third, efforts at senior government levels to co-ordinate export development were found in need of improvement. The lesson here is that while positive and proactive attitudes are essential, well-funded guidance and support systems at the EPO, government and enterprise levels need to be co-ordinated in order to serve export development goals. Programmes may be too ambitious and a more focused approach (such as realistic sectoral action plans in line with resources) is appropriate.[21]

Country C – Latin America A project aimed at strengthening trade-related training was evaluated. Among the elements of this programme were the exchange of teaching staff in the region, developing a nucleus for the creation and distribution of training materials, and contributing to the establishment of a regional co-operative effort for training in international trade. Data banks on curriculum programmes, teaching materials and teachers were developed and disseminated, leading to improved international trade curricula in several institutions. While the information exchange was implemented, the co-operative training effort and exchange of teachers in the region was not realized primarily due to insufficient funding. The lesson here is that well-conceived programmes, intended to benefit a given country or a region, have the potential of contributing to international trade consciousness and thus export awareness but are critically dependent upon governmental commitment through adequate funding. It is a positive indicator that the country as well as the region have co-operated in the mutual building of international trade expertise.[22]

Evaluations of this kind show that ITC is placing greater emphasis on the development of co-ordination for both the planning and implementation of export promotion programmes. It is apparent that EPOs are one element in the export development/promotion process and that other institutions and the enterprises themselves need to be integrated into the activities from the beginning.[23]

Developed country evaluations

As discussed in Chapter 2, several industrial countries have undertaken large-scale reviews of their overall export promotion activities. More often, however, industrial countries carry out evaluation studies of particular export promotion programmes. The scope and emphasis of such efforts varies widely. To demonstrate both the diversity of programme evaluation and the lack of a common methodology, recent evaluations undertaken in Ireland, Sweden, and the United Kingdom are outlined.

Ireland[24] The Irish Export Board, the national trade promotion organization, periodically conducts its own reviews while also being subject to external evaluations. These evaluations concentrate on the appropriateness of the services provided to company needs, the usage of services by exporters, and assessment of the effectiveness of specific services or programmes. In the process of conducting these evaluations, a number of points have surfaced:

1 the qualitative nature of certain services and programmes, and hence, the difficulty of measuring impact,

Table 6.3 Evaluation of trade fairs and retail store promotions of the Irish Export Board

Trade fairs: objectives

General

- To promote a favourable country image abroad.
- To increase the value and volume of exports to the chosen market.
- To assist *x* number of firms to overcome some of the disadvantages of exporting by improving seller/buyer relationships.

Specific

- To assist *x* participating companies in achieving £*x* million in export sales to the target market within a one-year period.
- To support the participating companies' existing importers/distributors in the market.
- To introduce *x* new products to the market and to obtain buyer reaction.
- To meet, hold discussion with, *x* number of current and new customers.
- To investigate new product opportunities.
- To gain publicity for the participating companies' products in important trade media.

Trade fairs: evaluation

The evaluation should provide answers, information, and recommendations under four main headings:

- Was the project effective in terms of the objectives and criteria set?
- Were the participating companies satisfied and what action will they be taking?
- Should the project be repeated and, if so, what changes, if any, should be made in the future?
- What new or alternative promotional activities should be undertaken by way of follow-up to the project?

The process of evaluation includes the use of the following:

- Company questionnaires;
- Report by the project manager;
- Formal review with participants;
- Qualitative research.

Retail store promotions: objectives

Primary

- Actual sales in the chosen store and to maximize opportunities for Irish suppliers; to obtain initial orders and to strengthen the purchasing relationship with the store concerned;
- Effective publicity for Irish consumer products in the market at both trade and consumer levels.

Secondary

To gain publicity for Ireland and 'things Irish' in the market by organizing ancillary events; to encourage and persuade other prominent retail stores and groups to consider mounting Irish product promotions, thereby increasing the overall volume and value of exports to the chosen market area.

Table 6.3 contd

Retail store promotions: evaluation

The evaluation process is mainly designed to:
- Compare the value of actual orders with the target;
- Hold a formal review with the store management of sales results and new product opportunities;
- Ensure continuity/follow-up suppliers and the store concerned;
- Consider undertaking qualitative research two years after the event.

Source: *Guide to the Evaluation of Trade Promotion Programmes*, International Trade Centre UNCTAD/GATT, Geneva, 1987, pp. 15–17, 19.

2 the issue of whether users should be charged for services or programmes and if so to what extent,
3 that a tendency exists to offer certain services and programmes because of their relative ease of organization and implementation,
4 the difficulty of defining clear and specific objectives for activities,
5 the problem of allocating limited resources across activities.

From the numerous programmes offered to companies each year trade fairs and retail store promotions are selected here to illustrate the criteria used to evaluate them (Table 6.3).

Sweden[25] The services provided by the Swedish Trade Council are generally limited to those not available elsewhere and have the overall aim to assist Swedish firms to establish an export presence in foreign markets. While the Swedish Trade Council does not have a regular and systematic evaluation of its programmes and services, trade promotion activities have been studied and shown to have contributed in a variety of ways, including

1 larger export revenues,
2 increased foreign market knowledge among exporters,
3 a greater international marketing emphasis among exporters,
4 more and longer lasting export initiatives.

There is an acute awareness by the Council that while some aspects of its export promotion activities can be measured with some precision, others cannot. Impact, then, can rarely be measured conclusively and may be judged only over time. On a broad scale, the collective performance of Swedish companies in export markets could suggest whether export promotion services have an effect. In a still more general interpretation, the Council views the increasing acceptance of its export promotion services among Swedish companies as an indicator of the perceived value of export support. It is surprising that questions of effectiveness of export promotion are addressed in such as general way when the financial performance of the Council and the efficiency of its programme implementation are measured in more detail (see Chapter 2). This is even more noteworthy since the issue of export promotion impact was first addressed comprehensively by a Swedish study.[26]

United Kingdom[27] With the goal of expanding exports, the British Overseas Trade Board (BOTB) is the umbrella organization which guides and supervises government export promotion. Its services are among the most comprehensive of all industrialized nations.

Programme evaluation is expected to indicate how export services can be provided more cost-effectively, how the allocation of resources to services can be improved, and how the major results of official export promotion efforts can be measured more reliably. Eight of BOTB's eighteen main services are evaluated by independent consultants using survey methods. The evaluators seek to determine the growth in export value that is linked to each of the eight services, and what share of this growth would have been foregone without BOTB's services. It is acknowledged that a significant source of error exists in such responses, and this, in turn, suggests that the results be acted on with some caution. Recent results indicate the following: (1) the ratio of total costs of export promotion relative to the total value of additional exports generated is 1:50; (2) individual programmes vary widely in their cost–benefit ratio, from 1:3 to 1:146; (3) technical help to exporters derived a cost–savings ratio of 1:7. In addition, typical survey evaluations yield a great deal of information on the behaviour and characteristics of programme users. This information tends to be valuable in assessing the impact of programmes at the firm level.

Implications for policy and programme management

The examples of programme evaluation from developing and industrialized countries considered, above – as well as others – lead to the conclusion that

1 the evaluation of programme performance is characterized by widely diverging views of need and evaluation objectives,
2 developing countries often benefit from assistance by international agencies such as the International Trade Centre,

which tend to be the driving force in evaluations of export promotion,

3 comprehensiveness and sophistication of programme evaluation is greatest in industrial countries,
4 evaluation methodology differs widely between countries and is often customized as opposed to standardized.

Programme evaluations are often carried out by outside consultants whose approaches vary depending on the scope and stated objectives of the study. In contrast, internally conducted evaluations are often covered by the rules and requirements of separate evaluation offices in government.[28] The broad approaches to evaluation include

1 generating specific cost–benefit ratios which show programme costs and benefits realized in export sales,
2 determining incremental export benefits from export promotion programmes in both quantitative and qualitative terms: this approach reflects the now widely held view that export support is complementary in impact and causality is difficult if not impossible to establish,
3 periodic assessments simultaneously of programme effectiveness relative to outcome goals and intended effects, as well as the determination of specific results and impacts at the user level.

Frequent changes in programmes – in both availability and content – prevent trends from being established. There are, however, programmes which seem to be consistently offered where regular evaluations allow base-line comparisons. A lot can be said for evaluations that use consistent impact measurement methods. This helps programmes to be viewed in the same light, rather than programme managers having to untangle the results obtained from the varying methods employed. To some extent, however, the process of tendering out evaluation studies to consultants works against consistency, as does the time that elapses between evaluations of a given programme.

Whatever the case, public policy-makers will benefit from well-conducted evaluations in two ways: first, they will have greater confidence in their funding allocation decisions, and second, they are able to justify the expansion of programmes that have the greatest impact and scaling down of those with little positive impact. In addition, the allocation of funds for new initiatives is sometimes suggested by comprehensive evaluations.

Impact from a company perspective

The impact of export promotion programmes on companies then can be considered in terms of the awareness of such programmes, usage and view of their helpfulness and criticalness.

Awareness and usage

Awareness of government export services among small and medium-sized companies (the main target group) is surprisingly low as revealed in recent research. For example, only 44 per cent of Canadian exporters were aware of the two major government export promotion programmes,[29] and among companies asked about fourteen individual services offered by the Dutch Export Promotion Service (EVD) awareness levels range from 42 to 88 per cent.[30] It seems as though company export experience influences how management reacts to exporting stimuli and indeed to externally available sources of export support. Another Canadian study reports that companies who began exporting in the last five years were significantly more aware of informational assistance services than their counterparts who have been exporting for more than five years.[31] Recent Dutch research corroborates this observation. Two-thirds of experienced exporters were aware of export support organizations while the ratio for inexperienced was nine out of ten.[32]

It is also clear that awareness does not necessarily lead to use. There must be a certain level of interest in programmes (of which the company is aware) by management.[33] From studies concerned with awareness of government export promotion programmes it is evident that companies must see such support as able to assist them with their particular export problems. This suggests that management attitude (towards government generally and government export programmes in particular) plays a role in a companies' propensity to use government programmes.

One reason why a company's perception of and attitude towards governmental export support is important is because it influences the expectation of the degree of helpfulness and thereby usage. Research on perception and attitude is not conclusive. Thus a Norwegian study shows that three-quarters of companies felt negatively about government export assistance.[34] In a US study negative image and government's perceived inability to assist exporters appears as the major reason for non-usage.[35] Yet in several other studies (e.g. UK, Australia, and West Germany)[36] results show that at least one-half of exporters interviewed regard assistance favourably. One consistent observation is made, however: the more a company knows about export support, the more helpful it perceives such programmes to be. Expressed differently, before one can given an opinion about helpfulness, one needs to know a programme (not just be aware of it).[37]

Although the evidence is far from consistent, management attitude appears to influence directly a company's usage of government services. A particular service tends to be considered in the context of company activity generally. For example, if an export support service is seen by the company as assisting in market entry then it may be considered as a positive and desirable element in the market entry decision.[38] If the company shows a favourable attitude towards such assistance, uses it, and concludes that the market entry was successful, the programme used may be perceived as having a favourable effect on the market entry (without necessarily demonstrating any direct programme impact.)[39]

Usage rates of export programmes have been observed by one study at 22 per cent or about one-half of the awareness rate for a major Canadian export promotion programme.[40] Another study analyzed nine different programmes and reports a usage rate among the exporter group of 36 per cent overall, with a range from 9 per cent (for trade information usage) to 79 per cent for use of trade commissioner services.[41] A further interesting factor should be noted: programme use was the result of an approach made by the government as often as an initiative of the company itself.[42]

Of related interest is the observation that as firms move from the pre-exporting stage to the exporting stage, and their experience and knowledge grows, their awareness and perceived usefulness of governmental export marketing assistance decrease.[43] Several possible explanations have been offered for this:

1 as companies gain competence in exporting, promotion programmes play a lesser role and perhaps are not specific enough to meet their needs,
2 companies planning to export may not have adequately developed their information needs and so their perception of support may be undifferentiated (i.e. they consider any help useful because they know little of programmes and exporting itself),
3 exporters' experience with programmes may have been marginal or unfavourable, or their own errors may be attributed to the programme.[44]

Helpfulness and criticalness

Relatively few studies have been concerned with how helpful or critical export promotion programmes are to companies' export operations. For the most part, studies falling into this area measure help or criticalness in terms of recorded opinions or qualitative responses, with more objective measurement attempts limited to a few cases. It is difficult to draw anything definite from these studies, since contrasting methods and measures are employed. A framework to show the breadth of possibilities is given in Table 6.4.

This framework shows that the four major problem spots in the interpretation of study results of the export promotion programme effects on companies stem from: (1) the way in which government assistance is measured, (2) the baseline against which results can be compared, (3) the stage of export involvement of the company, and (4) the type of variable measures used. We turn to this matter again later but now discuss some study findings on helpfulness and criticalness.

The nature and timing of export promotion programmes can play a significant role for companies who seek specific support to suit particular needs. Research shows that early in the exporting process when companies typically lack experience, their belief in the helpfulness of export support was highest.[45] The kind of help companies needed most seems to be of the experiential or learning kind.[46] This does not suggest that statistical data are not needed or useful, but intimates that meaningful interpretation of data depends on knowledge and experience. It is noteworthy that with growing export experience, companies' demand for statistical information becomes quite specific and the usefulness of general statistics decreases.[47] Clearly there are some companies who use export support as a matter of habit, despite having learnt from previous usage and acquired expertise.[48] Whether or not such regular users should be dissuaded from further use is a policy decision.

Indicators of awareness, use, or helpfulness provide some evaluative measure of government export promotion. The question, however, is whether such programmes have an impact on the exporting activity of the user and how such impact manifests itself. Very few studies consider the impact of export promotion on company performance. The incremental nature of export promotion programmes on company activity, as suggested earlier, complicates such impact measurement. In addition, measures of management opinion of export support are frequently inseparable from indicators of helpfulness. The methodological problems highlighted in the framework (Table 6.4) add to this dilemma with the result that attempts to show

Table 6.4 Framework for evaluation of government export promotion research

Methodology	
Government assistance construct	
– Global	measure combines all export marketing assistance services or programmes offered by government.
– Narrow global	measure combines similar-purpose services or programmes, for example those providing objective information for export planning and market entry etc.
– Individual	measure of individual assistance provided by a service or programme, for example the Canadian Trade Commissioner service which can assist with information, contacts, visits, etc.
– Specific	measure of specific assistance provided by a specific programme, for example a trade mission used to enter export market.
Contrast groups	
– Single group (no control or contrast group)	
– Ex-post group definition of exporters and non-exporters, assistance users and non-users	
– Ex-ante group definition of exporters and non-exporters, assistance users and non-users	
Export involvement phase (of respondent firms)	
– Pre-export	
– Preparation for export	
– Exporting	
Measurement	
Subjective measures	
– attitude, opinion, perception of assistance	
– impact or effectiveness measures	
Objective measures	
– export performance measures	
Scales	
– level	
– single or multi-item	

Source: F.H. Rolf Seringhaus, 'The impact of government export marketing assistance', *International Marketing Review*, 1986, vol. 3, no. 2, summer, p. 58, reprinted with permission.

how promotion programme expenditures generate export sales have been less than satisfactory. One part of this problem is knowing what to measure at the company level. This is the main reason why impact measurement is moving to a multiple measures approach. These include company performance indicators such as share of sales exported, and qualitative indicators, such as management's level of satisfaction with the results of programme participation. We now look at the results of research on trade missions to show both the applicability and importance of a multiple indicator approach to measuring impact on the company.

Trade mission research

Trade missions to foreign markets are prearranged and organized group visits by about one dozen companies for the purpose of exploring and developing market opportunities. In countries with government export promotion schemes, specific programmes often exist to mount trade missions to targeted market areas.

As one export marketing guide suggests,[49] trade missions can

1 help with market research,
2 create publicity for the company and international trade,
3 provide more effective contacts with business and government,
4 provide a learning experience and an opportunity to exchange views.

There is ample evidence that the personal involvement and contact with foreign markets made possible through a trade mission can be of foremost importance in developing greater competitive competence.[50] This is especially so in the early market entry stage of exporting when the need for learning and knowledge is great. Because the process that leads to export sales is often lengthy and complex, trade missions can play a facilitating role early on. Management's expectations about market entry can be favourably influenced by some of the positive characteristics of trade missions.

Results from a study comparing exporters using trade missions in an overseas market entry and those entering such markets on their own show some interesting contrasts. Companies that used missions are generally more aware of a broad range of government export promotion services and show greater willingness to use such external programmes in their international marketing efforts.[51] Not surprisingly non-users do not see trade missions as important to market entry.

Companies were seen to view trade missions as fulfilling specific objectives. Such objectives are either related to the process of market entry, such as gaining export market experience, establishing contacts for market development, evaluating what marketing effort is required, or concern performance, such as sales, agent/distributor appointment, gaining quoting/bidding opportunities. The process objectives suggest that companies use the mission as a learning experience. Interestingly, 70 per cent of trade mission users went on the mission with performance objectives, while only 30 per cent went for learning reasons. The opposite view exists among non-users, where 65 per cent see learning objectives as the most important reason for trade mission participation, while 35 per cent give performance objectives as the reason.[52] The latter suggests that non-users see performance objectives as relating to their own independent efforts (possibly supplemented by the support from a trade mission) and see missions mainly as a means to gather information and to learn about markets.

Two further indicators, namely events and results after market entry, and their attribution to the trade mission, round out our discussion of the role of missions in the company. First, eight different outcome measures were used, capturing both the nature and dynamics of results experienced by trade mission users and non-users over the year following market entry. (These outcome measures were: contact, enquiries, quotes, additional promotion, repeat visit, negotiation with agents, appoint agents, receive order.) It appears that the entire market entry process – over the period of one year beginning with a company's initial entry – is more systematic among companies using trade missions than those not using them. The obvious question is: To what extent were the results achieved by trade mission users due to the trade mission? This leads us to the second indicator. A qualitative approach to this question suggests that between 38 and 51 per cent of companies attributed the results entirely to the trade mission, while between 11 and 34 per cent said that the results would have occurred anyway.[53] Interestingly overall companies rate their market entry in which they used a trade mission as more effective compared to other market entry experiences.[54]

These results suggest that differences between companies using and not using trade missions lie in managerial characteristics such as learning and willingness to use government programmes, and the perceived importance of such programmes to exporting. While we cannot unequivocally say that trade missions caused companies' behaviour, it is apparent that some different attitudes and behaviours are associated with trade mission usage. The following implications are apparent:

1 trade missions are a more formal method of foreign market entry and hold the potential for better organized and implemented entry activity;
2 trade missions may help (through learning and experience) companies develop appropriate and competent international marketing activities.

Implications for management

Companies are concerned with performance, seeking sales and profits, whether at home or in foreign markets. If an export support programme can help in this process, then management may well use the support. It was seen earlier that awareness of programmes varies considerably. Awareness is a necessary but insufficient condition for programme use. Awareness may occur from searching for assistance, or it may result from being confronted with information, as in an unsolicited brochure from government. The former suggests a proactive and the latter a reactive motivation on part of the company. Awareness, in turn, does not mean that the company knows what a given service offers. Indeed, management must perceive a need (for information, experience, etc.) and desire a solution before a government programme merits attention.

A company's needs become more specific and custom as it gains exporting knowledge and experience. This appears to present a problem for some export promotion programmes in that companies express dissatisfaction because a service is unsuitable for their particular export situation. When companies use programmes and perceive them as helpful or useful then they are more likely to consider use of other such services as well. Some companies display the tendency of fairly regular usage of export promotion programmes.

A major issue for management, however, is how governmental export support impacts on the company. This is seldom formally evaluated. That is not to say management has no opinion or views about such programmes and their apparent effect. Researchers are concerned with the impact of export promotion at the company level and are preoccupied with such matters as deciding what to measure, how and over what relevant time period. Several studies highlighted suggest that this task is both comprehensive and complex. The idea of marginal or incremental impact, which we discussed earlier in this chapter, is relevant to the company. Amidst all the activities of the company, how can the effects of a government export promotion programme be separated from other influences? As the discussion of the trade mission example shows, comparison between programme users and non-users, combined with using several different indicators – both quantitative and qualitative – offers useful insights. Management, however, should more often offer practical feedback to agencies on how programmes appear to affect their company, how programmes can and should be tailored to fit the varying needs of companies over the exporting process, and how results (whether contacts established or customer orders received) might be attributed to specific actions of the company or programme.

Concerns about impact measurement

Main issues

As we showed in the earlier discussion, the main focus of export promotion programme evaluations is on the results these achieve. For government, or the programme agency, this helps to answer the question whether or not a given programme achieves its goals and to what extent. For companies, of interest is the degree to which potential offered by such programmes delivers actual benefits. A number of issues arise from these points. First, are companies' needs properly understood, and do programmes address such needs? Second, are companies aware that external resources to assist them are available and accessible? Third, is there a match of programme-specific support to company-specific needs? In other words, is there explicit targeting of programmes to companies?

These issues are interrelated and difficult to sort out. Whether or not companies' needs are understood by programme management, or policy-makers for that matter, is at least partially reflected by the extent to which companies use programmes and attribute results to them. Company management is pragmatic and generally not inclined to experiment unless it perceives a potential positive payback. Evidence shows that only a small proportion of companies use government export promotion programmes. As we saw in an earlier section, awareness of export support among companies is generally quite low, although levels can vary. Communication of availability and accessibility of programmes has been found lacking. While the latter does not speak to the suitability of programmes, it is an important hurdle in the way of programme usage. The international market environment as well as the companies competing in it are dynamic. Company needs change in line with markets and their own evolution through the exporting process. Low programme use points to a need for better and different programmes in addition to proven staple support such as trade missions and fairs. The onus for change and improvement, however, does not lie solely on the programme side.

Governments periodically evaluate their programmes and the impact they have on users; companies rarely formally assess the programmes' effects. Thus the performance impact of export government promotion on the company, although of considerable interest to management, is not widely studied. Researchers have recently become concerned with programme impact at the company level and most of the findings on this issue stem from the academic community. A recent comprehensive survey of such research concludes that no consistent answer can be given to the question whether export promotion programmes have any impact on firm performance. Indeed, the broadly uncertain results reported seem to be influenced, if not caused by conceptual and methodological problems as well as measurement effects.[55]

The situation with programme-specific evaluation has its problems. As a base line, programme development and management must acquire an ongoing and thorough understanding of companies' export processes. Then regular and methodologically consistent evaluation of programmes is required. Singular methodologies are insufficient and multi-measure, multi-indicator approaches are most promising towards this end.

Thus difficulty of impact measurement, whether at programme or company level, stems from poorly defined goals and objectives for programmes, the likelihood that impacts may be minor or incremental, and, as seen earlier, methodological problems.

Table 6.5 summarizes the main characteristics of impact research and suggests approaches through which impact evaluation can be improved. Many of the difficulties presently associated with export promotion programme evaluation and impact measurement can be overcome or at least improved upon. The benefits of using the approaches suggested would manifest themselves at both the public policy as well as company level, through a more accurate view of how export promotion contributes to exporting.

Integrated conceptual approach

In the earlier discussion of impact from a programme perspective, we noted ITC's evaluation approach and their attempts to disseminate 'good practice' in this area. While ITC's functions are specific to developing countries, their evaluation approach is of general applicability. ITC's basic methods include[56]

1 objectives and purpose of evaluation,
2 evaluation levels and timing,
3 measures of indicators of efficiency, effectiveness, and impact,
4 collection of information and quantification,
5 measurement and judgement,
6 cost and distortions,
7 integrating programming and evaluation.

Such an approach can be used to evaluate impact from a programme, activities, or user perspective.

We have recognized that export promotion impact is complex, multidimensional, and interactive. To render this complexity more approachable three main parameters have been suggested within

Table 6.5 Suggestions for improvement of research on impact of government export promotion

Methodology/ measurement	*Past studies*	*Recommended practice*
Government assistance construct	Global	Specific and individual
Contrast groups	None or ex-post	Quasi-experimental and ex-ante
Export involvement phases	Broad definition	Distinction of phases and companies' needs and activities
Geographic focus	Domestic companies only	Comparative, looking for similarities and differences in export assistance
Industry focus	Mainly non-stratified samples	Stratified, exploring export assistance within or across sectors
Research design	Descriptive, cross-sectional	Causal, longitudinal
Sampling techniques	Non-probability sampling	Probability sampling procedures
Data collection method	Single method with emphasis on personal interview	Combination methods including personal interviews
Impact measures	Single method, multi-item measures looking at opinion and performance	Multi-method, multi-item measures looking at opinion and performance. Recognize that management expectations and objectives condition appraisal and impact
Validity of measures	Little concern with threats to validity	Multiple measures, concurrent and discriminant validity, predictive validity in context of longitudinal research designs

Source: Adapted from R.H. Rolf Seringhaus, 'The impact of government export marketing assistance', *International Marketing Review*, 1986, vol. 3, no. 2, summer, p. 63, reprinted with permission.

which programme impact occurs and varies. First, impact may occur at the company or environment level. An industry sector may experience greater export orientation and companies realize export sales in some measure tied to programme usage. Second, impact may be intended, as in the case of contracts sought and found at a trade fair, or unintended as in devoting effort to a new market only to discover that third-country competitors have decimated the company's prospects for export sales. Third, impact can be primary, that is related directly to a company's objectives, or secondary, when participation in a trade fair leads to awareness of and ideas for product modification and innovation and hence improved market prospects in the future.[57] These are basic screening criteria to understand the complexity of impact. While an arsenal of measures and methods would be necessary for the full quantification of programme impact, it is clear that impact situations cannot be completely pre-specified and anticipated. Thus some aspects of impact may become apparent only after the fact. Whatever the nature of impact, evaluation is based on these assumptions:[58]

1 preconditions for programme delivery/use are appropriate,
2 a match of user need and programme output exists,
3 programme implementation is carried out as desired,
4 impact methodology and measures of high reliability and validity exist.

While evaluation of impact has been discussed from the two distinct perspectives, programme and user, there is a need to present an integrated view, namely that private and public sectors interact and are interrelated. A proposed model shown in Figure 6.4 underlines the integrated nature of public and private sector interest in export promotion programmes. It also shows the common area of impact measurement and its effect on decision-making in the respective sectors.

Frameworks such as the one shown in Figure 6.4 aim at creating a better understanding of the public-private sector interaction in the area of export promotion. The approach suggested should also help clarify the process of impact assessment generally. Two enduring characteristics of the context of export promotion, however, remain at the centre of the impact measurement problem. One is that company activity consists of human behaviour in a dynamic environment which rules out clinical, scientific analysis; the other that export promotion programmes probably offer only marginal and incremental benefits to the user's overall activity.[59]

Conclusions

This chapter has been concerned with the results of government export promotion programmes. Both public policy-makers and programme users are interested in the answer to a straightforward question, namely: What effects do these export support efforts have and how can they be measured? Although the question is straightforward, the answer remains elusive, for the reasons outlined.

The very concept of impact has been shown to be complex. On the one hand there are various aspects to impact; for example is it major or minor, positive or negative, immediate or lagged, intended or unintended, financial or behavioural? On the other hand, there is

Figure 6.4 Conceptual model of evaluation: integration of programme and users

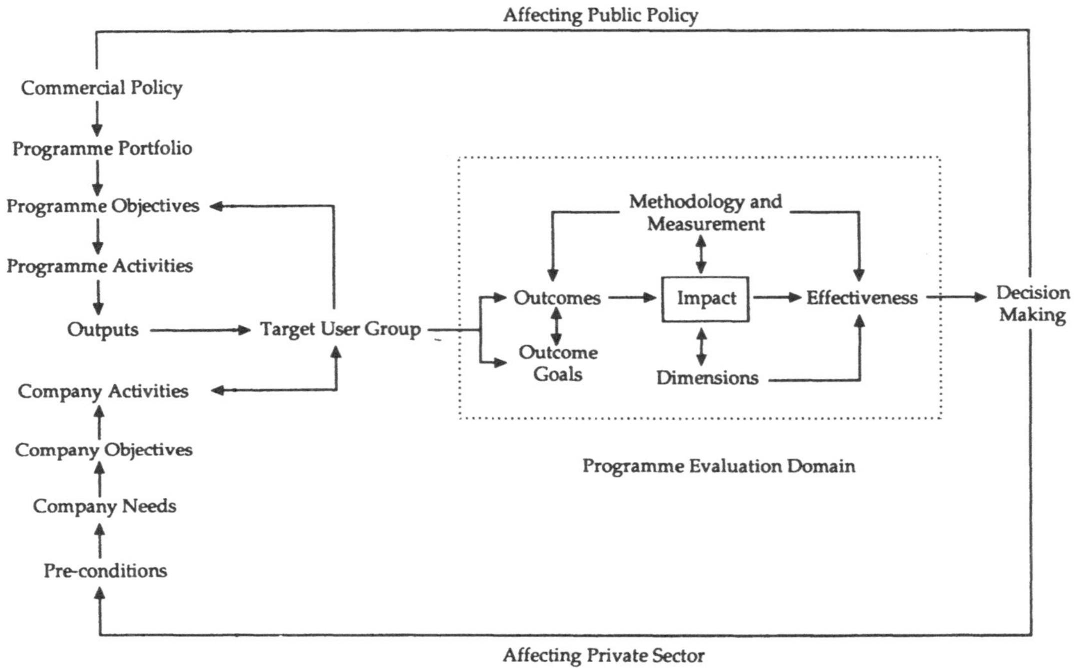

Source: F.H. Rolf Seringhaus, 'A methodological approach to the evaluation of government export promotion programs', Research Paper Series 1.88, School of Business and Economics, Wilfrid Laurier University, Ontario, 1988, p. 41.

the question of the size of the impact and the essentially incremental effect programmes can realistically exert.

Some key implications drawn from reviews of programme impact evaluations, in both developing and developed countries, show that cost–benefit ratios are used as macro indicators, incrementality of programme impact is widely accepted, and periodic evaluation against outcome goals and intended results is viewed as desirable. Furthermore, implications from research on the impact of programmes at the user level suggests that governments have not achieved adequate awareness of their programmes among companies, which has a direct influence on usage of such support. Furthermore, among companies actually using the programmes, insufficient tailoring of support to match changing company needs has taken place.

No consistent answer is possible then to the question of what impact programmes have. This is largely due to the varied approaches used by both governments and researchers in their respective attempts to evaluate export promotion programmes. Methodological and measurement problems abound and render many of the results inconclusive. Notwithstanding these difficulties, the comprehensiveness and sophistication of impact measurement is increasing. The recognition that programme development, delivery, use, and assessment are essentially integrated from a public policy and private sector perspective, is a step in the direction towards more valid and reliable approaches to measuring programme effectiveness and impact at the company level.

Notes and references

1 Treasury Board of Canada, *Guide on the Program Evaluation Function*, Minister of Supply and Services, Ottawa, May 1981, p. 4.

2 ibid., p. 6,

3 *Guide to the Evaluation of Trade Promotion Programmes*, International Trade Centre UNCTAD/GATT, Geneva, 1987, p. 1; *Enhancing the Effectiveness of Technical Assistance in Export Promotion*, Joint Advisory Group on the International Trade Centre UNCTAD/GATT, Eighth Session, Geneva, 6–17 January 1975, p. 2.

4 *Guide to the Evaluation*, p. 4.

5 ibid., F.H. Rolf Seringhaus 'A methodological approach to the evaluation of government export promotion programs', Research Paper Series no. 1.88, School of Business and Economics, Wilfrid Laurier University, Ontario, 1988.

6 H.C. Olson, *Studies in Export Promotion*, Acta Universitatis Upsaliensis, Studia Oeconomiae Negotiorum 10, Stockholm, Alqvist & Wiksell International, 1975, p. 30.

7 Olson, *Studies in Export Promotion*, p. 31.

8 F.H. Rolf Seringhaus 'The impact of government export marketing

assistance', *International Marketing Review*, vol. 3, no. 2, summer, 1986, p. 61.
9 F.H. Rolf Seringhaus, 'Government export marketing assistance to small and medium-sized manufacturing firms: the role and impact of trade missions on firms' off-shore market involvement', unpublished Ph.D. dissertation, York University, Toronto, 1984.
10 Seringhaus, 'A methodological approach', pp. 14–15.
11 ibid., p. 6.
12 ibid., p. 23. F.H. Rolf Seringhaus, 'The use of trade missions in foreign market entry of industrial firms', *Industrial Marketing and Purchasing*, 1987, vol. 2, no. 1, pp. 49, 51–53.
13 Seringhaus, 'A methodological approach', pp. 21–4.
14 *Guide to the Evaluation*, p. 2.
15 *ITC Manual on Programming, Project Design, Monitoring and Evaluation*, International Trade Centre UNCTAD/GATT, Geneva, August 1987, pp. 30–1.
16 ibid., pp. 33–4.
17 ibid., p. 38.
18 ibid., p. 37.
19 *Enhancing the Effectiveness*, p. 1.
20 *Annual Report on the Activities of the International Trade Centre UNCTAD/GATT 1987*, Joint Advisory Group, Twenty-first Session, International Trade Centre UNCTAD/GATT, Geneva, 25 January 1988, p. 23.
21 ibid., p. 24.
22 ibid., p. 24.
23 *Some General Conclusions from ITC Evaluations Carried Out in 1986*, International Trade Centre UNCTAD/GATT, Geneva, 23 September 1987, p. 1.
24 *Guide to the Evaluation*, pp. 12–19.
25 ibid., pp. 22–7.
26 Olson, *Studies in Export Promotion*.
27 *Guide to the Evaluation*, pp. 27–30.
28 Treasury Board of Canada, *Guide to the Program Evaluation*, p. 6.
29 S.D. Reid, 'Information acquisition and export entry decisions in small firms', *Journal of Business Research*, 1984, vol. 12, no. 2, pp. 141-57.
30 'Greater export opportunities for small and medium-size firms', Amsterdam-Rotterdam Bank Report, January 1983; 'Export: research and policy', Conference Report, EVD Netherlands Export Promotion & Information Service, The Hague, 1986.
31 Rolf Seringhaus, 'The role of information assistance in small firms' export involvement', *International Small Business Journal*, 1986/7, vol. 5, no. 2, winter, p. 31.
32 'Greater export opportunities'.
33 P.D. Grub, 'An export decision pattern: a management guide to successful export entry and expansion', in P.D. Grub and M. Kaskimies (eds), *International Marketing in Perspective*, Helsinki, Sininin Kirjia Oy, 1971, p. 166.

34 K. Gronhaug and T. Lorentzen, 'Exploring the impact of government export subsidies', *European Journal of Marketing*, 1983, vol. 17, no. 2, pp. 5–12.
35 C.L. Simpson, D.A. Roy, and D.L. Loudon, 'Use and perception of external support facilities in the initial export activity among smaller manufacturing firms in the southeastern United States', presented at the annual meeting of the Academy of International Business, Montreal, October 1981, pp. 15–17.
36 T. Pointon, 'Measuring the gains from government export promotion', *European Journal of Marketing*, 1978, vol. 12, no. 6, pp. 451–62; L.S. Welch and F. Wiedersheim-Paul, 'Export promotion policy – a new approach', *Australian Journal of Management*, 1979, vol. 4, October, pp. 165–77; U. Schwarting, C. Thoben, and M. Wittstock, *Nachfrageverhalten Kleiner und Mittlerer Unternehmen nach Aussenhandelsinformationen und Beratung*, Göttingen, Beitraege zur Mittelstandsforschung, Verlag Otto Schwartz & Co., 1982, Heft 83.
37 T.D.C. Cullwick and J.P. Mellallieu, 'Business attitudes to government export services and export marketing behaviour', *New Zealand Journal of Business*, 1981, vol. 3, pp. 33–54.
38 Reid, 'Information acquisition', p. 153.
39 F.H. Rolf Seringhaus, 'Market entry and the impact of export marketing assistance: a conceptual approach to causal modelling', *Finnish Journal of Business Economics*, 1986, vol. 35, no. 4, p. 280.
40 Reid, 'Information acquisition', p. 150.
41 F.H. Rolf Seringhaus, 'Empirical investigation of awareness, use and impact of export marketing support by government in manufacturing firms', in K. Moeller and M. Paltschik (eds), *Contemporary Research in Marketing*, vol. 1, Helsinki, European Marketing Academy, 1986, p. 259.
42 ibid., p. 260.
43 Seringhaus, 'The role of information', p. 33.
44 F.H. Rolf Seringhaus, 'Export promotion: the role and impact of government services', *Irish Marketing Review*, 1987, vol. 2, spring, pp. 110–11.
45 M.R. Czinkota, *Export Development Strategies*, New York, Praeger, 1982, p. 104.
46 Reid, 'Information acquisition', p. 151; P.G.P. Walters, 'Export information sources – a study of their usage and utility', *International Marketing Review*, 1983, vol. 1, winter, pp. 41–2.
47 Walters, 'Export information sources', p. 41, Seringhaus, 'The role of information', pp. 33–4.
48 C.S. Mayer and J.E. Flynn, 'Canadian small business abroad: opportunities, aids and experiences', *Business Quarterly*, 1973, vol. 38, winter, pp. 33–47; Seringhaus, 'Government export marketing assistance', p. 260.
49 E.P. Hibbert, *The Principles and Practice of Export Marketing*, London, William Heineman, 1985, p. 141.
50 Reid, 'Information acquisition', p. 151; S.T. Cavusgil and E. Kaynak,

'Success factors in export marketing: an empirical analysis', in B. Walker *et al.* (eds), *Assessment of Marketing Thought and Practice*, Educators' Conference Proceedings, American Marketing Association, Chicago, Ill., 1982, pp. 309–12; J.E. Denis and D. Depelteau, 'Market knowledge, diversification and export expansion', *Journal of International Business Studies*, 1985, vol. XVI, no. 3, pp. 86–7.

51 F.H. Rolf Seringhaus 'Using trade missions for export market entry', *Industrial Marketing Management*, 1987, vol. 16, no. 4, p. 252.

52 Seringhaus. 'The use of trade missions', pp. 49, 52, see note 14.

53 ibid., p. 56.

54 ibid., p. 52.

55 Seringhaus, 'The impact of government', pp. 62, 64.

56 *Guide to the Evaluation*, pp. 45–51.

57 Seringhaus, 'A methodological approach', p. 27.

58 ibid., p. 25.

59 ibid., p. 29.

Chapter seven

The impact of government export promotion programmes: a case study

Introduction

The threads of the arguments developed in the previous two chapters are drawn together here. In Chapter 6 a review of past attempts to measure the impact of government export promotion support programmes revealed no clear or consistent pattern of results. Yet large amounts of money are spent on such programmes and many companies clamour for assistance. This suggests that the programmes are believed to support exporters and, hence, boost their export earnings. A large part of the reason for the equivocal findings on export programme impacts is related to the evaluation procedures followed. In Chapter 6 we characterized previous studies as having a number of conceptual, methodological, and measurement problems. We went on to indicate how future evaluation research might be conducted so as to produce more accurate results. In the first part of this chapter we describe an evaluation study that largely employed these principles. Having highlighted the approach taken, in the second part we present the unequivocal findings resulting from the evaluation. This discussion shows that export promotion programme impacts can be determined. In a sense then, the early part of the chapter provides some 'how to do it' guidelines that others may find useful.

The same study also allows us to return to the argument developed in Chapter 5, namely the need for care in the targeting of companies that are to receive government export support. In other words, support programmes are likely to be more effective when they are designed and delivered to meet specific needs. These needs were held to be different for the five types of companies these programmes serve – 'non-exporters', 'first-time exporters', 'failed exporters', 'expanding exporters', and 'continuing exporters'. This idea is examined further in the third part of the chapter, and a determination made of the extent to which the appropriate targeting of companies discussed in Chapter 5 in fact takes place. By looking at the matching of companies to programmes, we reveal something about present practices. As well, since some unexpected results emerge, we are forced to reassess earlier arguments. Taken together, this gives us some idea of the room that exists for improvements in targeting programmes, and how this might best be done.

The study

Overview

Canadian federal government programmes are evaluated on a regular basis and the study in question was undertaken in 1987 to meet this requirement.[1] The programme evaluated was the Promotional Projects Program (PPP), which is briefly described in Table 7.1.[2] This highlights the way in which this programme is administered as well as its objectives. PPP is seen to span the full range of company export development, from developing an export consciousness among non-exporting companies to assisting companies already established overseas to maintain or enhance a position. The PPP activities considered here are trade fairs and outgoing trade missions,[3] namely those discussed in the final section of Chapter 5.

Of particular relevance to the present discussion were the following issues addressed in the study:

1 *Programme impact* What impact does trade fair and trade mission participation have on the export performance of individual companies and Canada as a whole?
2 *Programme targeting* What part does the programme play in companies' export plans and operations? Is assistance provided by the programme directed so as to best meet companies' needs?

Methods

The study was conducted in three major stages: (1) an exploratory research phase resulting in a planning report; (2) a mail survey of recent participants of trade fairs and missions; and (3) analysis of the survey data, culminating in a final report. The most important components of the evaluation, particularly as they describe the survey methodology, are detailed below.

Sampling

The target population for the study consisted of companies which

Table 7.1 The Promotional Projects Program

The federal government recognizes that there is a need for federal assistance in the exploitation of foreign markets by Canadian firms. The Promotional Projects Program is the funding vehicle through which the government underwrites some of the cost to industry of participating in promotional events that are organized by the Department of External Affairs. These events are designed to increase the knowledge of foreign buyers about Canadian products and capability and to undertake export market intelligence-gathering operations.

The program encompasses a wide variety of trade promotional techniques within three general categories: trade fairs abroad, trade missions and trade visitors. These projects are initiated by the government and reflect those events developed in consultations between the Departments of External Affairs and Regional Industrial Expansion.

The responsibility for selecting and planning specific projects, consultation with the Posts, Sector Branches, and Regional Offices of DRIE, as well as operational implementation is delegated to the Trade Development Division in the five Geographic Branches of External Affairs.

The objectives of the Promotional Projects Program are:

(a) to increase private sector effort on export marketing;
(b) to increase private sector consciousness of export market opportunities;
(c) to encourage additional firms to become (new) exporters;
(d) to encourage existing exporters to move into new markets (geographical and product); and
(e) to facilitate the establishment and development of international business contacts.

The intended effects are to maintain/increase Canadian export sales. These effects may be *immediate* (i.e. during the event), in the *near term* (i.e. during the following 12 months), in the *medium term* (i.e. in 12–36 months), or in the *long term*.

Source: From the Evaluation Terms of Reference, Department of External Affairs, Ottawa, 1986.

participated, with the Department of External Affairs' support, in trade fairs and missions in the period fiscal year 1984/5 to the first half of 1986/7. Sampling of this population was in two stages, first of the trade fairs and missions (or events), and then of participants within events. This meant that a detailed analysis of factors contributing to the success of events and companies was made possible.

The sampling of events was stratified by type of event (trade fairs, outgoing missions and incoming missions); geographic area (five categories); and industrial sector (eight categories). Some forty-nine trade fairs, eighteen outgoing, and eleven incoming trade missions were sampled. A random selection process within each sampled event led to a sample of 570 companies being drawn. On average, about nine companies per trade fair and five per mission were sampled. A response rate of 90 per cent was achieved, allowing for an overall accuracy of estimates to within ± 5 per cent for most variables examined.

Survey procedures

The draft questionnaire was developed after a review of the literature, consultation with Department of External Affairs (DEA) trade officers, and discussions with export companies and trade fair organizers. This was pre-tested with a sample of twenty-five companies, with return of the questionnaires by special delivery mail and telephone follow-up. The pre-test led to a number of changes in the final questionnaire.

The survey process ensured that the correct respondent for the survey was identified prior to the first mailing of the questionnaire. Verification of the correct respondent, full mailing address and telephone number, as well as the language of preference (English or French) for the questionnaire, was achieved through a telephone screening survey. Companies were not surveyed unless an appropriate respondent could be found, that is someone who could accurately report on the event in question.[4] The survey process included three mailings, including a postcard reminder, as well as a telephone reminder where necessary.

Respondents were guaranteed full confidentiality in both the covering letter and introduction to the questionnaire. Respondents were informed that, first, no one except the consultants would ever see the specific answers from any respondent, including DEA staff, who would be provided only with statistical summaries; and second, all questionnaires would be destroyed after the data had been entered into the computer. A supplementary survey of thirty companies was conducted after the survey proper, to test the reliability of survey results, especially for certain questions requiring judgmental (as opposed to categorical) responses. The test-retest reliabilities of these data were within acceptable bounds (75 per cent or greater) for surveys of this type.

The study and 'good practice'

In Chapter 6 we commented on past practices in evaluated government export promotion programmes, and made recommendations for the future. Here we show how the present study 'scores' on the various methodology and measurement criteria. To a large extent we regard the study as following these recommendations. Each of the criteria is discussed in the order of appearance in Table 7.2.

The recommendation regarding the government assistance construct was met, in that the study delved beyond global impressions.

Table 7.2 The present and past studies and good practice

Methodology/ measurement	*Past studies*	*Recommended practice*	*Does study meet recommendation?*
Government assistance construct	Global	Specific and individual	Yes
Contrast groups	None or ex-post	Quasi-experimental and ex-ante	No
Export involvement phases	Broad definition	Distinction of phases and companies' needs and activities	Yes
Geographic focus	Domestic companies only	Comparative, looking for similarities and differences in export assistance	No. Good idea but government unlikely to feature
Industry focus	Mainly non-stratified samples	Stratified, exploring export assistance within or across sectors	Yes
Research design	Descriptive, cross-sectional	Causal, longitudinal	No
Sampling techniques	Non-probability sampling	Probability sampling	Yes
Data collection method	Single method with emphasis on personal interview	Combination methods including personal interviews	No
Impact measures	Single method, multi-item measures looking at opinion and performance	Multi-method, multi-item measures looking at opinion, behaviour, and performance. Recognize that management expectations and objectives condition appraisal of impact	Largely
Validity of measures	Little concern with threats to validity	Multiple measures, concurrent and discriminant validity, predictive validity in context of longitudinal research designs	Some

Source: See Table 6.5

PPP was evaluated from the standpoint of its three constituent promotional events – trade fairs, outgoing and incoming trade missions. This survey was concerned only with past participants, and so is unable to speak from a non-participant perspective. Like other studies then, this one does not meet the criterion of using a contrast group approach. Consequently the views of two categories of company are excluded: (1) those that are unaware of the programme, and (2) those that may find the present programme unsuited to their needs. The study satisfies the next criterion. An appreciation of companies' differing export needs (related to their stage of development) is built into the survey. This will become apparent in the later discussion.

The recommendation that comparative evaluations of government export promotion be conducted is a laudable one. However, governments are unlikely to engage in such studies, for their interests are with their own rather than some other programme. Academics (singly or groups from different countries) and organizations whose interests extend beyond national boundaries (ITC, for example), will have less instrumental reasons for conducting only single-country studies, and will thus be more prone to carry out comparative evaluations. In light of these comments, the fact that this government study restricted itself to Canada should come as no surprise. Although not meeting the comparative nation criterion, the study did meet the recommendation regarding industrial sectors. As described above, industrial sector (eight categories) was one of the sample stratification factors employed.

The next criteria are research design, sampling techniques, and data collection method. Of these, the present study met only the sampling criterion, companies being drawn from the universe of participants on a probability basis. What of the research design criterion? Again, while meritorious, few evaluations will (ever) be designed to demonstrate that export promotion programmes categorically produce export sales or other impacts, that is causality. Longitudinal methods are perhaps more likely to be seen in the future, for so long as companies can be tracked, are accessible, and willing to provide appropriate data at various points in time, the technique is not a difficult one. The study described here was of the traditional cross-sectional kind, presenting a record of usage, views, and results in the mid-1980s. Data were collected though one method, namely a mail questionnaire. Again then, the study does not satisfy the criterion that combination methods be used.

Finally, we come to two criteria related to the measures employed. Generally the study design meets these criteria quite well. Impact was assessed through a number of methods, including the use of opinion, behaviour, and performance measures, often with more than one item for each measure. As to the validity of the measures, several of the indicators used show good face validity, that is similar ones have been used in previous studies with reasonable results. The technique of using several different variables seeking to assess a single behavioural dimension appears to have contributed to generally more acceptable and therefore better results in this study. The validity of measures of opinion or behaviour will always remain imperfect and the present study is no exception.

Having argued that the study was reasonably well conceived, designed, and implemented, we now turn to the results that were generated. We describe these in two parts, first looking at the measured impact of PPP trade fairs and outgoing trade missions, and second, examining the extent to which targeting of these programme events matches the expectations developed in Chapter 5.

Measuring impact

Impact at the company level

Four categories of company trade fairs and mission impact were envisaged: (1) the extent to which fair or mission objectives are met; (2) the number of agents, representatives, or distributors appointed; (3) the sales resulting from the fair or mission; and (4) the follow-up activities that have taken place. Sales are clearly the ultimate goal of a promotional activity, but the above categories recognize that there are intermediate steps along the way. These steps may involve satisfying non-sales objectives (making business contacts, for example), appointing foreign agents, representatives, or distributors, and making marketing changes as a result of the fair or mission. The detailed results are shown in Table 7.3 and are listed separately for trade fairs and outgoing trade missions.

Trade missions are seen in this case to be rather better than fairs at fulfilling companies' objectives. Of the ten objectives examined in the study (and listed at the bottom of Table 7.3), those most often achieved on trade missions were: introducing a new product to the market (74 per cent); maintaining presence in the market (51 per cent); meeting regular customers and agents/representatives/distributors (40 per cent); and making business contacts (39 per cent). All but the last of these are surprising since they would normally be expected to be dealt with through trade fairs rather than missions. We return to this later. As far as trade fairs are concerned, the objectives most often satisfied were: meeting regular customers and agents/representatives/distributors (47 per cent); maintaining

Table 7.3 Impact of programme participation on company

Impact measure	*Trade fair participants (n=342)*	*Trade mission participants (n=82)*
1 *Meeting objectives*		
Percent rating results of fair or mission as excellent compared with objectives[a]	6–47%	18–51%
2 *Number of agents/representatives/distributors appointed*	1.3	0.5
3 *Sales impact*		
– Total sales related[b] to fair/mission	$279,000	$756,000
– companies with sales greater than $1 million	4%	11%
– companies with no sales	51%	69%
– companies with sales greater than own costs	41%	20%
– companies *directly* attributing[c] sales to fair/mission	70%	55%
– attributed sales[d] net of companies' own costs	$96,000	$195,000
– ratio of attributed sales net of companies' own costs, to those costs	10.3	22.2
4 *Follow-up activities*		
– companies that have increased effort in market	34%	34%
– companies that have made changes in marketing[e] as a *direct* result of fair/mission	2–25%	2–32%
– companies that have made no positive follow-up	9%	14%

Source: 'The fairs and missions (promotional projects) program: Survey of past participants', Report by SPR Associates Incorporated/National Mail Surveys for the Department of External Affairs, Ottawa, 5 October 1987.

Notes:
[a] Objectives were: testing market for demand, acceptance, and competitiveness; identifying or appointing agents/representatives/distributors; obtaining quote or bid opportunities; making immediate sales to final users; making immediate sales to dealers; securing licensing/joint venture arrangement; making business contacts; maintaining presence in market; meeting regular customers and agents/representatives/distributors; introducing a new product to the market; other.
[b] Sales that followed participation in the trade fair or mission.
[c] Sales that would not have been achieved without participation in the trade fair or mission.
[d] Related sales weighted by attribution factor, using company *not* average values.
[e] Marketing changes were: modified product to better suit market; introduced new products to market; gone to additional trade fairs; gone on more trade missions; made additional business trips to market; established offices in market; purchased marketing studies; increased promotion/advertising; made organizational changes in firm to better focus efforts on this market; reduced level of effort in this market; withdrawn from this market; started to explore other markets.

presence in market (46 per cent); introducing a new product to the market (38 per cent); and making business contacts (37 per cent). These objectives are more in keeping with those expected of fairs. Trade fairs appear to be more effective events for the identification and recruitment of foreign selling partners, with companies on average appointing 1.3 agents, representatives, or distributors per fair as opposed to 0.5 per mission.

Turning to related sales, trade mission participants generate 2.7 times the sales of fair participants – on average $756,000 versus $279,000.[5] However, the picture is not so clear-cut as these aggregate figures suggest. The sales impact for trade missions is much more variable than trade fairs. Table 7.3 shows that more than one in ten trade mission participants achieve sales of greater than $1 million, but seven in ten achieve no sales, and eight in ten are unable to recover their mission costs. While producing less spectacular sales, about one-half of all trade fair participants achieve some sales, with four in ten more than offsetting their costs.

Trade fairs are also seen to be more instrumental in achieving sales than missions. On average, 70 per cent of trade fair sales were attributed directly to company participation, whereas the equivalent for missions was 55 per cent. This raises some questions about the membership of the trade missions in question, especially when the previously mentioned variability of sales is also considered. Despite this, the sales that companies attributed to trade missions ($195,000 on average) are still twice those for fairs ($96,000). Another measure of impact for companies is the return on their financial investment. With similar costs of participation for fairs and missions (about $9,000), missions again outperform fairs, attributable sales being twenty-two times the costs for mission versus ten for fairs.

A final impact measurement is couched in terms of follow-up activities. Given that companies stand to learn much from involvement in trade fairs and missions, the actions they have taken as a result of participation are useful pointers to the future. Here fair and mission impacts are more similar. One-third of companies surveyed reported increasing their effort in the market that was the focus of the fair or mission. Some marketing approaches were changed as a direct result of the promotional event. Of the twelve changes considered (see bottom of Table 7.3), trade fair participants most often reported: made additional business trips to market (25 per cent); modified products to better suit market (19 per cent); and introduced new products to market (19 per cent). For mission participants, the most frequent changes were: made additional business trips to the market (32 per cent), and started to explore other markets (19 per cent). Finally, some companies indicated that they had taken no positive actions in following up their trade fair (9 per cent) or mission (14 per cent) participation.

The above results show that the overall impact of trade fairs and missions is positive. Whether measured in immediate (sales) or future terms (marketing change), the impacts are highly acceptable. However, the impacts do vary and, although this is to be expected, the magnitude of variation may warrant further consideration.

Impact at the programme level

In light of the very positive impact of trade fair and mission participation for companies, similar results at the programme level should not be surprising. Table 7.4 shows three impact measures and programme performance under each. Although we saw in the previous section that trade missions generally outperform fairs in terms of average export sales, we see here that the greater number of companies participating in fairs means that overall sales within the programme are higher for fairs ($937 million) than missions ($734 million). This is accentuated further when, rather than simply including all sales that followed the trade fair or mission, we consider sales directly attributable to the event. Because trade fair sales resulted more directly from participation it is estimated that the total sales attributed to the programme were $350 million for fairs and $197 million for missions. Whichever of these sales measures is used, these are sizeable export earnings and reinforce the merit of government support programmes for exporters. This is further indicated by a crude cost–benefit measure. With approximate average programme costs of $9,000 per company/event, the return on each dollar of government spending is twenty-eight times for trade fairs and eighty-four times for missions. Clearly these programme-specific measures of impact are all highly satisfactory.

Summary

Many studies of government export promotion have yielded equivocal results. This is not the case for the present Canadian example. Very positive impact levels are evident for both participating companies and the economy as a whole. The return on investment – whether viewed from a company or programme cost standpoint – was seen to be at highly acceptable levels. This is not to suggest that there is no room for improvement. Indeed, although both trade fair and mission events produce good results, some of the results suggest that fine-tuning of the programme might be in order. For example, the percentages of companies that achieve no sales as a result of participation may point to closer screening of participants and/or better event/company matching. These and other points are pursued in the next section.

Programme targeting

In this section, the idea of matching export promotion programmes to companies is explored further, again in the context of the

Table 7.4 Impact at programme level

Impact measure	*Trade fairs*	*Trade missions*
1 Sales related to fairs/missions[a]	$937 million	$734 million
2 Sales attributed to fairs/missions[b]	$350 million	$197 million
3 Ratio of related sales to government programme costs[c]	28	84

Source: 'The fairs and missions (promotional projects) program: Survey of past participants', Report of SPR Associates Incorporated/National Mail Surveys for the Department of External Affairs, Ottawa, 5 October 1987.

Notes:
[a] Average company sales that followed the trade fair or mission in survey, multiplied by total number of companies participating in these events.
[b] Average company sales *directly* resulting from the trade fair or mission in survey, multiplied by number of companies participating in these events.
[c] Average company sales that followed the trade fair or mission, divided by government programme costs.

evaluation study described above. While five types of company targets for export promotion programmes were identified in Chapter 5, only three can be examined here. The two missing company types are 'non-exporters' and 'failed exporters', and this situation is explained as follows. Since the evaluation was to be conducted among users of the programme, non-exporters – those with no active interest in foreign markets – were not its focus. Regarding failed exporters, the evaluation was designed before this type of company had occurred to us. Such exporters, however, appear worthy of separate consideration. Consequently we are left with 'first-time exporters', 'expanding exporters', and 'continuing exporters' as the company types or targets that can be examined.

These company types were not identified directly during the study but rather through responses to two questionnaire items. These items, the qualifying responses, and the number of companies falling into each category are shown in Table 7.5. Thus the analysis which follows is based on 38 first-time exporters, 80 expanding exporters, and 129 continuing exporters. The balance of the sample is not part of this analysis since the company responses either did not meet the qualifying criteria set for a category, or were missing. Of immediate interest is the number of companies qualifying under each company type, with expanding exporters twice as numerous, and continuing exporters more than three times as numerous as first-time exporters. These data suggest that the trade fairs and missions under review are targeted more to established as opposed to new exporters, which seems contrary to the avowed policy of the export promotion

Table 7.5 Defining the three types of companies

Company type	*Length of time exporting to the market, prior to trade fair or mission*[a]	*Extent to which trade fair or mission provided a first learning opportunity about exporting*[b]
First-time exporter (n=38)	Not at all	To a great extent
Expanding exporter (n=80)	Not at all	Not at all
Continuing exporter (n=129)	More than 3 years	Not at all

Source: Prepared by the authors.

Notes:
[a] Six-point scale, ranging from (1) Not at all, to (6) More than 5 years.
[b] Three-point scale, ranging from (1) Not at all, to (3) To a great extent.

Table 7.6 Profiles of target companies

Characteristic	*First-time exporter (n=38)*	*Expanding exporter (n=80)*	*Continuing exporter (n=129)*
1 *Company type*			
- manufacturer	84%	84%	84%
- trading company/distributor	11%	11%	13%
- provider of services	13%	18%	15%
2 *Date of:*			
- establishment (average)	1972	1961	1951
- starting to export (aerage)	n.a.	1970	1965
3 *Current total annual sales*			
- less than $2 million	46%	23%	12%
- $2–50 million	51%	50%	66%
- more than $50 million	3%	27%	23%
4 *Current export experience*			
- number of senior managers with export experience	2	6	6
- number of countries exported to	4	16	17
5 *Current export/total sales ratio*	23%	40%	46%

Source: Prepared by the authors.

programme in question. This and other issues are taken up again in the discussion which follows.

Target companies and their profiles

Given the sample breakout, what are the characteristics of companies that make up the three types? Table 7.6 shows that quite sharp differences exist. Continuing exporters are longer established and more seasoned at exporting than expanding exporters, who are themselves older than first-time exporters. The dates referred to suggest that the average company enters export markets after a lag of ten to fifteen years during which, presumably, it has developed a secure position at home. The total annual sales data show that over time, as might be expected, the older, continuing exporters have built somewhat larger operations than expanding exporters, and substantially larger operations than first-time exporters.

It is clear that the amount of export experience should vary across the three types of companies and Table 7.6 shows this to be the case. There is almost no difference between expanding and continuing exporters' export experience (six experienced senior managers and sixteen or seventeen foreign markets served), but the contrast with first-time exporters (two experienced senior managers and four foreign markets currently served) is marked. Experience is also indicated by the *current* export-to-total-sales ratio for the three company types. Again, the obvious contrast is between first-time exporters and the other two categories, the latter doing twice the exporting in percentage terms, and when the sales base is considered, many times more volume than the former. The only area of similarity between the three company types lies in the nature of their business activities – 84 per cent of companies are manufacturers irrespective of the category considered, the balance accounted for almost evenly by trading companies and distributors, and service providers.

These data reveal important contrasts in the profiles of the three company types considered. Most dramatic is the more recent establishment, smaller size, and slimmer export experience of first-time exporters compared to the other two target groups for export promotion programmes. Expanding exporters also differ from their continuing counterparts, being more newly established, and somewhat smaller and less experienced. Although important, the contrasts here, however, are less pronounced. The clear implication to be drawn from the profiles is that first-time exporters have a greater need for the support offered through export promotion programmes. Since they are entering new markets, expanding exporters also benefit from support although, perhaps, in a less fundamental sense. Given their characteristics, continuing exporters are a surprisingly large element in the sample. In many respects, it might be felt that these companies have gone beyond the stage where they need the support government export promotion programmes provide.

Targeting of trade fairs and missions

In light of the fairly sharp differences that exist between the three types of company that export promotion programmes are targeted to, next we look at whether the profile of companies participating in trade fairs and missions also vary in a substantive way. In this analysis, the entire sample is considered (n=462).

Both differences and similarities are found when trade fair and mission participants are compared. Table 7.7 shows that manufacturers again make up the majority of participating companies, whether at fairs or on missions. For trading companies and distributors, and service companies, however, a different story is seen; trading companies and distributors are about twice as likely to attend a fair as go on a mission, while for service providers the exact reverse is true. An explanation for this situation could be that first, trading companies and distributors that export will tend to be dealing in relatively mature product fields where securing sales is the key objective, and second, because the nature of their offering is often intangible, service providers will be drawn less to fairs (where display and demonstration of the offering is important) than to missions. Turning to company size, trade fair participants are seen to be smaller on average than mission participants. The explanation for this will become apparent below.

Having looked at two general profiling factors, we now turn to factors more specific to export promotion support. The first of these concerns the pre-fair or mission activity in the relevant market. For both fair and mission participants, the most frequent response was that the level of marketing effort in the prior year was moderate. Only one point on the scale used reflected a greater level of activity ('major'), and so the similar responses are somewhat surprising in light of the earlier argument that missions are best used earlier in the export process (when no or minimal effort has been made). Although levels of marketing effort are most often similar for fairs and missions, participants at the former had double the prior-year sales in the market than companies going on missions ($40,000 versus $19,000 respectively). Clearly, given similar levels of effort, fair participants have been more successful in generating sales. Whether this results from a greater competence, or longer/more intense

Table 7.7 Targeting trade fairs and missions

Characteristic	*Trade fair participants (n=367)*	*Trade mission participants (n=95)*
1 *Company type*		
– manufacturer	85%	81%
– trading company/distributor	13%	7%
– provider of services	13%	24%
2 *Current total annual sales*		
– less than $2 million	32%	14%
– $2–50 million	54%	62%
– more than $50 million	14%	24%
3 *Activity in market year prior to trade fair or mission*		
– level of marketing effort[a] (modal response)	moderate	moderate
– annual sales (average)	$40,000	$19,000
4 *Objectives for trade fair or mission*		
– testing market for demand, acceptance and competitiveness	72%	72%
– identifying or appointing agents/representatives/ distributors	51%	40%
– obtaining quote or bid opportunities	31%	35%
– making immediate sales to final users	25%	20%
– making immediate sales to dealers	27%	17%
– securing licensing/joint venture arrangement	14%	20%
– making business contacts	79%	89%
– maintaining presence in market	52%	50%
– meeting regular customers and agents/ representatives/distributors	45%	39%
– introducing a new product to the market	45%	25%
5 *Role played by government*		
– most beneficial aspect of participation[b] (modal response)	subsidization	subsidization
– companies that would have participated in trade fairs without government support	15%	—
– companies that would have explored market without support of a government trade mission	—	30%
6 *Exporter type*		
– first-time exporter	20%	8%
– expanding exporter	23%	37%
– continuing exporter	57%	56%

Source: Prepared by the authors.

Notes:

[a] The range of responses available here was: no effort; minor effort; moderate effort; major effort; in business less than 12 months at time of trade fair or mission; don't know.

[b] Respondents were asked to check one of the following items: (1) motivation to exploit export markets; (2) the subsidization of our export marketing costs; (3) the consultant services provided by government trade officers; (4) the administrative services provided by government officers; (5) the prestige associated with a Canadian government trade show or mission; (6) obtaining a better booth location and publicity than we could get if we were on our own (for fairs only); (7) introductions to higher level business contacts than we could make on our own (for missions only); (8) other.

activity in the market is not clear. What is surprising, however, is that mission participants show the level of effort and prior-mission export sales in the market they do.

A similar percentage of participants at trade fairs or on a mission reported that their objectives included

1 testing the market for demand, acceptance, and competitiveness,
2 obtaining bid or quote opportunities,
3 making immediate sales to final users,
4 maintaining presence in market,
5 meeting regular customers and agents/representatives/distributors.

Some of these similar results were unexpected but, in the light of the profiling discussion above, are not surprising. Specifically, objective 1 would normally be associated with mission participation, while objectives 3–5 are most often thought of in the context of fairs. Objectives where larger differences emerged for fair and mission participants were

1 identifying or appointing agents/representatives/distributors,
2 making immediate sales to dealers,
3 securing licensing/joint venture arrangement,
4 making business contacts,
5 introducing a new product to the market.

In each case, the differences were in the direction anticipated; however, their magnitude is smaller than might have been expected. We comment more fully on this later.

Next we consider the role government export promotion programmes play for companies. The most frequently reported benefit of the government programme evaluated, whether in the form of a trade fair or mission, is the subsidization of companies' export marketing costs. But while subsidization is important for both, the criticality of this support varies. Only 15 per cent of trade fair participants indicated that they would have exhibited without government support, whereas 30 per cent of mission participants stated that they would have investigated the market anyway. These percentages are the opposite of those expected from previous reasoning. In other words, if trade missions are appropriate at earlier stages of company export activity than trade fairs, we might anticipate government support to be more critical to these companies. Thus we might expect a smaller (not larger) percentage of trade mission than fair participants to have been active without government support.

A possible answer to some of these paradoxical results emerges when we consider the breakdown of trade fair and mission participants by exporter type. As was the case in Table 7.5, relatively light overall participation by first-time exporters and heavy participation by continuing exporters is shown in Table 7.7. Our earlier comment about providing support to those most in need is again relevant. As well as these general levels of programme participation, the take-up of fair and mission places by these two exporter types shows unexpected results. For example, first-timers make up 20 per cent of all fair participants and only 8 per cent of mission participants. Exhibiting in a trade fair is more appropriate when the decision has been made to enter a given foreign market, capacity is available to meet customer orders, and distribution channels have been put in place. For the company that wants to investigate a foreign market for possible entry, and to develop contacts that will be useful later, trade missions are usually more effective. Another unanticipated result was that for trade missions, where 56 per cent of participants are continuing exporters. Given the fact that these companies have been exporting to the market covered by the mission for three or more years, a trade fair would seem to be a more relevant vehicle to promote and sell their product or service.

Some recapping of the discussion seems appropriate at this point. The data presented in Table 7.6 showed that the profile of first-time, expanding, and continuing exporters are quite different. Following the reasoning developed in Chapter 5, one might then expect the varying characteristics and needs of these three exporter types to be mirrored in the trade fair and mission data. Table 7.7 showed this not to be the case. Although some contrasts between trade fair and mission participants are evident, these are fewer in number and often not the kind that were anticipated. In other words, the fair and mission company profiles are much 'fuzzier' than was expected. An important follow-up question then arises – why is this so? The anticipated results can potentially be explained in one of two ways. First, the benefits offered by fairs and missions are not matched to company export needs carefully enough (i.e. programme targeting is imprecise, either for procedural reasons or because companies apply pressure to be included when this is not ideal). An alternative second explanation is the trade fairs and missions do not serve different needs but, in fact, largely act as substitutes for one another (i.e. our theory is too restrictive). We explore these questions in the next section.

Examining the 'fuzzy' promotional event/company profiles

Two particularly surprising results were noted above: first, many

Table 7.8 A comparison of trade fair participants

Impact measure	*First-time exporter (n=33)*		*Continuing exporter (n=93)*	
1 *Top three objectives for trade fair and their realization*				
Per cent responding 'yes' to objective/ (per cent stating results 'excellent')				
– testing market for demand, acceptance and competitiveness	91%	(24%)	—	—
– making business contacts	76%	(31%)	83%	(37%)
– identifying or appointing agents/ representatives/distributors	73%	(15%)	—	—
– maintaining presence in market	—	—	82%	(46%)
– meeting regular customers and agents/ representatives/distributors	—	—	77%	(56%)
2 *Number of agents/representatives/ distributors appointed*	0.4		0.3	
3 *Sales impact*				
– Total sales related[a] to trade fair	$82,000		$731,000	
– companies with no sales	52%		40%	

Source: Prepared by the authors.

Note: [a] Sales that followed participation in the trade fair.

first-time exporters participate in trade fairs rather than missions; second, while in the minority, more continuing exporters participate in trade missions than would be expected. Through further analysis, we attempt to provide a better explanation for these contrary results.

First-time exporters at trade fairs

Some thirty-three of the thirty-eight companies classified as first-time exporters participated in a trade fair rather than a mission. Since this runs against the argument made in Chapter 5, it is important to examine this matter further. This is somewhat difficult to carry out. The preferred method, of course, would be to compare first-time exporters participating in trade fairs and missions; however, the very small number of companies using trade missions (n=5) rules out this approach. Since trade fairs were earlier argued to be 'most appropriate' for continuing exporters and 'least appropriate' for first-time exporters as promotional vehicles, some insight is gained from analysis of these exporter types. Table 7.8 presents summary statistics along these lines, specifically the trade fair objectives, the extent to which these were achieved, and a number of other performance measures.

Considering trade fair objectives first, Table 7.8 shows the three most frequently stated objectives for each exporter type. With one exception, sharp differences are evident. First-time exporters are most often preoccupied with matters of market assessment and location of an overseas sales/distributor partner. In contrast, continuing exporters stress objectives concerned with maintaining a market position. One objective – making business contacts – is a common objective for both exporter types. These differing objectives make sense when the varying export stages of the companies are considered. Given our interest in programme targeting, however, more important than the objectives themselves, is their level of realization. Substantial differences are seen here, with continuing exporters reporting 'excellent' trade fair results much more often than first-timers. We begin to get a picture of less than stellar performance here, for two-thirds to three-quarters of first-time exporters are unable truly to achieve their leading trade fair objectives.

When attention turns to harder measures of impact, this picture is detailed further. Continuing exporters achieve related trade show sales of $731,000 on average while the equivalent for first-timers is $82,000. These performance levels should be seen in the context of the $71,000 sales achieved by continuing exporters and no sales by first-time exporters in the twelve months prior to the trade fair. Trade fairs are thus seen to be a very effective promotional tool for continuing exporters, producing a substantial increase in sales. First-time exporters also generate sales, but at understandably lower levels given their newness to the market in question. A further consideration is that more than one-half of all first-time exporters achieve no sales whatsoever, greater than the (still high) 40 per cent for continuing exporters. Set against these lower level sales impacts, first-time exporters appoint slightly more agents, representatives, and distributors than do continuing exporters. This result is to be expected; in fact, the average of 0.3 partners appointed by continuing exporters is surprisingly high for companies with market maintenance priorities. This probably reflects the need for exporters of all types to review and strengthen their overseas networks on a regular basis.

While it has already been stated that the above analysis is not ideal for the matter at hand, it does suggest that few first-time exporters get good results when their initial activity is to exhibit at a foreign trade fair. One interesting additional statistic is that one in five first-timers who exhibit at a trade fair follow this up by participating in a trade mission to the market covered by the fair. Perhaps this should have been their beginning step.

Table 7.9 A comparison of continuing exporters using trade fairs and missions

Impact measure	*Continuing exporters using*			
	Trade fairs (n=93)		*Trade missions (n=29)*	
1 *Top three objectives for trade fair or mission and their realization*				
Per cent responding 'yes' to objective/ (Per cent stating results 'excellent')				
– testing market for demand, acceptance and competitiveness	—	—	59%	(22%)
– making business contacts	83%	(37%)	90%	(50%)
– maintaining presence in market	82%	(46%)	76%	(56%)
– meeting regular customers and agents/ representatives/distributors	77%	(56%)	59%	(58%)
2 *Number of agents/representatives/ distributors appointed*	0.3		0.2	
3 *Sales impact*				
– total sales related[a] to trade fair or mission	$731,000		$1,614,000	
– companies with no sales	40%		48%	

Source: Prepared by the authors.

Note: [a] Sales that followed participation in the trade fair.

Continuing exporters on trade missions

Of the 129 companies classified as continuing exporters, 29 participated in trade missions rather than fairs. This runs against the reasoning developed in Chapter 5 and so merits closer analysis. Again, we look at the participation objectives of companies, the degree to which these are realized, and other performance measures.

It is interesting to note in Table 7.9 that whether participating in a trade fair or mission, continuing exporters have the same major objectives. The top three stated objectives are identical and show a concern for maintaining a foreign market position. The only difference between fair and mission users is that the latter hope to test the market somewhat more than the former. To what extent are these objectives realized? It appears that continuing exporters are rather better able to satisfy their objectives through trade missions as against fair participation. This point is reinforced by the sales data, which show that average sales for mission participants are more than twice those of companies going to fairs. There is somewhat more variability in sales performance for companies on missions, with almost one-half achieving no sales at all. Another concrete way to measure the impact of these promotional events is the number of foreign agent, representative, or distributor appointments made. Here, mission participants do marginally less well, appointing an average of 0.2 partners versus 0.3 for fair exhibitors. However, only 28 per cent of mission companies stated appointing such a partner to be an objective, compared to 38 per cent of fair participants.

This analysis reveals that trade fairs and missions are mostly employed by continuing exporters to achieve the same objectives, but that mission participation generates better results. These results cast further doubts on the Chapter 5 argument that fairs serve the needs of continuing exporters better than missions. Additional comparisons lead to some clues about these usage patterns.

Continuing exporters that participate in trade missions seem not to be very different in their general characteristics from those using fairs (see Table 7.10). Both are well established and seasoned in exporting – with many years of foreign selling, a group of experienced senior managers, and customers in numerous countries. One general point of difference, however, is size, with one-third of all mission participants having total sales of more than $50 million, as opposed to one-fifth for companies exhibiting at fairs.

While the differences in general characteristics between fair and mission users appear small, those for situational characteristics are larger. For example, continuing exporters who sell services are more likely to participate in missions than fairs. An earlier comment is relevant here, namely that missions may be better promotional vehicles for companies with offerings that cannot be easily displayed and demonstrated, i.e. services. This appears borne out by our data, which show the average sales of continuing exporters of services to be $21,000 at fairs and $1.8 million on missions. Two other factors which may well affect the choice between participating in a fair or mission are shown in Table 7.10. It is interesting that the industrial sectors that dominate the listing for fairs and missions are mostly different. This suggests that these promotional vehicles may vary somewhat in their usefulness to companies from different industries. Finally, note that although most continuing exporters had exerted the same moderate level of effort in the relevant market in the twelve months prior to fair or mission participation, those going on missions had sales at one-fifth the level of their trade fair counterparts ($13,000 and $71,000 respectively). How do we then account for the $1.6 million resulting from mission participation and the $13,000 sales levels in the year prior to the event? We suppose that some companies were able to revitalize their exporting operations through mission participation but believe the disparity in sales too large to explain in this fashion. Another interpretation is that for

Table 7.10 Further profiling of continuing exporters

Characteristic	*Continuing exporters using*	
	Trade fairs (n=93)	*Trade missions (n=29)*
General		
1 *Date of*		
- establishment (average)	1952	1948
- starting to export (average)	1966	1961
2 *Current export experience*		
- number of senior managers with export experience	5	9
- number of countries exported to	17	17
3 *Current annual sales*		
- less than $2 million	14%	4%
- $2–50 million	67%	62%
- more than $50 million	19%	35%
Situational		
1 *Company type*		
- manufacturer	85%	79%
- trading company/distributor	13%	14%
- provider of services	8%	32%
2 *Industry sector* [a] (top three)	industrial and machinery (30%), consumer goods (23%), defence and electronics (16%)	defence and electronics (28%), transportation (21%), agriculture (17%)
3 *Activity in market year prior to trade fair or mission*		
- level of marketing effort[b] (modal response)	moderate	moderate
- annual sales (average)	$71,000	$13,000

Source: Prepared by the authors.

Notes:

[a] The sectors used were: agriculture; defence and electronics; transportation; mines, metals, and petroleum; consumer products; industrial and machinery; others.

[b] The range of responses available here was: no effort; minor effort; moderate effort; major effort; in business less than 12 months at time of trade fair or mission; don't know.

some companies the trade mission was a vehicle simply to consummate a sale that had been some time in the making. This would explain both the high prior effort levels of mission participants and the sales gap.

We have attempted to uncover reasons for the superior performance of continuing exporters using trade missions over those using fairs. As in the previous discussion in this section of first-time exporters, no proof of a position can be tendered. At best we offer some possible explanations for the results. We have suggested that certain situational factors may predispose a continuing exporter to choose a mission as against a fair. These situations include (1) companies selling services, (2) companies from certain industrial sectors, and (3) companies that can finalize a protracted export transaction through a trade mission. Of course, for some companies more than one of these situations may simultaneously apply.

We began this section with the view that either imprecise targeting or an overly restrictive theory explained the 'fuzzy' promotional event/company profiles seen in Table 7.7. Further analysis indicates that both explanations may apply. We feel that the frequent use of trade fairs by first-time exporters in this study is a reflection largely of poor targeting. In contrast, since the participation by some continuing exporters in trade missions is seen to be highly productive, some modification of our ideas seems in order.

Summary

The above discussion shows that room exists for improved targeting of government export programmes to companies. At a general level, it appears that too many trade fair and mission places are taken up by continuing exporters, that is companies whose experience and resources should mean that such assistance is unnecessary. Although many of these companies gross large export sales as a result of participation, many more achieve no sales at all, and through participation block off places that others with greater needs might have benefited from. Because they lend visibility and prestige to a government-sponsored trade fair or mission, the participation of some large, experienced companies may be regarded as imperative. However, inviting too many companies of this type should be guarded against.

On a more specific note, the 'over-use' of trade fairs by *first-time exporters* was discussed. This certainly seems to be one area for closer examination and possible adjustment. What of *expanding exporters*? Because of their special characteristics – similar in some respects to first-timers and in others to continuing exporters – these companies make for more difficult analysis. We have avoided this group here, feeling that the companies at either extreme deserved our attention. Clearly, however, the very mixed nature of companies of this type means that there is an onus on programme officials to invite them to events which are appropriate to their needs. Finally, we turn to *continuing exporters*. Here we saw that the event/exporter type framework developed in Chapter 5 needs some further detailing, for trade missions seem to play an important role for certain companies.

Conclusions

We began this chapter by stating that it would provide some closure on the question of the impact of government export promotion programmes. The practical setting of an evaluation study enables our ideas to be tested in the 'real-world' we are concerned with. In the first part of the chapter we described the methods used to conduct the study and showed that, although a complex subject, with knowledge of the exporting process in companies, and care in the design, data collection, and analysis stages, programme impact can be measured. The present study demonstrates that the trade fairs and missions in question generated very satisfactory returns on the company and programme investments made. Of course, these results provide only a 'snap-shot' at one point in time, but the dynamics of programme impact can be assessed with appropriate longitudinal methods. The most important point then is that in contrast to other studies, these results are unequivocal – the programme pays off in participant company (micro) terms, as well as for the economy as a whole (macro). Despite these positive findings, however, room for improvements in programme/company targeting appear to exist. A number of analyses were presented in the last section of the chapter and these indicate that 'fine-tuning' might improve programme impacts further. As is so often the case, some of the findings raise almost as many questions as they answer. However, a data base of this kind permits programme officials (and others) the opportunity better to understand the role and impact of government export promotion programmes.

Notes and references

1 'The fairs and missions (promotional projects) program: survey of past participants', Report prepared by SPR Associates Incorporated/National Mail Surveys Incorporated for the Department of External Affairs, Ottawa, 5 October 1987. We appreciate the Department of External

Affairs' permission to use data generated in this evaluation study. The programme evaluation included other elements, such as a survey of companies which won Canada Export Awards, a detailed survey of two events, and a literature review.

2 In April 1987 the PPP ceased to exist. The trade fair and trade mission activities of this programme continue, however, as part of an expanded Programme for Export Market Development.

3 Outgoing missions are those where Canadian companies travel to the foreign market. This contrasts with incoming missions (or trade visitors in Table 7.1), where foreign buyers and key influencers are brought to Canada to visit companies. Both types of missions were evaluated in the study.

4 Where possible, the screening survey sought to verify the person (or persons) who had attended the event or, in the case of an incoming mission, received a delegation. If this was not possible, efforts were made to locate the person most knowledgeable about the event and its results for the company.

5 Related sales include those made on-site (customer orders); made within twelve months of the fair or mission; and other firm and committed future sales.

Part IV

Conclusions

Chapter eight

Government export promotion: present and future

Introduction

This book has described the supportive role played by government export promotion in international trade, and assessed the impact of the programmes through which assistance is made available to companies around the world. Although numerous bodies and writers have covered aspects of this subject previously, to our knowledge this is the first book to deal comprehensively with this important subject.

As befits a final chapter, we now take stock of the present state-of-the-art in government export promotion before concluding with a look to the future. The first section reviews the role played by government export promotion in the developed and developing world, the export assistance needs of companies, and the difficulties experienced in evaluating the impact of export promotion programmes. The second section speaks to the future, pointing to certain trends affecting government initiatives and looking at the key challenges facing public policy makers and programme officials.

The present state-of-the-art

The developed world

The concept of export promotion is as old as trade itself. Over the years, countries in the developed world have established export promotion programmes to the point where, today, these are comprehensive and often embody sophisticated and innovative features.

The idea of export promotion continues to be highly relevant to international trade and is generally viewed as an instrument of economic development on the one hand, and of strengthening the competitive competence of business on the other. In the former context export promotion is mainly of relevance to the developing world, while in the latter context it is important to both the developed and the developing countries.

The pertinence of export promotion is clear. Economic development as a process towards greater prosperity is heavily dependent on foreign trade and exporting. Export competitiveness, the vehicle to ensure that a country's products or services produced find international market acceptance, is no longer a simple matter of factor endowment. Rather, competitiveness today increasingly reflects technological and managerial prowess. In the current international trade environment developed and developing countries – their governments and business community – are acutely aware of this fact of life.

Export promotion is generally a part of governments' foreign trade policy, although, as we have seen earlier, the approach taken in various developed countries is not always a direct one. The concept of export promotion has been adapted to different philosophies of government intervention and ideas about business–government interaction. Furthermore, the strategies underlying export promotion efforts vary, that is export promotion systems serve similar ends through sometimes different means.

Because of increasing internationalization of business and competition, often accompanied by converging market needs and opportunities, the export promotion activities of developed countries show similarities in emphasizing the needs of small and medium-sized companies, especially as far as export planning and market entry are concerned. Assistance often includes standard services for information, market research, and market contact through trade missions and fairs.

Although there is a trend towards similar export promotion offerings, philosophies and strategies differ from country to country. This is not surprising in that export promotion evolves in a particular country setting (culture, economic, and political environment) and seeks to respond to the needs of the business community in a manner consistent with that setting. It therefore would be inappropriate to expect extensive government-led initiatives in export promotion in Germany where the government attitude towards the business community has traditionally been *laissez-faire*. Likewise, expecting to find the private sector dominating export promotion efforts in a country such as Canada, where different levels of government have a history of providing extensive export support, would be equally unrealistic.

Although in some cases export promotion efforts are led by the government or the private sector, this does not mean the other is excluded. In countries with a clear government-led export promotion system, for example, private sector organizations, such as chambers of commerce or industry and trade associations, participate and provide services complementary to those available from government. Conversely, private sector-led systems benefit from certain governmental services and support. There is no evidence to conclude that government-led export promotion excels over private-sector-led or vice versa. Nor is it possible to say that mixed approaches fare better or worse than either of the other two.

With international competition becoming increasingly intense, countries with a strategically focused export promotion system (i.e. a comprehensive and programmatic approach) may be able to offer more effective export promotion support to the business community. Countries with a loose or unsystematic approach may find that their support may not provide the same degree of effectiveness. We know from the business world and the business literature, however, that strategic and systematic management assures a competitive advantage at the company level. If one extends this premise to international trade, and indeed economic development (namely Japan), then it would be reasonable to expect better performance from an export promotion system operating under a strategic-integrated approach over one that is loosely co-ordinated, because the former provides the right programmes, to the right companies, to do the right things, at the right time.

Some of these concerns lie at the root of reviews of export promotion systems undertaken by several countries. The implications of these reviews are clear: a strategic and systematic focus for export promotion and international market involvement is needed by both, the export promotion system (whether government, private sector, or mixed), and the business community.

The developing world

If one takes a look (admittedly simplistic) at the population-to-trade ratio of the developing and industrialized worlds, a gross imbalance is apparent. This indicates the scope for increased trade that exists for developing countries. On a positive note, however, developing countries have dramatically increased their participation in global trade. Both output and exports have expanded at nearly twice the rate found in developed countries, over the past two decades. As well, developing countries recently passed an important milestone in their development, when for the first time export earnings from manufactured products exceeded those from agricultural exports.

As noted earlier, export promotion in developing countries must be seen in its context. Specifically economic development, export development, and export promotion are deeply intertwined and thus interdependent. This is quite different from export promotion in developed countries, where its task is to pursue international trade objectives through government-enhanced export management competence and competitiveness.

In the period following the Second World War a number of developing countries have demonstrated that when public policy emphasizes domestic economic development, it can retard international trade involvement, and so lead to slower rather than faster industrial and commercial progress. The framework of inward or outward orientation, suggested by the World Bank, has been useful in understanding the dynamics of public policy and economic development. It is clear that the developing countries' economies are tied to international trade, largely in the form of exports. Countries that have recognized this and shaped their public policies accordingly have developed faster than others.

The prosperity of developing countries depends, in large measure, on their own efforts (their will and attitude), and to a much lesser extent on what help developed nations can and will provide. It should be noted, however, that many obstacles continue to stand in the way of harmonious trade relations between developing and developed nations, more effective market access to the latter being one important area. As discussed in the context of developed countries, the approach taken to the development and expansion of exports is important, as is the structure put in place, but even more so in developing countries. Often the resources in their business communities must be marshalled with concerted effort so as to create an export base. ITC was seen as making a vital contribution by focusing its efforts on fostering an export orientation in the public sector and among the business community, and providing organizational as well as managerial guidance for export development. Export promotion organizations are designed and employed as comprehensive and important tools which place great emphasis on these elements.

Proven export promotion structures and approaches help but do not guarantee success in export development. It is important to understand this difference. A simple grafting of export promotion approaches used by developed countries will not suffice, because the latter have a sophisticated export base as well as, by and large, an outward-looking and aggressive business community. As experience has shown, developing countries sometimes merely go through the motions of export development and promotion. They set up an export structure, often with the co-operation of the ITC, but lack what might be called basic export commitment, that is they fail to create a co-operative approach between the business community and the institutional infrastructure. Regions and countries in the developing world are diverse. Accordingly, in the same way that developed world models may not be appropriate, it is a mistake to expect one developing world export promotion approach always to work. The diversity of export promotion approaches is readily apparent when one examines specific efforts in, for example, Latin America and Caribbean countries, and South-East Asia.

Whatever approach is taken, a number of points seem of universal importance. These include having

1 sufficient autonomy and influence at both the governmental and business community level,
2 a clear role in the development of trade policy,
3 defined responsibilities and jurisdiction in export development objectives and export promotion functions.

This requires that a clear mandate be given and adequate resources made available so that the EPO can fulfil its task. The size of the resources made available is a tangible expression of government commitment to exporting.

Overall, the appreciation of the interrelationship of export development and export promotion seems imperative. Thus the process of developing an export base should not be seen as isolated from the process of developing export market opportunities. The two activities should work in parallel to ensure a true export orientation in a particular developing country. Finally, we emphasize again the ability governments have to retard development. Adoption of an outward orientation, and development of suitable export promotion strategy and activities, serve to foster economic development.

The needs of companies

International markets play an increasingly important part in the development plans of both nations and companies. Various factors account for this trend: technology, for example, has 'shrunk' the separation of production and consumption points and permitted many products (such as kiwi-fruit and lobsters) and services (financial, informational) to be marketed more widely. Lower import tariffs and, hence, greater market access – resulting from the GATT rounds – have also played a key part in drawing more companies into exporting. Although these and other factors have led to a more conducive trade environment, many companies remain within the confines of their own local, regional, or national home market. Others do export, but not to their true potential. In both cases this is often a consequence of export barriers – either perceived or, in the case of those with an export track-record, actual barriers that have been experienced. The point being made here is that while many international trade opportunities exist, achieving foreign market sales is no easy matter. Whether they are going international for the first time, expanding their foreign market coverage, or maintaining existing operations, companies often need assistance. Governments around the world have responded to this need with a multitude of programmes and services. An unresolved question, however, concerns how well company needs are understood by those responsible for establishing export promotion policies and running the resulting programmes.

Company needs are not uniform, rather they are shaped by the stage of the export development that has been reached. This suggests that major efforts should be made to ensure that appropriate programmes are designed for, and delivered to, user companies. Five types of user companies were proposed – 'non-exporters', 'first-time exporters', 'failed exporters', 'expanding exporters', and 'continuing exporters', and the varying needs of each type described. Clearly a non-exporting company will have quite contrasting export promotion requirements from its more seasoned counter-part whose major pre-occupation is with expanding into, say, its twentieth foreign market. Although this point may seem obvious, existing programmes often seem not to reflect these distinctions. Indeed, a case study example in Chapter 7 showed that room exists for improved targeting of programmes, even in countries that have a long history of export promotion support, stated goals for programmes, and a sizeable complement of well-educated programme officials.

In summary, while many programmes exist to help companies deal with the problems involved in exporting, we believe there is scope for improvements in design and delivery, using the targeting approach described. How much scope can be determined only from well-designed and well-conducted evaluation studies – itself a thorny issue.

Effectiveness issues

The need to evaluate government export promotion efforts serves two purposes. First, governments need to show that public funds are put to effective use and that both country and industry benefit. Second, a positive impact on programme users needs to be demonstrated, through which the benefit to both industry and country becomes apparent. It would be naive, however, to suggest that evaluations should serve only government. The programme users, the target for such government export promotion efforts, are the other important reason for attempting to measure the effect of programmes. Companies need to know and understand that export promotion programmes can and do contribute to exporting competence. The methodology of evaluation and impact measurement is multi-faceted and thus very complex. This is so whether a programme or company perspective is taken. Impact measurement then is approached from these two directions and the results of both have been far from consistent.

Programme evaluations are often hampered by a lack of specific goals or targets against which to compare results. Programme design and management, however, stand to gain a great deal from competent evaluations. Notwithstanding the problems, the latter is an important reason why, in developed countries, more or less comprehensive evaluation procedures are in place. Those developing countries whose export promotion is systematic tend to have their programmes evaluated, often with the support of organizations such as ITC or ESCAP. Although the comprehensiveness and sophistication of government export promotion in developed countries is greater than in developing countries, many of the evaluation problems are similar, as indeed are the lessons for improving export promotion efforts.

An especially disturbing aspect of efforts to measure impact at the company level is management's apparent ambivalence as to the benefit of export promotion. The finding that many companies are not aware of governmental programmes should alarm programme and EPO management. Clearly a 'user perspective' based on both the needs of the target audience and the best-suited communications methods to reach them seems required. The relatively low usage rate of export programmes then may in part be attributed to lack of awareness. Another likely factor is business attitudes towards governmental or external intrusion in company affairs. In developed countries such attitudes may be long-standing and are part of the prevailing philosophy of business. In developing countries, however, where export promotion efforts and the creation of an export base in the business community are emerging, much greater flexibility prevails with respect to creating a co-operative working relationship between public and private sectors.

Evaluations suggest that, at best, export promotion programmes might have a marginal effect on export activity. This is not altogether surprising in light of the myriad of activities companies routinely undertake to carry on their business. Because of the incremental role played by government export promotion in company operations, it is difficult to separate out programme effects from others. This marginal effect problem, combined with the methodological complexities, is a continuing challenge to those evaluating government export promotion.

As suggested, approaches to evaluation and impact measurement are becoming more sophisticated in an effort to produce more reliable results. While the measurement of results can be undertaken from either a programme or company (user) perspective, it must be realized that evaluation will yield the best results when it is viewed as an integrated activity. In other words, more meaningful and useful results are likely when each sector's views and concerns are built into the evaluation approach and there is an appreciation of each party's role in the export promotion process.

The future

Trends and directions

If the above comments summarize the present state-of-the-art, what of the future? A number of discernible trends are shaping the way governments will promote exports in the future. These include

1 intensifying international competition,
2 changes in the scale and role of government,
3 increasing knowledge about how companies internationalize,
4 more sophisticated trade fairs.

We review these trends below and note some export programme implications. We then move on to look at the broader challenges facing those responsible for establishing and managing government export promotion programmes.

There can be little disagreement that today's world is an increasingly competitive economic arena. The confluence of numerous changes – more open markets, manufacturing capabilities in the developing world, shorter product life-cycles, converging tastes and the emergence of certain global markets, technology advances, to name a few – poses threats to industries and their member companies. While threats of this kind are not new, the pursuit of competitive advantage – *the* critical business activity – seems more difficult now and in the future. In this business environment a convincing argument can be made for a continuing or even enhanced role for government export promotion programmes. Further, it could be argued that the more intense competition becomes, the more selective programmes should be, supporting only those companies and efforts with the greatest probability of success. Politically, however, such an approach would be difficult to implement.

Governments around the world are under pressure to change their ways. Triggered by spending deficits, downsizing is one manifestation of this trend, while another is withdrawal from certain types of activities which are regarded as inappropriate for government. Export promotion activities have not been immune from these moves, even though trade development is almost universally regarded as important to a nation's well-being. Thus export budgets have often been trimmed, and/or conscious decisions have been made that others should shoulder more of the promotional load. These trends appear to contradict the previous point that intensifying competition will require more government support for exporters. One solution to this dilemma is for government programmes to become more efficient and effective. We comment on this more below. While at first glance the situation may seem impossible, it gives those in favour of change and improvement a chance to test and demonstrate their ideas. The situation should prompt more and better evaluation of programmes and, one hopes, speed the adoption of computerized management information systems which are noticeably lacking today.

As noted earlier, although company export assistance has been provided by governments for centuries, the system of export promotion programmes we are familiar with today is much more recent. Despite being relatively new, the establishment of export programmes preceded any significant accumulation of knowledge about why and how companies expand overseas. The huge trade increases from the 1960s onwards drew more researchers to the study of international business, but their preoccupation was mostly with the multinational corporation. It is only since the mid-1970s that much effort has gone into studying the internationalization process in the small and medium-sized companies that are the declared major focus of export programme attention. Much of this work has taken place in universities and, while it is increasingly recognized and used by government, greater collaboration could benefit both parties. From a government standpoint, there are gains that can be made from the involvement of programme officials with persons who are formally trained and experienced in international marketing and business research. The design of better promotion programmes and evaluation studies could result. This is not to say that government personnel know little about these matter. However, programme officials come from diverse educational backgrounds and relatively few have direct, personal international trade experience to draw from, so that most of their knowledge is gained on-the-job. When export promotion organizations are part of a foreign affairs or diplomatic ministry, and intra-organizational transfers are frequent, the problem of experienced manpower is further exacerbated.

As an important activity (and a major line item in most export promotion budgets) international trade fairs deserve attention, the more so since there are changes afoot here.[1] The number of trade fairs is increasing, as is their level of specialization and complexity. Established fairs are becoming larger, and due to product specialization, there is a growing number of vertical fairs, some of which have been spun-off from large, horizontal fairs. Pressure for space at the best fairs is increasing. Fair organizers are benefiting from electronics/computer technology that allows better tracking of fair attendance and sales results. This will ultimately help governments and companies in their selection of the most appropriate fair for their purpose, a major factor in the light of the numerous fairs mounted annually. Electronics technology is playing an even larger role in fairs – product or equipment displays being replaced by electronic media presentations and the view is expressed that, in the longer-term, such technology may make fairs redundant. This trend may develop only partially because of the need for, and importance of, personal contact and interaction between buyer and seller. These trends impact on government programmes in a number of ways: increasing the pool of fairs at which to exhibit; making fair/company selection processes somewhat easier; allowing for more accurate evaluations of fair activities; and drawing attention to the fact that the objectives companies currently seek to satisfy through fairs, in the future may be achieved through alternative means.

Challenges for government

We have intimated that governments face challenges in their export promotion support activities. International trade is regarded as crucial to economic development and many companies need export promotion support so as to enter foreign markets, to expand or maintain their existing overseas business. Because of intensifying international competition, the need for support seems to be increasing, but this has come about at a time when government budgets are under pressure. Other changes also make for a dynamic and sometimes uncertain environment. The challenge for government, then, is to generate better export sales in a harder economic climate. We conclude by highlighting some of the ways this might be achieved. Figure 8.1 shows five areas in which government might consider change: a bigger export promotion budget; better allocation of the budget; more careful selection of events and companies; more efficient operations; more effective monitoring and evaluation.

Before it seems that we have contradicted ourselves about budgets, let us point out that not all export promotion budgets are being

Figure 8.1 Achieving export sales gains in a tough economic climate

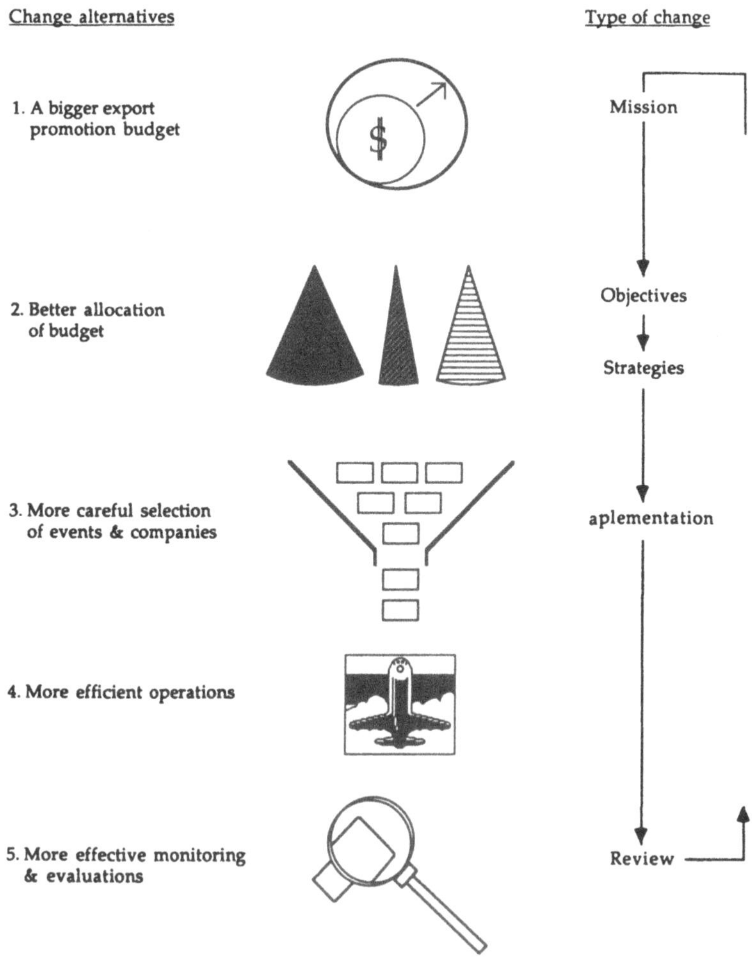

Source: Prepared by the authors.

trimmed. Although this is a fact of life in many countries, in others government budgets in general continue to grow or, because of the importance accorded to trade development, export promotion budgets have been spared. To the extent that export promotion budgets can be increased, export sales gains are obviously that much easier to achieve. There are other means, however, through which government can improve export performance and, while generally applicable, these are of special interest to those experiencing static or shrinking promotional budget allocations.

A second area for improved performance is in the allocation of the export promotion budget. Three types of allocations are often made within overall export promotion budgets, to (1) programmes, (2) industrial sectors, and (3) foreign markets/regions. Arguably a fourth allocation is also important, namely to company types (along the lines developed in Chapter 5), but this is usually not explicitly made. The allocation of resources is always a political process and so one fraught with problems. To some extent this, as well as the simplicity of the approach, explains the frequent practice of using historical levels to guide allocations. This approach and problem is, perhaps, found most often in large, established EPOs where 'empires' are defended against any form of encroachment. For other EPOs, allocations which depart from traditional levels should be less problematical. While zero-based budgeting is probably unrealistic as an approach in EPOs, allocations should be expected to change as the export objectives and priorities vary over time. Where EPOs or other associated government agencies go to the trouble of developing sectoral and market plans and priorities, it appears senseless then largely to ignore these in the allocation of promotional funds. Like other bureaucratic organizations though, EPOs often seem to fall into this trap. A final point is that the programme/sector/market/company allocation units are not totally independent of each other. For example, if computer software is selected to be a high export priority sector for a given nation, then that will transpose into market (Europe, North America, and Japan, for the most part) and company (often small) emphases. This should be recognized in the allocation process, where there is room for practices which are more closely tasked to objectives and strategies.

A third area where improved practice is possible is in the way that the allocated budget is spent. Using the government-initiated trade fair and mission examples again, we can say that the budget is used well when appropriate fairs are chosen or missions planned, and the right companies chosen to participate. Results from the study of trade fair and mission participation reported in Chapter 7 showed great variability. Whether this results from ill-chosen fairs/missions, poorly selected companies, or some combination of the two, is not clear. What is clear, however, is that if this case study is remotely typical, then considerable room exists for better management of the screening processes involved.

Another area in which improvements might be sought is operational. Where government takes on the responsibility for actually running a particular export promotion event (e.g. trade mission), efficiency gains can conceivably be made. When government merely provides export promotional assistance in an arm's-length manner (e.g. partial funding of a foreign market visit for a company), then it has little control of expenditure and so is not in a good position to make efficiency improvements. It is difficult to determine the scope that exists for improved practice in operational matters, but it deserves mention.

A final, fifth area is more straightforward. We have commented at numerous points in the book that the impact of government export promotion programmes is not well understood. This in itself indicates that these programmes are not sufficiently well monitored or evaluated. When programmes cost the equivalent of millions of dollars, and involve large numbers of companies annually, an urgent need exists for more comprehensive review. The EPO in a developed country can expect to be dealing with thousands of applications for assistance, with company files often 'active' for long periods due to the time-lag between the export promotion initiative and the results that (hopefully) flow and are recorded. This means that the EPO operational/review function is often a very large-scale undertaking. Audits show that this function is seldom run very effectively: companies continue to be assisted when ten or more previous initiatives have produced no export sales; companies do not file the reports that are required of them, and so on. Yet, well organized and operated, this function could provide a very rich source of information and insight into the role and impact of government export promotion, with positive repercussions at all levels of activity. Considerable opportunities exist for improvements in this area.

We have argued that even though international competition is intensifying, government can improve the pay-off from export promotion through changes at several decision-making levels. Of course, it is often easier to point to what change is necessary than to implement these in the setting of an organization. We recognize this, but for the sake of simplicity have deliberately chosen not to deal with organizational barriers (structural and behavioural) to change, focusing instead on what might be done. One point deserves mention, however. Making changes could be complicated by the fact that in some countries the EPO is part of a larger governmental unit, while in others more than one public agency is involved.

Conclusions

This final chapter assessed the state-of-the-art of government export promotion and took a look towards the future suggested by several trends. The mechanism and support structure for international trade are very sophisticated in the developed world. Export promotion systems are generally well integrated into the government policy framework and the mode of conducting international business. We saw that the needs of companies for exporting are similar if not identical and that export market entry and expansion poses the same challenges to all companies, regardless of their origin or target market. Similarity in government export promotion efforts speaks to the fact that both government and business community have recognized this convergence in the key dimensions of international trade generally and exporting in particular. This notwithstanding, review and self-assessment has been a characteristic of government export promotion in a number of countries seeking greater effectiveness of programmes and services.

The developing world shows impressive signs of acknowledging the importance export development plays in economic development. Although it is impractical to prescribe an export development and promotion process to developing countries, there are encouraging signs that, on the whole, their learning curve is accelerating because of

1 better communications systems,
2 better models of EPOs,
3 international, regional, and national organizations willing and able to guide export development.

It is also clear that, while outside guidance is useful, export development cannot be decreed from outside but must take hold within a developing country through forceful commitment and a proactive attitude and collective will.

We said that government export promotion assists companies. Of ongoing concern is, on the one hand, understanding how companies operate and in which area export promotion can and should offer assistance, and, on the other, what the effect of export promotion is at the company, industry, or country level. Our understanding of the process of exporting has broadened considerably since the 1970s and with it our knowledge of the needs to which governments can respond. Although efforts to determine the impact of export promotion programmes are evolving and improving, creating better measures remains challenging.

The future environment for government export promotion will be one of still greater intensification of international competition. This is spurred by technological capabilities crossing developed/developing country boundaries, globalization of certain markets, and accelerating life-cycles of products and services. The pressure on both researchers and government fully to grasp and understand these dynamics is substantial. As the commercial environment changes so are governments pressed to change their ways. Through constraints on budgets, demand for better management of resources, and the need for ever greater international trade linkages, governments continue to emphasize the distinct role export promotion plays, albeit under more effective management and return-on-expenditure criteria. While there are likely to be changes in some of the traditional tools of export promotion, such as the influence of electronic technology on trade fairs, others, catering to the need for personal experience and contact will remain relatively unchanged. Where governments will be challenged most is in creating and managing EPOs that function as committed and effective facilitators for the development of export management competence. The requirement to meet this challenge is a co-operative attitude by both government and business, an integrated framework to increasing exporting competence, and appreciation and understanding of their respective roles, responsibilities, and contributions to this process.

Notes and references

1 This information is drawn from a survey of ten international trade fair organizers conducted as part of the evaluation study referred to in Chapter 7: 'Trade fairs and missions: present and future', prepared for the Department of External Affairs by SPR Associates, September 1987.

Appendix

Import promotion organizations

We have seen that developing countries are increasingly emphasizing exports in their development plans. They face many obstacles in this process including: restrictive trade policies, lack of technical and organizational know-how, infrastructural inadequacies, and risk aversion on the part of exporters.[1] Increasing exports from developing countries require that a sequence of events takes place:[2]

1 development of export production,
2 elimination of export restrictions in developing countries,
3 marketing of exportable products to developed countries,
4 elimination of import restrictions in developed countries.

In 1972 UNCTAD requested that developed nations set up organizations (national agencies) to help developing countries in their export drive, specifically to provide market information, to assist in marketing products, and to help in making contacts with importers. In recent years, a number of industrial countries have responded to this request, creating import promotion organizations (IPO). Their mission is to provide developing countries with improved access to their market. While, at this time, import promotion organizations are mainly in western countries, several Eastern European countries also have created such organizations. A recent study by ITC provides an overview of the general kinds of assistance such organizations offer to developing countries (Table A.1).[3]

Most of the work of IPOs can be categorized as information assistance which includes

1 statistical information on domestic market and sales opportunities,
2 information on import requirements and procedures,
3 publications on domestic market,
4 information on marketing techniques and business practices,
5 lists of importers, wholesalers, distributors, agents by product line,

Table A.1 Services provided by import promotion organizations to developing countries

Types of services	*Import Promotion Organization in*	
	Western countries	*East block countries*
Information assistance	59%	64%
Marketing assistance	19%	17%
Contact assistance	12%	12%
Other assistance	10%	7%
Total	100%	100%
Number of countries	16	7

Source: Adapted from 'Import promotion offices', International Trade Centre UNCTAD/GATT, Geneva, 1987.

6 names of buyers seeking specific products in specific quantities,
7 information on training seminars and co-operation with other organizations,
8 lists of foreign exporters for importers,
9 responding to initial enquiries regarding exports,
10 library services.

The emphasis on information is logical and complements developing country export promotion organizations' efforts in this area. Marketing and contact assistance is much less prevalent among IPOs. The former includes such services as

1 trade fair and exhibition assistance,
2 showrooms for product display or exhibitions,
3 seminars or audio-visual services on trade promotion,
4 assistance in locating showrooms for product display,
5 active promotion for selection exporters,
6 advice on product adaptation and development,
7 free advertisements in trade information bulletins.

Contact assistance occurs primarily in the areas of

1 arrangements for visit contacts,
2 exchange visits,
3 assistance to visiting trade missions.

Various other services address specific needs of patenting information, translation, and interpretation as well as training activities.

To expand on this general profile of IPOs, we now describe in more detail three particularly well-thought-out and comprehensive approaches to promoting imports from developing countries: the Japanese External Trade Organization (JETRO), the Netherland's Centre for the Promotion of Imports (CBI), and Sweden's Promotion Office for Products from Developing Countries (IMPOD).

Japan

Import concerns are in the purview of JETRO which, through various approaches and activities, may be viewed as the umbrella organization for import policy and its implementation. These import promotion activities are influenced, on the one hand, by foreign exchange rate policy and adjustments and, on the other, by the stimulation of domestic demand. Although JETRO's import promotion activities cover both developing and developed nations, it is noteworthy that in the 1986 fiscal year nearly three-quarters of the budget of about $10 million was devoted to the latter.[4]

As outlined in Figure A.1 Japan's import promotion activities are in three main areas. First, the promotion of understanding and dissemination of information; second, development of the import market and importable products; and third, support and assistance to importers.

Promotion of understanding and dissemination of information

Activities consist mainly of publicity such as making import trade awards to companies that excel in importing, and the holding of some 20,000 imported products bazaars across Japan to stimulate interest and demand in foreign products. The Prime Minister's office issues appeals to the public for the support and acceptance of imported products.

Development of import market and importable products

Apart from some general publicity and information activities referred to in the previous section, JETRO undertakes the main import promotion efforts. However, there are other programmes, described in more detail below, with a distinct focus that operate either under JETRO or separately, although not independently. As Table A.2 shows, JETRO's activities for import promotion can be broadly divided into those concerned with import promotion activities primarily in Japan, and those which focus on foreign companies and countries. Clearly both aim at improving market access and the acceptance of foreign products and services in Japan.

In broad terms, the domestically focused efforts involve creating and meeting demand for products and services and both to facilitate and to harmonize the process of bringing these to the Japanese market. The outwardly focused efforts seek to promote awareness of opportunities in Japan and to encourage both foreign companies as well as governments to pursue such opportunities. One key aspect in the latter are market access missions which aim to foster an understanding of the Japanese market by explaining the role of trading companies, the distribution system, and how business is transacted.[5]

One of the additional programmes mentioned earlier, the Manufactured Imports Promotion Organization (MIPRO), is a dedicated exhibition facility reserved for the showing of foreign products to Japanese consumers and businessmen. MIPRO is also an information resource on foreign products, and plays a role in introducing foreign industries and other cultures to Japan and assists with business negotiations.[6] A further effort, the Specific Product Trade Expansion Programme (STEP), provides highly focused market information on product opportunities to foreign companies. Sometimes such activities are undertaken together with exhibitions in conjunction with MIPRO.[7]

Support and assistance to importers

A variety of individual measures exist to accommodate the financing needs of import transactions. These include finance services (including preferential interest rates) provided by the Export-Import Bank of Japan for product imports, and Japan Development Bank's financing of an importer's physical facilities, as well as financial support particularly aimed at but not limited to smaller companies (subsidiaries of major international companies have also benefited from these scheme).[8]

The lack of financing for a proposed transaction can threaten the deal unless appropriate institutions, such as the Export-Import Bank of Japan, lend support to the importer. The example of a Japanese natural resource import transaction (Figure A.2) shows that characteristically most of the interaction is between the Export-Import Bank and the Importer.[9] It is relevant that the exporter be familiar with this process so as to have realistic expectations about the consummation of a trade transaction.

In addition to these import promotion activities Japan undertakes market access measures. These measures, while vital to the import promotion process, are much broader in scope and are related to the efforts towards trade liberalization which are ongoing under GATT negotiations. Under a three-year action programme, initiated in

Figure A.1 Structure of import promotion activities in Japan

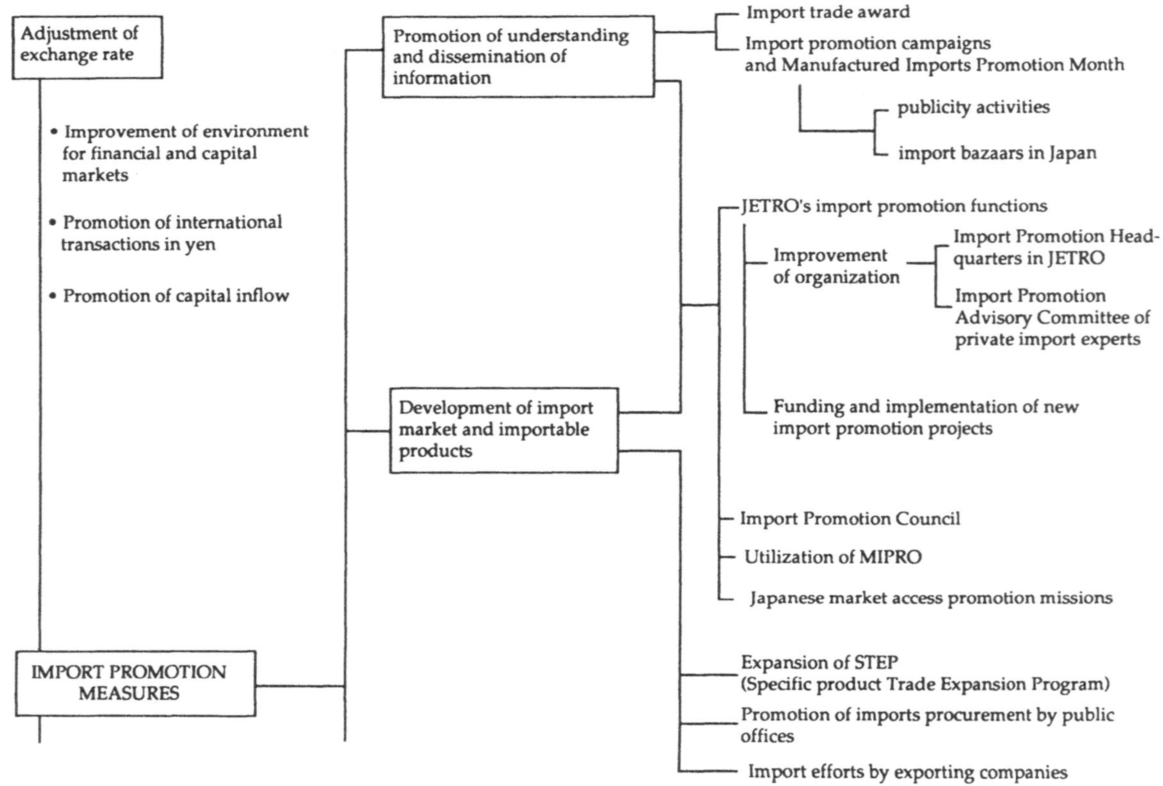

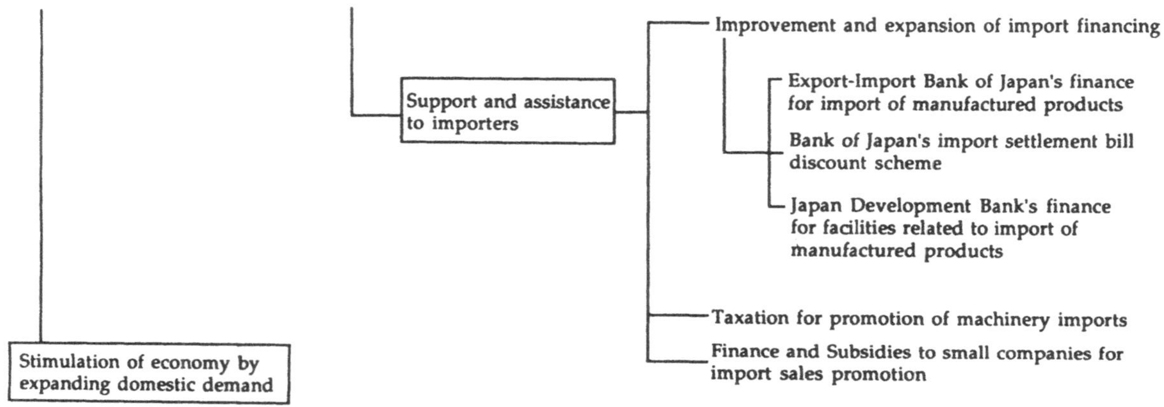

Source: Adapted from The Japanese Import Market, Tokyo, JETRO, 1987, p. 34.

Table A.2 Main activities of JETRO for import promotion

	JETRO activities for import promotion in Japan	*JETRO support to foreign companies and government to export to Japan*
Missions	Japanese buying missions to foreign countries	Market access promotion missions to foreign countries
		Consulting missions to developed and developing countries
		Reception of overseas missions to Japan
Exhibitions/fairs	Specific foreign country fairs (such as 'Made in USA' fair)	Special exhibitions by developing countries
	Product or region-oriented exhibitions (including catalogue and sample exhibitions)	
	Import bazaars	
Consulting	Introduction of foreign exporters to Japanese companies	Consultants with specific industry expertise available to foreign exporters
		Overseas seminars on market access and opportunities
Information	Market research for imported products (both potential and actual)	Information/report audio-visual material
	Import product information	Specific market aspects (target market, product, etc.)
		Trade sales enquiry system

Source: based on *The Japanese Import Market*, Tokyo, JETRO, 1987, pp. 54, 58.

1985, particular objectives were set for tariff reduction on some 1,853 import items. While 80 per cent of machinery items, for example, are stated to be tariff-free, this clearly depends on the type of product and the competitive situation in Japan. For instance, tariffs are levied against 32 per cent of machinery imports from the EEC.[10]

Import restrictions as well as standards and procedures are undergoing changes to ease market access. In some cases self-certification by manufacturers or importers has been introduced. Problems and complaints that fall under market access can be brought before the Office of Trade and Investment Ombudsman. Here specific complaints about import barriers can be lodged.[11]

It should also be recognized that the government maintains an International Trade Conference exclusively concerned with trade

Figure A.2 A natural resource import transaction involving Export–Import Bank

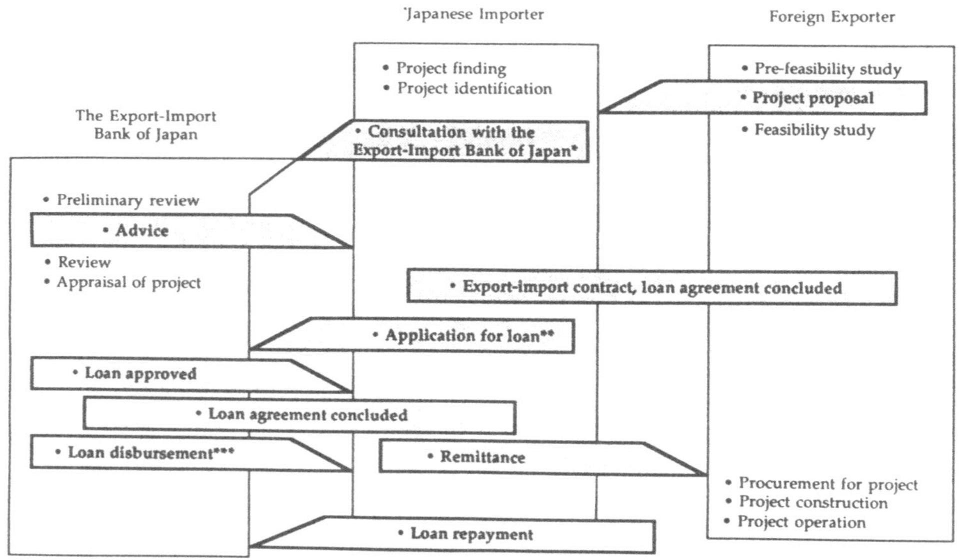

Source: *Japan's Trade Finance*, Tokyo, JETRO, March 1984, Figure 16.10, p. 28.

Notes:

* The prospective borrower begins consultations with the Bank at the earliest possible stage of project planning.

** After examination of the details of the project, the Bank accepts the formal loan application through the agent bank among the co-financing institutions when the import contract is concluded and the necessary approvals from the governments concerned are received.

*** In principle, disbursement is made at the time of remittance to the exporter.

policies and trade-related agendas. The purpose of this conference is to address trade impediments, whether export- or import-related, as far as specific industry sectors are concerned.[12]

Netherlands

The Centre for the Promotion of Imports from Developing Countries (CBI) was established in 1971 by the Netherlands government. CBI is a part of the government's foreign trade policy framework, with its own general director, advised by a council of government officials and representatives from the private sector.[13] Its main purpose is to promote the import of industrial products and services from developing countries to the Netherlands, and more generally, to western Europe. It does this by helping to stimulate the market demand for exportable products and services. This is undertaken through an integrated programme of marketing services whose essential purpose it is to match exports with the requirements of importers. Figure A.3 shows the four main elements of this approach.

Market information

A number of focused information services are available, including

1 a comprehensive guide for exporting to the Netherlands which profiles the country's trade rélationship with developing nations, industry sector opportunities, as well as practical hints on both market access and approaching the market,[14]
2 product surveys on the Netherland's market with specific emphasis on product categories most suited to developing countries,
3 a news bulletin with comprehensive coverage of CBI's activities and specific market opportunities as well as information on related international agencies such as ITC or other trade promotion organizations,[15]
4 a trade documentation centre which acts as a resource on information on trade with developing countries.

Market product testing

A permanent product display area is used for specially selected product groups with serves as an ongoing exhibition to importers. CBI undertakes both product tests (concerned with quality, finish, packaging, pricing) and surveys of importers (or their reactions to and reception of displayed products). This information is channelled

Figure A.3 Framework for import promotion CBI Netherlands

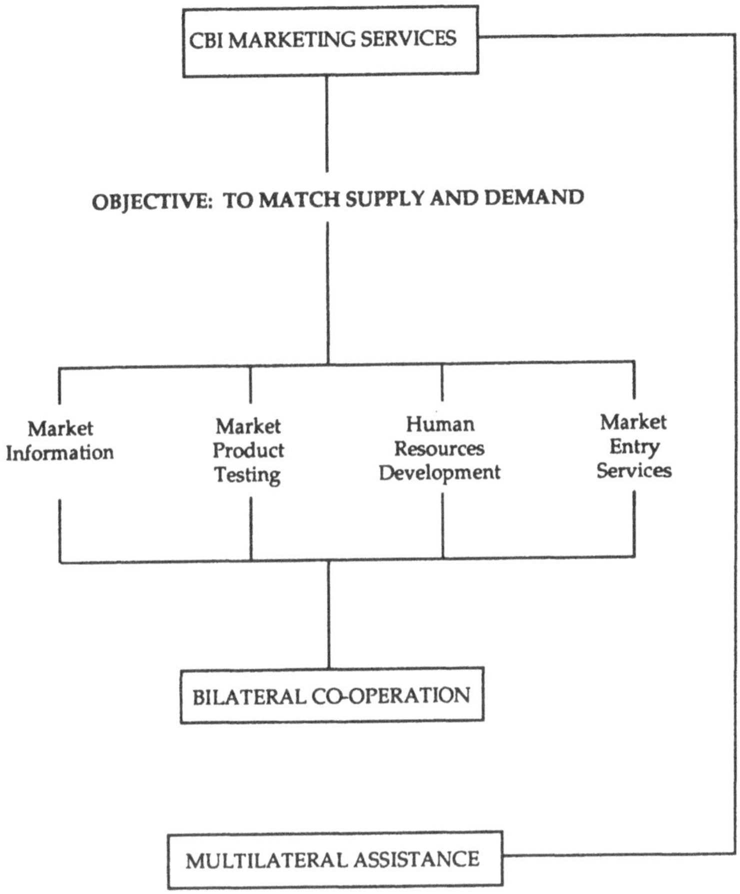

Source: *This is CBI*, Centre for Promotion of Imports from Developing Countries, Rotterdam, undated, p. 2.

to the exporter to establish business contacts and to provide feedback as to the adequacy of products for importation.[16]

Human resources development

Seminars and workshops for both company executives and trade promotion officials from developing countries focus on techniques of trade promotion for western Europe as well as developing specific

Figure A.4 Integrated market entry programme of CBI

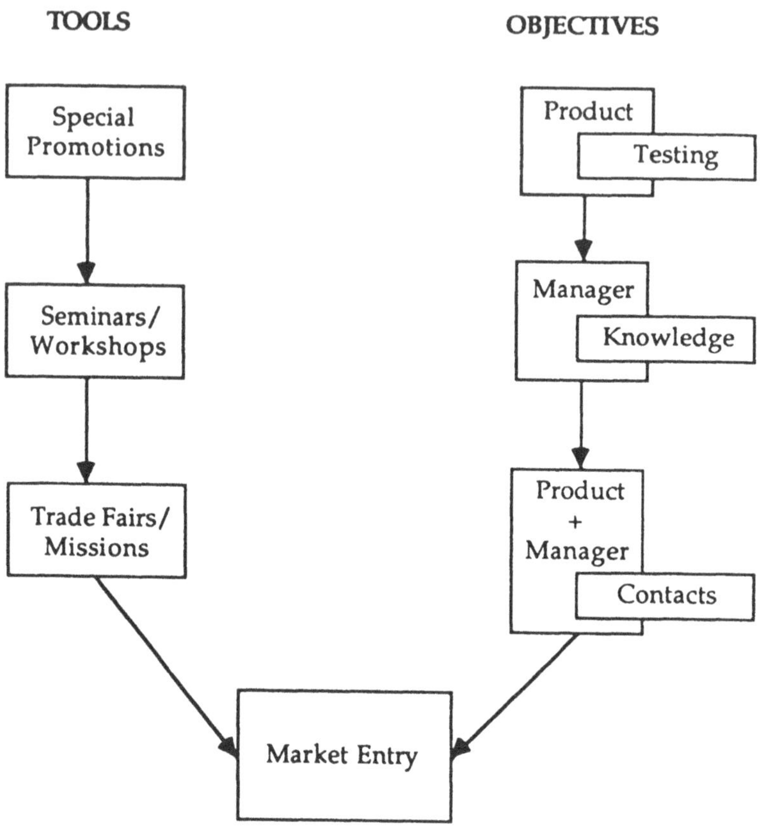

Source: *This is CBI*, Centre for Promotion of Imports from Developing Countries, Rotterdam, undated, p. 14.

action plans for marketing their products. Also offered are in-service training programmes for trade promotion officials on using CBI's programmes and on developing detailed demand studies for developing countries' products.[17]

Market entry services

Participation in Dutch trade fairs is supported both technically and financially. Such help usually follows successful display of products at the products display centre of CBI. Trade missions are organized

Figure A.5 Framework for Import Promotion IMPOD Sweden

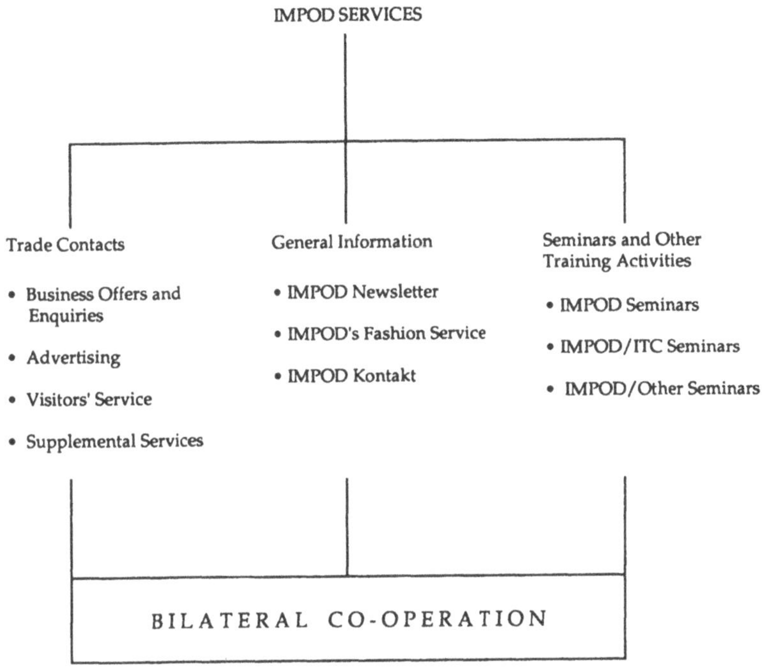

Source: Based on *Exporter's Guide to Sweden*, Stockholm, IMPOD, Import Promotion Office For Products from Developing Countries, 1985, p. 4.

for exporters from developing countries, as well as for Dutch importers visiting the latter. Participants from developing countries usually have undergone training through CBI-organized workshops. Market entry proceeds in a strategic manner, as shown in Figure A.4.

This recent strategic approach to market entry requires that prospective exporters successfully pass through a process of participating in special promotions (by using the market product testing), seminars, and workshops (to develop both understanding of the market, its requirements, and managerial knowledge to export to the Netherlands), and trade fairs or missions (for the purpose of contact development and pursuing concrete market opportunities). The aim of this approach is to help exporters to be more effective in entering western European markets.[18]

Bilateral and multilateral co-operation further enhances CBI's efforts by entering into specific co-operation agreements with trade promotion organizations in developing countries, and by maintaining a close relationship with ITC, the World Bank, and others, for the purpose of increasing the effectiveness of CBI efforts.[19]

Sweden

The Import Promotion Office for Products from Developing Countries (IMPOD) fulfils a role similar to CBI in the Netherlands. IMPOD, established in 1974, acts as an intermediary, a service and advisory body to assist government authorities, special-interest organizations, and companies in developing countries to gain access to the Swedish market. It operates under specific guidelines set by the Swedish parliament. While all non-European developing countries may request IMPOD's general services, specific trade promotion assistance efforts are usually restricted to a small group of such countries due to limited resources. IMPOD's services comprise four distinct sets of activities: trade contacts, general information services, seminars and other training activities, and bilateral co-operation (Figure A.5). A brief summary of the main facets of these services follows.[20]

Trade contacts

Business Offers and Enquiries handles both offers from exporters in developing countries and enquiries from Swedish importers, and thus helps in establishing contacts. Computerized data banks are maintained of prospective exporters and Swedish importers. Access to the data banks is available to both groups. Prospective exporters can use the advertising service to publicize products and business offers in IMPOD's *Kontakt* magazine. A visitor's service is available to foreign businessmen or trade delegations visiting Sweden, and assists in developing a suitable programme. Supplemental services include Product Notes (mini market surveys), help in the distribution of product samples, and, on a small scale, the provision of consulting, and the carrying out of product tests or small promotion projects.

General information

The main purpose of this service is the dissemination of information on the Swedish market and various product opportunities suitable to developing countries. A detailed Exporter's Guide, a regular newsletter with market trends, a special fashion service publication, and IMPOD *Kontakt* with a focus on business opportunities, are provided. In addition, a resource library is available for use by both exporters from developing countries and Swedish importers.

Seminars and other training activities

Seminars on the Swedish market are offered to specific audiences, including commercial attachés, officials from export promotion organizations, or marketing personnel of companies. Depending on the scope of seminars and the needs of particular developing countries they are offered by IMPOD alone, in conjunction with ITC, or jointly with other import promotion organizations of Nordic countries.

Bilateral co-operation serves to provide greater depth to selected import promotion efforts with specific developing countries. Such concentrated efforts are an extension of IMPOD's general services and typically include market surveys, purchasing and sales delegations, and promotional campaigns. Prerequisites for such bilateral efforts include the developing country pursues a general development policy compatible with IMPOD assistance, there is a need for assistance, and the country can offer some products of commercial interest to Sweden.

Notes and references

1 J. Reichel, 'The importer's role in co-ordinating the marketing effort of developing countries', Stockholm, IMPOD, 1987, p. 4.
2 ibid., p. 5.
3 *Import Promotion Offices*, International Trade Centre, UNCTAD/GATT, Geneva, 1987.
4 *The Japanese Import Market*, Tokyo, JETRO, 1987, p. 34.
5 ibid., p. 56.
6 *Guide to Japan's Import Activities*, Tokyo, JETRO, 1986, p. 118.
7 *The Japanese Import Market*, p. 56.
8 ibid., p. 52.
9 *Japan's Trade Finance*, Tokyo, JETRO, March 1984, p. 28.
10 *The Japanese Import Market*, p. 36.
11 *Guide to Japan's Import Activities*, p. 56.
12 ibid., p. 110.
13 'CBI News Bulletin', Centre for the Promotion of Imports from Developing Countries, Rotterdam, November 1987, p. 2.
14 *Exporting to the Netherlands*, Centre for the Promotion of Imports from Developing Countries, Rotterdam, 1987.
15 'CBI News Bulletin', November, p. 1.
16 'This is CBI', Centre for the Promotion of Imports from Developing Countries, Rotterdam, undated, pp. 6, 8.
17 'CBI News Bulletin', Centre for the Promotion of Imports from Developing Countries, Rotterdam, October 1987, pp. 15–16.
18 'This is CBI', p. 15.
19 ibid., pp. 18–19
20 *Exporter's Guide to Sweden*, IMPOD, Import Promotion Office for Products from Developing Countries, Stockholm, August 1985, p. 5.

Bibliography

Amsterdam-Rotterdam Bank (1983) 'Greater export opportunities for small and medium-size firms', Amsterdam-Rotterdam Bank Report, January.

Australia-New Zealand: Closer Economic Relations – Trade Agreement, (1983) 28 March, 22 I.L.M. 945.

Barrett, N.J. and Wilkinson, I.F. (1985) 'Export stimulation: a segmentation study of the exporting problems of Australian manufacturing firms', *European Journal of Marketing*, vol. 19, no. 2, pp. 53–72.

——— (1986) 'Internationalisation behavior: management characteristics of Australian manufacturing firms by level of international development', in P.W. Turnbull and S.J. Paliwoda (eds) *Research in International Marketing*, Beckenham, Croom Helm.

Beamish, P.W., Goerzen, A. and Munro, H. (1984), 'The export characteristics of Canadian manufacturers: a profile by firm size', Working Paper Series 8284, School of Business and Economics, Wilfrid Laurier University, Ontario.

Betro Trust (1975) *Concentration on Key Markets*, 2nd edn, Royal Society of Arts, London, December.

Bilkey, W.J. (1978) 'An attempted integration of the literature on the export behavior of firms', *Journal of International Business Studies*, vol. 9, no. 1, spring/summer, pp. 33–46.

2 BISD 39 (1952).

2 BISD 44 (1952), para. 29(a).

9 BISD 33 (1961).

9 BISD 191 (1961), para. 10.

9 BISD 192 (1961), para. 12.

10 BISD 207 (1962).

26 BISD 171 (1978–79).

26 BISD 333 (1980), para. 14.

28 BISD 77 (1982), paras 26, 33–5.

29 BISD 81 (1983), paras 18–21.

33 BISD 24 (1987).

Bodur, M. (1986) 'A study on the nature and intensity of problems experienced by Turkish exporting firms', in S.T. Cavusgil (ed.) *Advances in International Marketing*, Greenwich, Conn., JAI Press, pp. 205–32.

Brady, D.L. and Bearden, W.O. (1979) 'The effect of managerial attitudes

on alternative exporting methods', *Journal of International Business Studies*, vol. 10, no. 4, pp. 79–84.
Brooks, M.R. and Rosson, P.J. (1982) 'A study of the export behavior of small and medium-sized manufacturing firms in three Canadian provinces', in M.R. Czinkota and G. Tesar (eds) *Export Management: An International Context*, New York, Praeger.
Buckley, P.J. (1982) 'The role of exporting in the market servicing policies of multinational manufacturing enterprises: theoretical and empirical perspectives', in M.R. Czinkota and G. Tesar (eds) *Exporting Management: An International Context*, New York, Praeger.
Bundeskammer der Gewerblichen Wirtschaft (1982) *Export Services – Ein Leitfaden durch das Service fuer Exporteure*, Vienna, Ungar Druckerei GMBH.
Cabot Corporation v. United States, (1985) 620 F. Supp. 722 at p. 730.
Canadian Anti-Dumping Tribunal, *Colour Television* (Anti-Dumping Inquiry No. ADT-4-75).
Cavusgil, S.T. (1980) 'On the internationalisation process of firms', *European Research*, November, pp. 273–81.
——— (1982) 'On the nature of decision making for export marketing', in *Proceedings*, Marketing Theory Conference, American Marketing Association, Chicago, Ill., pp. 177–80.
——— (1982) 'Public policy implications of research on the export behaviour of firms', *Akron Business and Economic Journal*, vol. 14, summer, pp. 16–22.
——— (undated) 'Differences among exporting firms based on their degree of internationalization', unpublished paper, University of Wisconsin-Whitewater.
Cavusgil, S.T. and Kaynak, E. (1982) 'Success factors in export marketing: an empirical analysis', in B. Walker *et al.* (eds) *Assessment of Marketing Thought and Practice*, Educators' Conference Proceedings, American Marketing Association, Chicago, Ill., pp. 309–12.
CBI (1987a) 'CBI News Bulletin', Centre for the Promotion of Imports from Developing Countries, Rotterdam, October.
——— (1987b) 'CBI News Bulletin', Centre for the Promotion of Imports from Developing Countries, Rotterdam, November.
——— (1987c) *Exporting to the Netherlands*, Centre for the Promotion of Imports from Developing Countries, Rotterdam.
——— (undated) 'This is CBI', Centre for the Promotion of Imports from Developing Countries, Rotterdam.
Certain Fresh Atlantic Groundfish from Canada, ITA 51 FR 1010 (1986).
Certain Nails from the Republic of Korea, ITA 47 FR 27397 (1982).
Certain Pig Iron from Brazil, ITA 44 FR 67544 (1979).
Certain Red Raspberries from Canada, ITC 731-TA-196 (GOP, Jan. 86-1408).
Certain Steel Products from Belgium, ITA 47 FR 39304 (1982).
Certain Steel Products from Spain, ITA 47 FR 51438 (1982).
Clough, S.B. and Cole, C.W. (1952) *Economic History of Europe*, 3rd edn, Boston, Mass, D.C. Heath.

Co. Dec. 73/391, 1973 OJL 346.
Co. Dir. 70/509, 1970 OJL 254.
——— 70/510, 1970 OJL 254.
——— 71/86, 1971 OJL 36.
Co. Reg. 228/85, 1698/85.
——— 1191, Art. 12(1).
——— 2176/84, Art. 2A(2), 3(1), 4(1, 5), 5(1), 7(1), 11(1), 12(1), 13(2, 3, 9), OJL 201.
Colour Television Receiving Sets from Japan, Taiwan and Singapore, 1 CER 262 (1980).
Comm. Rec. 2129.83.ECSC, 1983 OJL L205, p. 30.
Convention Establishing the European Free Trade Association, 4 January 1960, 370 UNTS 3.
Convention on the Organization for Economic Cooperation and Development (1960), 888 UNTS 179, December.
Crespo-Blanco, J., Senior Officer, Trade Promotion Latin America (1987) Personal Interview, International Trade Centre UNCTAD/GATT, Geneva, 9 December.
Cullwick, T.D.C. and J.P. Mellallieu, (1981) 'Business attitudes to government export services and export marketing behaviour', *New Zealand Journal of Business*, vol. 3, pp. 33–54.
Czinkota, M.R. (1982) *Export Development Strategies: US Promotion Policy*, New York, Praeger.
Czinkota, M.R. and Johnston, W.J. (1981) 'Segmenting U.S. firms for export development', *Journal of Business Research*, 9, pp. 353–65.
Dam, K.W. (1970) *The GATT: Law and International Economic Organization* University of Chicago Press, Chicago, Ill.
Declaration Giving Effect to the Provisions of Article XVI:4 of the General Agreement on Tariffs and Trade, November 1960, 9 BISD 32 (1961).
Denis, J.-E. and Depelteau, D. (1985) 'Market knowledge, diversification and export expansion', *Journal of International Business Studies*, vol. XVI, no. 3, pp. 86–7.
Deutsche Aussenhandelskammern – Informationen, Anschriften (1982) Bonn, Deutscher Industrie- und Handelstag.
Dichtl, E., Koglmayr, H.G. and Muller, S. (1986) 'Identifying export potential: a comparative analysis of German and Japanese firms', in S.T. Cavusgil (ed.) *Advances in International Marketing*, Greenwich, Conn., JAI Press.
DM-CFME *Promosalons*, (undated).
Economist (1987a) 4 July, p. 75.
——— (1987b) 'A survey of the world economy', 26 September, pp. 6–56.
——— (1987c) 3 October, p. 115.
——— (1987d) 26 December, pp. 11–16, 20–2, 88.
Eiteman, D.K. and Stonehill, A.I. (1982) *Multinational Business Finance*, 3rd edn, Reading, Mass., Addison-Wesley.
Encyclopedia of European Community Law (1974) vol. 8, III, K.R. Simmonds (ed.) 'Agreement between the European Economic Community

and the Republic of Austria', 22 July 1972, London, Sweet & Maxwell, pt. B12, 13 12 369.
Engblom, G.M. (1987) Executive Director, Personal Interview, International Trade Centre, UNCTAD/GATT, Geneva, 8 December.
ESCAP (undated) *ESCAP Trade Promotion Centre*, Economic and Social Commission for Asia and the Pacific, United Nations, Bangkok.
Eurochambers (undated) Association of European Chambers of Commerce and Industry, Brussels.
EVD (1986) 'Export: research and policy', Conference Report, EVD Netherlands Export Promotion & Information Service, The Hague.
Export Development Board and its Activities (undated) Sri Lanka, p. 2.
Export Promotion Review Committee (1979) *Strengthening Canada Abroad*, Department of Industry, Trade and Commerce, Ottawa.
Fabric and Expanded Neoprene Laminate from Japan, ITC 731-Ta-206 (GOP, January 86-1412).
Ferroalloys from Spain, ITA 45 FR 25 (1980).
Filippi, J.-P. (1983) Deputy Commercial Counsellor, Consulate General of France, Toronto, personal interview, March 4.
Ford, D. *et al.* (1987) 'Managing export development between industrialized and developing countries', in P.J. Rosson and S.D. Reid (eds) *Managing Export Entry and Expansion: Concepts and Practice*, New York, Praeger.
French Chamber of Commerce (undated) *French Chamber of Commerce in Canada*.
Frenkel, O. and Fontheim, C.G.B. (1981) 'Export credits: an international and domestic legal analysis', *Law and Policy in International Business*, vol. 13, p. 1,078.
GATT, *Understanding Regarding Notification, Consultation, Dispute Settlement and Surveillance*, BISD 26th Supp. 210 (1978–9).
——— *Working Party Report on Suspension of Customs Liquidation by the United States*, 24 BISD 134 (1976).
——— *Working Party Report on Broader Tax Adjustments*, 18 BISD 97 (1970–1).
General Agreement on Tariffs and Trade, Basic Instruments and Selected Documents, vols I–IV, supps 1–34.
Government of Canada (1986) *Directory of Canadian Trading Houses*, 1986 edn, Distribution Services Division, Service Industries Branch, Department of Regional Industrial Expansion, Ottawa.
Grey, R.de C. *United States Trade Policy: A Canadian View* (1982) Institute for Research on Public Policy, Montreal.
Gronhaug, K. and Lorentzen, T. (1983) 'Exploring the impact of government export subsidies', *European Journal of Marketing*, vol. 17, no. 2, pp. 5–12.
Grub, P.D. (1971) 'An export decision pattern: a management guide to successful export entry and expansion', in P.D. Grub and M. Kaskimies (eds) *International Marketing in Perspective*, Helsinki, Sininin Kirjia Oy, p. 166.
Hartland-Thunberg, P. and Crawford, M.H. (1982) *Government Support for*

Exports – A Second-Best Alternative, Lexington, Mass., Lexington Books.
Hibbert, E.P. (1985) *The Principles and Practice of Export Marketing*, London, William Heineman.
House Subcommittee of the Committee on Government Operations (1977) *Commerce and State Department Export Promotion Programs*, 95th Congress, 1st Session.
House of Commons (1980) *Proceedings of the Special Committee on a National Trading Corporation*, First Session of the Thirty-Second Parliament, Supply and Services Canada, Hull.
Hufbauer, G.C. and Erb, J.S. *Subsidies in International Trade* (1984) Institute for International Economics, Cambridge, Mass.
Illustrative List of Export Subsidies (1979) Appendix in *Subsidies and Countervailing Duties*, Agreement on Interpretation and Application of Articles VI, XVI and XXIII of the General Agreement on Tariffs and Trade, 26 BISD 56 (1978–79) April.
IMPOD (1985) *Exporter's Guide to Sweden*, Import Promotion Office for Products from Developing Countries, Stockholm, August.
Income Tax Practices Maintained by Belgium, 23 BISD 127 (1975–76), para. 34.
Income Tax Practices Maintained by France, 23 BISD 114 (1975–76), para. 47.
Income Tax Practices Maintained by The Netherlands, 23 BISD 156 (1975–76), para. 34.
Industrial Wood Cutting Band Saw Blades from the US, 5 CER 207 (1984).
Industry, Trade and Commerce (1981) 'Update on Government Response to EPRC (Hatch) Report Recommendations', Department of Industry, Trade and Commerce, Canada.
Institutional Systems for Export Promotion in Latin America and the Caribbean – A Comparative Analysis (1984) document No. 1, International Trade Centre UNCTAD/GATT, Geneva.
International Trade Centre UNCTAD/GATT (1975) *Enhancing the Effectiveness of Technical Assistance in Export Promotion*, Joint Advisory Group, Eighth Session, Geneva, January.
——— (1986) *Annual Report on the Activities of the International Trade Centre UNCTAD/GATT 1985*, Joint Advisory Group, Nineteenth Session, Geneva, April.
——— (1987) *Annual Report on the Activities of the International Trade Centre UNCTAD/GATT 1986*, Joint Advisory Group, Twentieth Session, Geneva, April
Israel-United States: Free Trade Area Agreement, 22 April 1985, 241 ILM 653.
ITC (1982) *Making the Most of Trade Fairs – How Chamber of Commerce can Assist Members in Participating in International Trade Fairs*, International Trade Centre, UNCTAD/GATT, Geneva.
——— (1984a) *The Role of Chambers of Commerce in Trade Facilitation*, International Trade Centre, UNCTAD/GATT and International Chamber of Commerce, Geneva.

——— (1984b) *Trade Information Services of Chambers of Commerce*, International Trade Centre, UNCTAD/GATT and International Chamber of Commerce, Geneva.

——— (1986a) *Trade Promotion Institutions: Monograph on the Role and Organization of Trade Promotion*, International Trade Centre UNCTAD/GATT, Geneva.

——— (1986b) *Selected Export Promotion Organizations: Structures, Functions and Activities*, International Trade Centre UNCTAD/GATT, Geneva, 25 September.

——— (1986c) *Trade Data Analysis at Enterprise Level for Trade Promotion*, International Trade Centre UNCTAD/GATT, Geneva, December.

——— (1987a) *ITC Activities and Services in Trade Information*, International Trade Centre UNCTAD/GATT, Geneva, 17 March.

——— (1987b) 'ITC Information', International Trade Centre, UNCTAD/GATT, No. 23, 6 Apr.

——— (1987c) *ITC Manual on Programming, Project Design, Monitoring and Evaluation*, International Trade Centre UNCTAD/GATT, Geneva, August.

——— (1987d) *Some General Conclusions from ITC Evaluations Carried Out in 1986*, International Trade Centre UNCTAD/GATT, Geneva, 23 September.

——— (1987e) 'Report on enterprise-oriented approach in ITC's technical co-operation for export development and promotion', International Trade Centre UNCTAD/GATT, Geneva, November.

——— (1987f) *Import Promotion Offices*, International Trade Centre UNCTAD/GATT, Geneva.

——— (1987g) *Guide to the Evaluation of Trade Promotion Programmes*, International Trade Centre UNCTAD/GATT, Geneva.

——— (1988) *Annual Report on the Activities of the International Trade Centre UNCTAD/GATT 1987*, Joint Advisory Group, Twenty-first Session, Geneva, April.

——— (undated) *ITC Promoting Trade*, International Trade Centre UNCTAD/GATT, Geneva.

——— (undated) *Market News Service*, International Trade Centre UNCTAD/GATT, Geneva.

Jackson, J.H. *World Trade and the Law of GATT*, (1969) New York, Bobbs Merril, SS13.5 and 15.7.

Japan Electrical Manufacturers' Association v. Anti-Dumping Tribunal, 12 CER 260 (198), p. 267.

JETRO (1976) *The Role of Trading Companies in International Commerce*, Jetro Marketing Series.

——— (1984) *Japan's Trade Finance*, Japan External Trade Organization, Tokyo, March.

——— (1986) *Guide to Japan's Import Activities*, Japan External Trade Organization, Tokyo.

——— (1987) *The Japanese Import Market*, Japan External Trade Organization, Tokyo.

Johanson, J. and Vahlne, J-E. (1977) 'The internationalization of the firm: a model of knowledge development and increasing foreign market commitments', *Journal of International Business Studies*, vol. 8. no. 1, spring/summer, pp. 23–32.
Jouvin, J.-J. (1987) Chief, Office for Europe, Mediterranean and the Middle East, personal interview, International Trade Centre UNCTAD/GATT, Geneva, 9 December.
Kaynak, E. and Stevenson, L. (1982) 'Profile analysis of Nova Scotia exporters', *Proceedings*, Administrative Sciences Association of Canada-Marketing Division, University of Ottawa, pp. 98–108.
Kleinschmidt, E.J. and Ross, R.E. (1984) 'Export performance and foreign market information: relationships for small high-technology firms', *Canadian Journal of Small Business and Entrepreneurship*, vol. 2, no. 2, pp. 8–23.
Korth, C.M. (1985) *International Business – Environment and Management*, 2nd edn, Englewood Cliffs, NJ, Prentice-Hall.
Leather Wearing from Uruguay, ITA 46 FR 19288 (1981).
Lee, W.-Y. and Brasch, J.J. (1978) 'The adoption of export as an innovative strategy', *Journal of International Business Studies*, vol. 9, no. 1, pp. 85–93.
Lidskog, N. (1983) Acting Trade Commissioner, Swedish Trade Office, Toronto, personal interview, March 4.
Lifting Australia's Performance as an Exporter of Manufactures and Services (1985) Report of the National Export Marketing Strategy Panel, Australian Government Publishing Service.
Live Swine and Pork from Canada, ITC 701-TA-224 (GOP, January 86-1403).
McGovern, E. (1986) *International Trade Regulation*, 2nd edn, Exeter, Globefield Press.
Mattson, J. (1986) 'Initial penetration of European continental markets by small and medium-sized firms', in S.T. Cavusgil (ed.) *Advances in International Marketing*, vol. 1, Greenwich, Conn., JAI Press.
Mayer, C.S. and Flynn, J.E. (1973) 'Canadian small business abroad: opportunities, aids and experiences', *Business Quarterly*, vol. 38, winter, pp. 33–47.
Ministerie Van Economische Zaken (1980) *Regelingen Voor De Export*, The Hague, Augustus.
Ministry of Commerce (undated) 'Export promotion and export development plan of the Department of Export Promotion', Bangkok.
MOCI (1982a) 'Promotions sur les marches porteurs', no. 533/13, December.
——— (1982b) 'L'accueil au CFCE', no. 533/13 December.
——— (1982c) 'Une assistance sur mesure', no. 533/13 December.
——— (1982d) 'Les informations en libre acces', no. 533/13 December.
——— (1983) 'Services publics de l'exportation', no. 537/10 January.
Moldex Limited v. Anti-Dumping Tribunal, 7 CER 323 (1985) p. 324.
Mori, Y., Chief, Trade Information Service (1987) personal interview, International Trade Centre UNCTAD/GATT, Geneva, 9 December.

Moulded Pulp Egg Filler Flats from Canada, ITC 731-TA-201 (GOP, January 86-1410).
National Swedish Industrial Board (1985) *Export Promotion by Government in Nine Countries*, Stockholm, Liber Tryck AB.
Neghandhi, A.R. (1987) *International Management*, Boston, Mass., Allyn & Bacon.
G.S. Nichols & Co. v. United States (249 US 34, 1919).
Nulty, P.J. (1972) 'Predecessors of the multinational corporation', *Columbia Journal of World Business*, May–June.
OECD (1973) *Code of Liberalization of Current Invisible Operations*, Paris.
——— (1986) Doc. TD/CONSENSUS, 86.33.
Ogger, G. (1977) *Kauf Dir einen Kaiser, Die Geschichte der Fugger*, Munich, Droemer Knaur.
Oil County Tubular Goods from Argentina and Spain, ITC 731-TA-191 (GOP January 86-1407).
Olson, H.C. (1975) *Studies in Export Promotion*, Acta Universitatis Upsaliensis, Studia Oeconomiae Negotiorum 10, Stockholm, Alqvist & Wiksell International.
Ortner, E. (1977) *Glueck und Macht der Fugger*, Munich, Ehrenwirth Verlag K.G.
Pasco Terminals, Inc. v. United States, 477 F. Supp. 201 (1979).
Paterson, R.K. *Canadian Regulation of International Trade and Investment* (1986) Toronto, Carswell.
Paumgarten, H. (1982) Deputy Trade Commissioner, Austrian Consulate General, Toronto, personal interview, 22 December.
Pointon, T. (1978) 'Measuring the gains from government export promotion', *European Journal of Marketing*, vol. 12, no. 6, pp. 451–62.
Program for Export Market Development (1987) *PEMD Handbook*, Department of External Affairs, Ottawa.
Protocol of Provisional Acceptance (October 1947, 55 UNTS 308), Article 1(b).
Rabino, S. (1980/1) 'An examination of barriers to exporting encountered by small manufacturing companies', *International Management Review*, vol. 20, pp. 67–73.
Railcars from Canada, ITA, 49 FR 6569 (1983) (*The Bombardier Case*).
Reichel, J. (1987) 'The importer's role in coordinating the marketing effort of developing countries', Stockholm, IMPOD.
Reid, S.D. (1981) 'The decision maker and export entry and expansion', *Journal of International Business Studies*, vol. 12, no. 2, fall, pp. 101–12.
——— (1984) 'Information acquisition and export entry decisions in small firms', *Journal of Business Research*, vol. 12, no. 2, pp. 141–57.
Reid, S.D. and Rosson, P.J. (1987) 'Managing export entry and expansion: an overview', in P.J. Rosson and S.D. Reid (eds) *Managing Export Entry and Expansion: Concepts and Practice*, New York, Praeger.
5th Report of Committee on Anti-Dumping Practices, 20 BISD 43 (1973).
Room, S. (1987) Written communication, Public Information Office, International Chamber of Commerce, Paris, 23 November.

Root, F.R. (1971) 'The elements of export promotion', *International Trade Forum*, July–September, pp. 118–21.

——— (1978) *International Trade and Investment*, 4th edn, Cincinnati, Ohio, South-Western Publishing.

Rosson, P., Brooks, M., Kamath, S., and Patton, D. (1985) *Excellence in Exporting: Advice and Comments from Canada Export Award Winners*, Department of External Affairs, Ottawa.

Roy, D.A. and Simpson, C.L. (1981) 'The decision to discontinue exporting: the experience of the smaller manufacturing firm in the Southeast United States', *Proceedings*, Academy of Marketing Science Conference, pp. 101–4.

Rugman, A.M. and Anderson, A.D.M. (1987) *Administered Protectionism in America*, London, Croom Helm.

Rules of the Canadian Import Tribunal, SOR/85-1068, s.36(a)-(c).

Schitzer, M.C., Liebrenz, M.L., and Kubin, K.W. (1985) *International Business*, Cincinnati, Ohio, South-Western Publishing Co.

Schwarting, U., Thoben, C., and Wittstock, M. (1982) *Nachfrageverhalten Kleiner und Mittlerer Unternehmen nach Aussenhandelsinformationen und Beratung*, Göttingen, Beitraege zur Mittelstandsforschung, Verlag Otto Schwartz & Co., Heft 83.

Seringhaus, F.H. Rolf (1984) 'Government export marketing assistance to small and medium-sized manufacturing firms: the role and impact of trade missions on firms' off-shore market involvement', unpublished Ph.D. Dissertation, York University, Toronto.

——— (1986a) 'The impact of government export marketing assistance', *International Marketing Review*, vol. 3, no. 2, pp. 55–66.

——— (1986b) 'The process, problem and management perspective of export involvement: a review of the export marketing literature', Working Paper Series 6.88, School of Business and Economics, Wilfrid Laurier University, Ontario.

——— (1986c) 'Empirical investigation of awareness, use and impact of export marketing support by government in manufacturing firms', in Moeller, K. and Paltschik, M. (eds) *Contemporary Research in Marketing*, vol. a, Helsinki, European Marketing Academy, pp. 249–67.

——— (1986d) 'Market entry and the impact of export marketing assistance: a conceptual approach to causal modelling', *Finnish Journal of Business Economics*, vol. 35, no. 4, pp. 275–85.

——— (1986/87) 'The role of information assistance in small firms' export involvement', *International Small Business Journal*, vol. 5, no. 2, winter, pp. 26–36.

——— (1987a) 'The use of trade missions in foreign market entry of industrial firms', *Industrial Marketing and Purchasing*, vol. 2, no. 1, pp. 43–60.

——— (1987b) 'Export promotion: the role and impact of government services', *Irish Marketing Review* vol. 2, spring, pp. 106–16.

——— (1987c) 'Do experienced exporters have market entry problems?' *Finnish Journal of Business Economics*, vol. 36, no. 4, pp. 376–88.

——— (1987d) 'Using trade missions for export market entry', *Industrial*

Marketing Management, vol. 16, no. 4, pp. 249–55.
——— (1988a) 'A methodological approach to the evaluation of government export promotion programs', Research Paper Series 1.88, School of Business and Economics, Wilfrid Laurier University, Ontario.
——— (1988b) 'The relationship of knowledge and firm behaviour in exporting: test of a conceptual model', Working Paper Series 5.88, School of Business and Economics, Wilfrid Laurier University, Ontario.
Simmonds, K. and Smith, H. (1968) 'The first export order: a marketing innovation', *British Journal of Marketing*, summer, pp. 93–100.
Simon, D. (1983–4) 'Can GATT export subsidy standards be ignored by the United States in imposing countervailing duties?', *Northwest Journal of International Law and Business*, vol. 5, p. 201.
Simpson, C.L., Roy, D.A., and Loudon, D.L. (1981) 'Use and perception of external support facilities in the initial export activity among smaller manufacturing firms in the southeastern United States', presented at the annual meeting of the Academy of International Business, Montreal, October, pp. 15–17.
Siriphand, P. (1987) Export Service Division, Department of Export Promotion, written Communication, Bangkok, 4 November.
Softwood Lumber Products from Canada, ITA 48 FR 10395 (1983).
Softwood Lumber Products from Canada, ITA 51 FR 37453 (1986).
Special Import Measures Act, S.C. (SIMA) 1984, c25, art, 2(1, 7), 3(1)(a, b), 15–30, 31(1)(a), 35(a)(ii), 38(1)(b)(iii), 41(1)(a), (b)(iv), 42(1)(a), (3).
SPR Associates Incorporated/National Mail Surveys Incorporated (1987) *The Fairs and Missions (Promotional Projects) Program: Survey of Past Participants*, report prepared for the Department of External Affairs, Ottawa, October 5.
Sir Lanka Export Development Board (1987) 'Annual Work Programme, Budgeting and Evaluation Procedures Adopted by the Sri Lanka Export Development Board', 31 October.
Steed, G.P.F. (1982) *Threshold Firms – Backing Canada's Winners*, Science Council of Canada, Background Study 48, Canadian Government Publishing Centre, Supply and Services Canada.
Steel Belted Tires from Canada, ITA 39 FR 1018 (1973).
Swedish Trade Council (1981) *Introduction to a New Export Market*.
——— (1986) *Annual Report 1985/86*, Stockholm.
Subsidies and Countervailing Duties. Agreement on Interpretation and Application of Articles VI, XVI, and XXIII of the General Agreement on Tariffs and Trade, (1979), 26 BISD 56 (1978–79), April.
Surgical Adhesive Tapes and Plasters from Japan, 10 CER 174 (1986), p. 183.
Tax Legislation: United States Tax Legislation (DISC), 23 BISD 98 (1975–76), para. 76.
Thailand's Department of Export Promotion: At Your Service Around the World (undated) Department of Export Promotion, Bangkok.
Treasury Board of Canada (1981) *Guide on the Program Evaluation Function*, Minister of Supply and Services, Ottawa, May.

Treaty Establishing the European Economic Community, 25 March 1957, 298 UNTS 4.
Tsurumi, Y. (1984) *Multinational Management – Business Strategy and Government Policy*, 2nd edn, Cambridge, Mass., Ballinger.
United Nations (1946) *Yearbook of the United Nations*, New York.
Uruguayan Recourse to Article XXIII, 11 BISD 95, (1963), 105, 111, 113 and 116.
US Congress House (1978) *Export Stimulation Programs in the Major Industrial Countries: The United States and Eight Major Competitors*, Congressional Research Service, 95th Congress, 2nd Session, Washington DC, October 6.
19 USCS SS 1673, 1671a(A, B), 1671b(B), 1677–1, 1677(4)(A), (5)(B), (7) (A, B, C), (9), 1677a, b, 2112.
US Department of Commerce (1980) *Report of the President on Export Promotion Functions and Potential Export Disincentives*, US Government Printing Office, Washington, DC.
——— (1980) *The Export Imperative*, Report to the President Submitted by the President's Export Council, vol. I.
——— (1986) *A Basic Guide to Exporting*, International Trade Administration, US Government Printing Office, Washington, DC.
——— (undated) Industry and Trade Administration, Seven Surprising Facts About Exporting', Government Printing Office, Washington, DC.
Varaldo, R. (1987) 'The internationalization of small and medium-sized Italian manufacturing firms', in P.J. Rosson and S.D. Reid (eds) *Managing Export Entry and Expansion: Concepts and Practice*, New York, Praeger.
Verzariu, P. (1985) *Countertrade, Barter, and Offsets*, New York, McGraw-Hill.
Von Amerongen, O.W. (1983) 'Maerkte Oeffnen und Faehigkeit am Wettbewerb Ueberpruefen', *Welt Report*, Heft 28, 14 December, p. 11.
Waldman, R.J. (1986) *Managed Trade: The Competition Between Nations*, Cambridge, Mass., Ballinger.
Walters, P.G.P. (1983) 'Export information sources – a study of their usage and utility', *International Marketing Review*, vol. 1, winter, pp. 34–43.
Weisbert, H.L. and Rauch, C. (1979) *A Comparative Study of Export Incentives in the United States, France, the United Kingdom, Germany and Japan*, Chamber of Commerce of the United States, International Division, Washington, DC.
Welch, L.S. and Wiedersheim-Paul, F. (1980) 'Initial exports – a marketing failure?', *Journal of Management Studies*, vol. 17, no. 3, October, pp. 332–44.
Wilkinson, I. and Barrett, N. (1986) 'Australian management's attitudes to exporting – past and present', unpublished paper presented to the Market Research Society of Australia's Annual Conference, Canberra.
World Bank (1987) *World Development Report 1987* New York, Oxford University Press.
Wortzell, L.H. and Wortzell, H.V. (1981) 'Export marketing strategies for

NIC and LDC-based firms', *Columbia Journal of World Business*, spring, pp. 51–60.
Young, A.K. (1974) 'Internationalization of the Japanese General Trading Companies', *Columbia Journal of World Business*, spring, pp. 74–85.
Zenith Radio Corporation v. United States, 437 US 443 (1978), p. 455.
Zimmerling, D. (1976), *Die Hanse – Handelsmacht im Zeichen der Kogge*, Düsseldorf, Econ Verlag.

Index

For Product Safety Concerns and Information please contact our EU representative GPSR@taylorandfrancis.com Taylor & Francis Verlag GmbH, Kaufingerstraße 24, 80331 München, Germany